SAT
PERFECT
SCORE

*Also by Tom Fischgrund*

The Insider's Guide to the Top Ten Business Schools
Barron's Top 50: An Inside Look at America's Best Colleges

# SAT
## PERFECT
## SCORE

### *7 Secrets to Raise Your Score*

# Tom Fischgrund, Ph.D.

**1● ReganBooks**
**Celebrating Ten Bestselling Years**
*An Imprint of HarperCollinsPublishers*

HarperCollins books may be purchased for educational, business, or sales promotional use. For information please write: Special Markets Department, HarperCollins Publishers Inc., 10 East 53rd Street, New York, NY 10022.

FIRST PAPERBACK EDITION PUBLISHED 2004.

*Designed by Nancy Singer Olaguera*

Printed on acid-free paper

---

**The Library of Congress has cataloged the hardcover as follows:**

Fischgrund, Tom.
    1600 perfect score : the 7 secrets of students who aced the SAT / Tom Fischgrund.—1st ed.
      p. cm.
    Includes bibliographical references.
    ISBN 0-06-050663-6 (alk. paper)
    1. Scholastic Assessment Test—Study guides. I. Title: Sixteen hundred perfect score. II. Title.
LB2353.57.F57 2003
378.1'662—dc21

2003047209

---

ISBN 0-06-050664-4 (pbk.)

04 05 06 07 08 ❖/RRD 10 9 8 7 6 5 4 3 2 1

*To my family, who supported me*

# Contents

## PART III: RAISING SAT SCORES: PRACTICAL ADVICE AND LEARNING FOR LIFE

# Acknowledgments

This book is about a group of really smart kids, distinguished not just by their intelligence or SAT scores, but more importantly by their thinking, their passions, and their views on life. I learned a tremendous amount from my discussions with them. First of all I would like to thank all those students I spoke with, for their time and participation in the study. Second, the College Board, specifically Brian O'Reilly, Ellen Sawtell, and Jeri Ann Cook, were very instrumental in helping me establish contact with students who scored 1600, and in sharing their research. To their credit, they never asked nor attempted to influence the outcome of this research. Third, great thinking is never a solitary venture, so my thanks go to all those educators and researchers who shared their ideas and time with me. In particular Page Boyer and David Sackin, who provided research and technical assistance, were of enormous benefit. I would also like to thank Walker Smith and Yankelovich for the use of the Yankelovich MONITOR®'s insights. Others who helped were: Steve Silbiger, Jeff Duval, Fran Linnane, Paige Arnof Fenn, Steve Jones, Iris Leo, Amanda Lombardi, Bonnie Lee, Jody Ogle, Pat Siegert, Gerry Toner, Scoot Diamond, and Hank Bangser.

Anyone who has written a book knows that editors make a huge difference. David Groff helped develop the original book proposal. The main editing in the book was done by Debbie Kotz, who, I like to joke, translated the book into English. Cal Morgan, my editor at ReganBooks, understood the promise of the book and provided clear direction. Susan Ginsburg, my agent, was my alter ego, keeping the idea and the book alive and on track.

It is impossible to do a book on education without thanking your kids; after all, parents and teachers learn most from their children. My daughter, Beth, was interviewed as I developed the original questionnaire. My son Ted was my research assistant in exchange for sending him to one of those elite private colleges. Finally, my third child, Sam, gets to be the recipient of all that I have learned—or maybe it still will be the other way around. In any case, my thanks to my kids.

# Preface to the New Edition

## THE NEW SAT: WHAT YOU NEED TO KNOW

What does a Korean clerk, who works in a dry cleaner and speaks little English, have in common with the host of a TV morning talk show watched by millions of people each day? They're both concerned about their kids' future performance on the SAT. While I was in New York to promote this book when it first came out last September, I stopped by a dry cleaner the day before my appearance on the *Today Show*. The clerk asked me why I was in New York and I told her briefly about my book and the Perfect Score Study. She immediately asked what kind of preparation was best for the SAT and what her son, a junior in high school, could do to raise his score. The next morning, after my interview on the *Today Show*, Katie Couric asked me privately about how she could apply the findings of my study to her own daughter. She wanted to know more about the habits of high academic achievers and whether her daughter was following those habits.

Two weeks later I had a phone conversation with the dean of admissions at one of the top colleges in the country. We were supposed to discuss the findings of the Perfect Score Study and how certain characteristics of perfect score students were consistent with the criteria he used to determine whether or not to accept particular college applicants to his university. He did mention that he was gratified to learn that my study verified his own methods of selecting students given that 15,000 students pass through his selection process every year. But what he was most interested in discussing was his own teenage daughter and what he could do as a parent to motivate her to do her best in high school.

What's fascinating here is that these three people, who vary widely in terms of background, ethnicity, income, and lifestyle, all share a common interest: their desire to raise a child who fulfills his or her potential—not just on the SAT or in school, but in life. I found this same thread running through all the conversations I had with parents across the country while discussing the findings of this book. I have yet to meet a parent who doesn't want to help his or her child do better academically, socially, and emotionally in all aspects of life. After all, we only want what's best for our children.

When I originally conceived of the Perfect Score Study, I thought its findings would prove most useful to students who were capable of getting stellar SAT scores of 1400 or above. They could use my study, I reasoned, to push their scores that much higher. While this is true, it's certainly not the most useful way to use the findings of the Perfect Score Study. I now know that all students can benefit from this study and that all can raise their SAT scores simply by following the 7 secrets of perfect score students.

I have to say I spoke to a greater number of students during my travels who scored in the 900 to 1200 point range than those who scored in the 1400 to 1500 range. These students were most interested in raising their scores by 50 or 100 points, enough to gain them acceptance to their college of choice. I told them that my book could give them the extra nudge they needed to excel academically and raise their SAT scores. They could still have a shot at getting into that state university in New York or California. They could still get the advantage they needed to overcome the tighter admission standards put in place to deal with the current increase in applicants.

Today colleges have no shortage of students. The number of college applicants continues to grow and will reach its peak in 2008.

Students today need that extra boost to make attending their dream school a reality. By taking advantage of the results of the Perfect Score Study, these students can do just that.

○

On top of everything else that parents and students have to deal with, another issue is well on the way. That's right folks, a new and improved SAT. You've probably heard by now that the SAT is changing. A new version will be rolled out in March 2005. This may have left you wondering, "What do I do now?"

Of course, the short answer is: Be prepared.

Reading this book will help you do just that. It addresses some of your most fundamental questions:

**How is the SAT changing?**

**How can students improve their scores?**

**What can parents do to help motivate their kids?**

It also addresses specific questions that I encounter over and over again such as:

○ What is a good score?

○ When should a student first take the SAT? Freshman, sophomore, junior, or senior year?

○ What kind of preparation is better: Kaplan, Princeton Review, an SAT computer program, or individual tutoring?

○ Can studying improve SAT scores? Isn't it supposed to be an aptitude test?

○ Will taking the test repeatedly help raise scores? Will it count against a student on a college application?

○ Are students doomed if they didn't start preparing for the SAT at least a year or two ahead of time?

○ What are some useful tips if the test is next week?

This thirst for information and advice is unquenchable. Let's start with the most pressing question:

## HOW IS THE SAT CHANGING?

To address critics who have complained that the SAT didn't reflect the current high school curriculum, the College Board decided to revise the SAT. The new SAT is more closely aligned with material taught in high schools nationwide. The biggest change is the inclusion of a new writing section. This section will include multiple choice questions that test a student's grammar, usage, and word choice. It will also require students to compose an essay stating their position on an issue with relevant examples to make their point.

The math and verbal sections have changed only slightly. The math section includes more difficult concepts from third year math (Algebra II) and no longer includes quantitative comparison questions. The verbal section—now called critical reading—will contain short reading passages in addition to longer passages, and will no longer contain word analogies.

It's important to keep these changes in perspective. The math and verbal sections are evolving slightly rather than changing radically. Thus, the habits and tips gleaned from perfect score students on SAT preparation (found in Part 3) are just as applicable. The writing section will require additional preparation. The good news is that the 7 Secrets of perfect score students, which are contained in this book, will give all students who read it an even greater advantage. All of the tools necessary to ace this section are found in the 7 Secrets. Developing good reading skills is one of the 7 Secrets. Expressing creativity is another, as well as developing a passion. Cultivating these qualities can help students organize and express their ideas effectively and develop a mastery of the English language. Anyone looking to achieve these goals need only read this book.

Many parents and students I've spoken to have expressed the concern that the essay will eliminate fairness on the exam. How can the

College Board grade two million essays each year with a standardized scoring system that's fair to all students? Won't subjectivity come into play on the part of the essay readers? The answer is that the College Board isn't setting a new precedent here. Essays are already found on the SAT II writing exam, which is recognized as a fair test by college admissions officers. What's more, the College Board has established highly specific grading criteria and writing samples reflecting these criteria at all levels, which will be provided to essay readers. The readers are teachers trained to evaluate essays on a consistent basis, and their scoring will be continually reviewed.

So, let's assume that the writing test will be graded fairly. The bigger question is: How can students get the best score possible on the new SAT?

○

The advice and insight offered by students who achieved a perfect score is a good place to start.

## Short-Term Tips

- ○ Read the instructions
- ○ Take practice exams
- ○ Decide the score you need to get into the school of your choice and establish your goal
- ○ Develop a personalized plan of attack
- ○ Do some kind of review, whether it's Kaplan, Princeton Review, individual tutoring, or computerized programs
- ○ Relax and keep things in perspective

## Long-Term Advice

- ○ Read, read, read
- ○ Take challenging courses

○ Pursue your passions

○ Be proactive

○ Remember the goal is to succeed in life

For the new writing section, the habits of perfect score students are even more relevant. Why? As I mentioned, this section is designed to specifically reflect what students learn in high school. Essay writing is a crucial part of the high school curriculum. So, too, is knowledge of the English language. Perfect score students not only aced the SAT but 97% of them also maintained a 4.0 average in high school. So, yes, they mastered what they learned in high school as well as the SAT.

I know many students will be approaching the new SAT with trepidation. Those taking it for the first time in the spring of 2005 will be the guinea pigs. They simply won't know what to expect. Still, they can take some comfort in the fact that everyone is in the same boat. They can also do their best to prepare for the completely new section. Here's how:

○ **Familiarize yourself with the essay.** Review any and all materials provided by the College Board about the new writing section. Understand what is required, learn how the essays will be scored, and see what differentiates the superior essay from the mediocre one. Check out the college board website at *www.collegeboard.com.*

○ **Write, write, write.** Yes, do an actual draft of an essay based on a sample question. In fact, do drafts of any and all essay questions that you can get your hands on. The more you write, the better your writing will become. Also, learn to edit yourself. Rewrite what you've written to get a feel for good phrasing and organization. On the new SAT, you will be asked to write an essay in a mere twenty-five minutes. The College Board recognizes that this will be written as a first draft. Still, they expect it to be a good first draft with proper grammar and punctuation, sound organization, and thoughtful examples. My advice? Set aside five minutes at the end to edit your work.

This means you should aim to get a draft down in twenty minutes to allow for a quick revision.

○ **Read voluminously.** Writing is an acquired skill often improved through reading the works of others. Best-selling author John Grisham was asked what he read most recently and he replied, "Mark Twain; I keep reading his works over and over again."

○ **Take a review course.** Though it allows for some creativity, the essay can be mastered by following a certain formula. Hiring a private tutor or taking a review course can help you improve your writing skills. Learning the art of organizing an essay and making a point effectively through examples are specific skills that can be taught through a course.

○ **Look at the larger gain.** Developing good essay writing skills will benefit you during the remainder of high school, throughout college, and possibly your career. Approach the essay preparation for the SAT as a critical life skill that you'll always have rather than a skill to be learned for the test. You'll be more likely to take your task more seriously and will see a bigger improvement in your writing skills.

## MOST COMMON QUESTIONS ABOUT THE SAT

Over the past year, I've participated in more than one hundred speaking engagements and done countless TV, radio, and newspaper interviews. The most common questions I received are these:

### What is a good SAT score?

A good SAT score is one that can get students into the school of their choice. I call this "Ted's Rule" named for my son who invoked it after I tried to get him to take the SAT a second time. He got the score he needed to get into his top choice school the first time around and basically told me to butt out when I approached him about increasing his score. With all the best intentions, parents often put too much pressure on their kids to do well on the SAT without considering what their child's goal score should be. In fact, a girl once approached me with her parents during a book signing and asked if I thought she should retake the SAT. I asked her what her score was and she told me it was 1200. "Will this get you into the college of your choice?" I asked. "Yes," she replied. "So why would you want to retake the SAT?" I answered. She smiled and felt relieved while her parents looked at me quizzically. Nevertheless, I probably saved her needless worry and time, since she already had a "good" score.

One last thought. Although I call this "Ted's Rule," my son Ted calls it "Ted Rules." And it's true. Students rule when it comes to determining what a "good score" is, since a good score is determined by their choice of college.

### Which test, the new or the old, should students take if they're in the transition year when both tests are offered?

This question for the graduating class of 2006 isn't so clear cut. First, contact colleges you're considering and see which test they will accept. If the college will accept either or doesn't require a writing score from the SAT II Writing, then my advice is this: Try the old version in the fall of 2004 and if you aren't happy with your score, take the new version of the test in the spring of 2005.

### What year in high school should a student take the SAT?

The advice of perfect score students on this is crystal clear. Students should not take the SAT before their junior year. The only exception is those students who need the SAT to apply to a gifted program. Often these students need to take the test in seventh grade in order to be eligible to participate.

### What kind of preparation is best?

This is a $1,000 question. Should you spend upward of $800 to take a Kaplan or Princeton Review course, to hire a private tutor, or to take a review course offered at the local high school? Or should you spend $50 to buy a computer program and some review books? It all depends on how you learn best and how much preparation you need. Some perfect score students took a Kaplan or Princeton Review course. Some just bought a review book. Others merely read the instructions and took one practice test. Regardless, one thing is clear. Do something! One of the biggest differences between those who did extremely well on the SAT and those who didn't is whether or not they did some preparation.

### Can studying improve SAT scores?

Absolutely. Even the College Board, which has long argued that the test is not coachable, now admits that, on average, students' scores go up 20 to 30 points each time they take the test. The private review companies usually guarantee a certain increase, up to 200 points, if you follow their programs.

### Should I retake the SAT if I don't get the score I want? How do colleges view multiple attempts?

You should definitely retake the SAT if your score is not what it needs to be to get into the college of your choice. Most schools will look at your best score. This does not mean you should take the SAT a dozen times. Two or three attempts should be enough. Also, be realistic. One mother told me her daughter scored 1050 and wanted to go to a school with average SAT scores of 1200. Her daughter had been to three review courses, memorized 2000 vocabulary words and studied math with a private tutor. After three attempts, she still couldn't raise her score above 1050. Her mother asked what her daughter should do next and I replied, "get a life." The SAT is a means to an end and should not become an obsession. The mother wasn't happy, but I'm sure her daughter appreciated my advice.

### What should I do if the SAT is in two weeks and I'm just starting to prepare?

Don't give up, and don't stress out. Even if you have only two weeks to go, you still have time to read the exam instructions, take a practice test, and review an SAT prep book. If you spend only five hours preparing—think of it as one night out with your friends—your score will definitely improve.

Perfect score students teach us two important life lessons. First, parents, students, and educators control their own destiny. Students who ace the SAT are far more than great test takers. They are hard workers who are focused, self-motivated, and passionate. Failing students, parents, and schools need to look in the mirror at themselves. Like the cartoon character Pogo once said, "We have met the enemy and he is us." The second lesson is that success is so much more than doing well on the SAT. Success in life is about finding a passion and pursuing it. Perfect score students don't obsess over SAT scores or grades. They would rather spend their time talking endlessly about their passions and interests, whether these passions are the piano, baseball, string theory, or volunteer work. Those are the ultimate lessons from this study, the keys to creating success not only on the SAT but in college and in life.

—*Tom Fischgrund, Ph.D., September 2004*

# Introduction

It's every parent's dream: to have a child who scores a perfect score on the SAT. But even at our most conscientious and optimistic, we know the chances must be pretty slim. Sure, we all know kids who've scored in the 1400s and 1500s. But a perfect score? How often does *that* happen?

Actually, every year a handful of students do manage to achieve this extraordinary academic feat. In the year 2000, 2.3 million students took the SAT, and 1.5 million of these were college-bound seniors. Of these seniors, just 541 of them got a perfect score of 1600. That's 0.03 percent of the seniors tested, or three students out of every ten thousand—a minute percentage. What are these students like? Are they natural prodigies? Are they total nerds, who spend their childhoods chained to their desks? What kind of trade-offs do they have to make in order to make the grade?

In short, the SAT has been a preoccupation of parents and students alike for decades. But no one has ever come close to cracking the secrets of perfect score success—until now.

*SAT Perfect Score* reveals the results of the first comprehensive survey of students who have achieved the Holy Grail of college-bound kids everywhere: perfect 800s on both the verbal and the math portions of the SAT, the nation's gold standard for college applications. At its core is the Perfect Score Study, the first of its kind to look at the highest academic achievers in the United States. The study offers an in-depth analysis of who these top-notch students are, how they think, what they do, and what they aspire to. It dispels the myths and preconceptions many of us share about these high academic achievers. And it answers the question that ambitious high school students and their parents ask every year:

*What does it take to get a great SAT score?*

We all grew up taking the SAT. It was a rite of passage. Thirty years ago, it helped determine where I applied to college (Williams, Tufts, and Hamilton) and where I got in (Tufts and Hamilton). Back then I took the test twice, and on my second attempt I scored a satisfying 1320. And I remember keenly how important these scores were made to seem. The administrators in my school district boasted constantly of how high our scores were, reminding us all that they were a reflection of the education the students were receiving. Plenty of things have changed in our culture since those days, but the importance of the SAT has only grown. Parents today are more likely to start thinking about the SAT when their kids are in grade school than they are to wait until the eleventh hour.

When the oldest of my three children entered high school, all of my memories of the SAT flooded back—along with new concerns for my kids. I wanted them all to do well on the SAT, for the same reasons I want them to do well in school: so that they'd have the best possible chance to succeed in life. I began to wonder: Was there anything they could be doing to better their chances? Was there anything *I* could be doing as a parent to help? Or was it all a big crapshoot, as it often seemed?

Then I learned that the son of a friend of mine had scored 1600 on the SAT. And a light went off in my head. By studying this boy, I thought, perhaps I could gain a little insight into what it takes to achieve that level of academic success. My mind filled with questions: *Who is this kid? Is he naturally brilliant, or did he study his pants off? Did his parents push him excessively, or did he do it all on his own?*

As a former educator, I had always been fascinated with the best and the brightest. As the author of a number of guidebooks to top business schools and top colleges, and as an executive recruiter, I was interested in how to identify talented and promising young men and women. And now, with my children's future before me, I had a practical reason to learn more.

What I learned was surprising, thought provoking, and inspiring. The students who score 1600, it turns out aren't obsessed about academics. They don't sacrifice their social lives, or their happiness, in an all-out drive to reach 1600. In fact, it turns out, that the kids who do best on the SAT are the kids who do best across the board—in school, in social circles, in pursuing their dreams and passions. And there's every reason to suspect that they're the kids who will do best in life.

The Perfect Score Study could not have been completed without the full cooperation of the College Board, the organization that administers the SAT. When I first conceived of the study, I approached the Board—with more brashness than hope—and asked whether they would be willing to supply a list of students who had scored 1600 that year. They turned down that request, citing their policy of protecting the confidentiality of the students. To my excitement and relief, though, they offered to send out a letter on my behalf, asking each of the perfect-scoring students to contact me if they were interested in participating in such a study.

I ended up interviewing 160 students, or one out of every three seniors who scored 1600 that year. I also spoke with many parents of the perfect score students. And, finally, I looked extensively at data concerning the 2.3 million students who took the exam each year—statistical information collected by the board, and a more focused survey of average-scoring students conducted for this study.

## WHAT I WAS LOOKING FOR

At the most basic level, I wanted to understand the academic habits of these bright students. How many times did they take the SAT?

How long did they study for them? What kind of preparation did they do? I also wanted to understand what kind of education they had received. Did they go to public or private school? How many kids were in their class? How many hours did they spend studying? What courses did they take? And I wanted to learn more about their families and family life: Were their families wealthy? Were their mothers and fathers professionals? How smart were their brothers and sisters? What did they do growing up?

On a second level, I wanted to understand who these students were as individuals. How would they describe themselves? What were their likes and dislikes? What were their sources of motivation and inspiration? I wanted to get to know them as real-life people, not just a collection of statistics and exam scores.

Finally, I wanted to know what made them successful. Was there something special about their upbringing? Did they all pursue the same activities growing up? Did their parents interact with them in special ways? Were there any inherent traits that enabled them to achieve their score? I also was interested in looking at whether they shared common habits. Did they all read a set number of hours per night? How many hours of TV did they watch? What did they do with friends? How were they different from the average academic achievers? Did they study more or less? Were they more interested in certain subjects? Were they equally adept in all academic areas?

And I knew the study wouldn't be complete until I could talk with their parents, to see what they had to say about their children's achievement. Was it expected? Was it celebrated? What did they feel they had to do with it? What advice would they give other parents?

## WHAT I FOUND

The findings of the Perfect Score Study were surprising. They challenged the common beliefs of countless parents, students, and educators who think that spending untold hours studying and preparing for the SAT will improve academic performance. The study uncovered a different view of how to succeed academically. Succeeding on the SAT is not a short-term approach but takes a lifetime approach to learning. It refutes the notion that academic achievement is grounded solely in practice tests and prep courses. It is based on what real kids in the real world—and their parents—have to tell us about stimulating academic performance. As hundreds of perfect score students show us, true academic achievement goes far beyond memorizing hundreds of vocabulary words or practicing math problems ad infinitum.

The Perfect Score Study identified some specific traits that you would expect to find in high academic achievers. Students who scored a 1600 on the SAT typically spend several more hours a week reading than those who get an average SAT score. The students with perfect scores spend less time watching TV than their average-scoring counterparts, and are less likely to have a part-time job.

But the study also revealed some myth-shattering information about those who ace the SAT. No more than a handful of them (less than 5 percent) describe themselves as brainy kids who are focused solely on academics. These young men and women don't spend every waking hour studying, nor do they speak in quadratic equations. They don't lie awake at night obsessing about what they are going to get on the SAT. In fact, most of them put the SAT in perspective, recognizing the importance of the test but realizing it's not the defining moment of their lives.

What's more, the vast majority of perfect score students participate in multiple activities outside of the academic realm. They pursue these endeavors with passion and won't settle for halfhearted attempts to learn a new skill. Instead, they go all out to master their passion, whether it's playing tennis, performing in theater, or learning the oboe. They also tend to focus on one or two extracurricular activities rather than a smattering of six or seven. They are less interested in making a long list of the various clubs they participated in for a college application than they are in describing how their passions define them.

Perfect score students tend to be leaders, not followers. If they paint scenery for the school play, they're likely to be the stage manager. If they're in the orchestra, they're likely to be first chair in whatever section they play in. If they're active in the honor society or student council, they're more inclined to hold a leadership position, such as president or vice president.

## THE IMPORTANCE OF PARENTS AND FRIENDS

Some of the perfect score students described themselves as belonging to the in-crowd, but the bulk of these students said they gravitate toward kids who have similar interests. Regardless of whether they are part of the cool group or are just part of the masses, all of these students said they had friends, and that they relied on their friends for emotional support throughout high school.

Friendships, of course, can take you only so far. These perfect score students don't rely on their friends for academic motivation. Nor do they rely on their parents. Whom do they rely on? A whopping 90 percent of these students rely on themselves, according to the Perfect Score Study. They weren't pushed by their parents or teachers to overachieve. Their drive comes from within. They have their own will to succeed, and they achieve for themselves, not for anyone else. What's fascinating, though, is that perfect score students weren't necessarily born with this self-motivation. Perfect score students nearly all agreed that their parents motivated them to learn in their early years and then gave them the tools to motivate themselves through high school.

In delving into the lives of students who scored 1600, the Perfect Score Study actually uncovered beneficial ways that parents can shape their child's ability to learn. While it's true that some children are more naturally motivated to learn than others, parents play an instrumental role in fostering this motivation in their child.

Perfect score student Josh G.'s mother described her parenting philosophy this way: "My husband and I were strong role models for our children, and we provided a lot of family time. We valued a sense of calm; family meals were important. We took a monthlong vacation every year and went to places like the Galápagos Islands and Australia. We did a lot that was educationally oriented, but not necessarily outwardly so. We had a strong commitment in our relationship with each other."

But Josh's mother gives her son full credit for achieving his full academic potential: "When it comes to doing so well on the SAT, first and foremost, it was all Josh's doing. He's passionate about living, and he's an avid reader. Josh always strives to do his best job. He had excellent schooling and good role models, not to mention good friendships. He had a solid ground from which to flower."

## HOW EVERY STUDENT CAN BENEFIT FROM THE PERFECT SCORE STUDY

Many of us assume that academic performance is in the genes—that brilliant children are born that way. Albert Einstein was born a genius; the average pro athlete may be equally gifted, but in a different way. Scientifically speaking, genes do play a role in determining our intelligence. They set the potential for what we can achieve and determine our likelihood for excelling in specific areas. I'm sure Einstein would have dreaded a game of one-on-one against Michael Jordan, just as Jordan might dread sitting through a course on quantum mechanics.

So while genes do play some role in determining how well students perform in school, on the SAT, and in life, they only provide the raw potential. Students who ace the SAT are able to take their natural potential and make the most of it. They actively seek out friendships, and participate in clubs, in sports, and in life. The Perfect Score Study is the first study of its kind to put to rest the myth that supersmart students can't be socially successful.

Yes, students who ace the SAT tend to have high grades and rank at or near the top of their class. Yes, these students go on to top colleges. Most parents want their kids to excel academically, but not at the expense of having friends or a date to the prom. They want their kids to be socially accepted by their peers as much as they want them to be near the top of their class. They know that to succeed in the real world, their kids have to be both.

In fact, the Perfect Score Study found this to be true for the SAT as well. Students who aced the SAT overwhelmingly showed both academic smarts and social adeptness. Students who lock themselves in their rooms studying encyclopedias day after day just aren't likely to ace the SAT. Nor will those who forgo their schoolwork to spend all their time hanging out at the mall with friends. The secret to acing the SATs lies in finding the proper balance in life, a balance between studying and socializing, between reading and sports, between seeking the advice of friends and seeking the counsel of parents. Students who score 1600 on the SAT have managed to find this balance in their lives. All students, no matter what their academic potential, can find this balance as well. This book will show them how.

## MY PERSONAL INTEREST IN PERFECT SCORE STUDENTS

While I was doing this research on perfect score students, I realized that what I was learning might be of real use to my own kids. When my younger son Sam entered high school, I knew he was bright and had a lot of potential for academic success. Sam applied himself, studied as much as he thought he needed to, and achieved a high grade-point average, ranking near the top of his class. Yet, if you asked Sam to recall some important events from his high school years, he'd probably mention a roller hockey game, or a big date he had with some girl he had a crush on. Sam didn't let his academics get in the way of his social life.

I had just finished analyzing the results when Sam was preparing to take the SAT. I wanted to see if I could apply some of the secrets of perfect score students I had learned from this study to help my son achieve a higher score.

The first thing I did was take a step back. I didn't want to put too much pressure on my son to study and take practice exams. Too much nudging from me might backfire and turn Sam off the whole process. So instead I just provided Sam with a handful of practical suggestions. He took some and ignored others. When he told me he had prepared enough, at first I balked and told him he needed more prep time, but then I decided to trust him and allow him to be his own guide. In effect, I had to shift to a lower gear to model myself after the perfect score parents I had talked with. I was a little nervous about giving up some control, but I knew that Sam had to use his own best judgment.

In the end, I saw that Sam knew best when it came to what Sam knew for the SAT. He took the SAT in the spring of his junior year, and scored a 1560. Sam was pleased. I was ecstatic. I learned a lot from Sam.

The lessons to be learned from the Perfect Score Study are really applicable to all parents—regardless of a child's academic potential. In fact, I wish I had known them earlier in my children's lives, when they were just beginning elementary school. After completing my study and showing it to some research and marketing experts for review, I concluded that parents and students throughout the country could learn something from the stellar students who achieved a perfect SAT score.

Doing well on the SAT, achieving good grades, and being happy and successful in high school are neither easy nor intuitive. This study provides insight and direction to help students and parents alike navigate through this difficult time. If it changes the way we act and in some way improves either our academic performance or the quality of our lives, this book will have provided a valuable service.

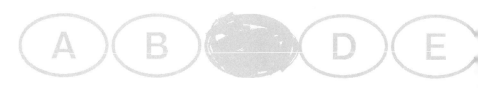

# PART I

The Perfect Score
Next Door

# What Does It Take to Get a Perfect Score?

On a given Saturday seven times throughout the year, 330,000 high school students will wake up after what we hope was a good night's sleep. Some will be able to swallow their breakfast; others won't. With two no. 2 pencils and a calculator in hand, they will head off to one of the test centers. After months of practice and in some cases thousands of dollars spent on Kaplan or Princeton Review prep courses, it will all come down to three hours of intense test taking. Then they and their parents will spend weeks waiting nervously for the results—results that, like it or not, bear massive importance in determining the academic fates of college-bound American students today.

Only 541 college-bound seniors achieved a perfect SAT score in 2000. Just 587 seniors performed this feat in 2001, and 615 seniors in 2002. With a million and a half seniors taking the SATs each year, it's remarkable that the number of students who obtain a perfect score doesn't vary much from year to year. The test is designed to ensure that nearly all students make a number of mistakes—all but those exceptional few.

Getting a high score on the SAT has always been a key goal of most college-bound high school students. But today it's even more important than ever before. The number of students applying to colleges is at a record high, and this larger pool of students must compete with one another for the same number of admission slots.

As a result of this increased competition, colleges have raised their standards for admission, including raising the average SAT scores for incoming students. Over the past ten years, New York University raised its SAT requirements from an average score of 1190 to an average score of 1334. Harvard raised its average SAT requirements from 1370 to 1485. And Yale University raised its requirements from 1365 to 1450. These scores are based on the current 1600 maximum score. With the new SAT, colleges will adjust these scores upward to reflect the new writing section and the overall maximum score of 2400.

State colleges have also become more demanding. Unable to shell out $25,000 a year for private college tuition, thousands of high school students have been turning to state-funded schools. As a result, these schools have experienced a huge increase in applicants in recent years and have also increased their admission requirements. A decade or two ago, achieving a decent SAT score was important but not necessarily vital to earning admission to many state universities and other "second-tier" schools. Now many students are finding themselves closed out of these schools if they don't meet the more stringent admission requirements.

Yes, it's true that a new curve system instituted in 1995 has caused SAT scores to rise by an average of 50 to 100 points, but this still doesn't account for the entire increase in SAT score requirements. Today's high school students have to increase their efforts to excel academically if they want to get into the college of their choice.

Results from the Perfect Score Study suggest that doing well on the SAT isn't all about what kind of prep work a student does. In fact, investing in private SAT tutors or spending a small fortune on an SAT review course isn't necessary to get a perfect score. (Only a handful of perfect score students used these methods.) And although taking practice exams and memorizing vocabulary words can be excellent ways to improve an SAT score, they comprise just a small part of most perfect score students' preparation.

In fact, the results of the Perfect Score Study turn the idea of SAT preparation on its head. Instead of cramming for the SAT two or three months before the test, perfect score students come by their learning naturally through a strong foundation laid by their parents. This foundation enables these students to learn to the best of their abilities. When it comes time to take the SAT, these students then draw on the vocabulary they absorbed from reading extensively. They might memorize additional vocabulary words, but that's just a supplemental part of their SAT preparation.

So who is the perfect score student?

If you saw seventeen-year-old Susan D., from South Peoria, Illinois, walking down the street, you would probably say she looks like an all-American girl. She has long, shiny brown hair, freckles splattered across her nose, and brown eyes that sparkle with intelligence. In high school, she did the ordinary kinds of things that most girls her age do—hanging out with her friends, performing in plays at her small high school, and surfing on her computer. But she also participated in some activities that were more exceptional: heading up her school's Model UN, playing violin in the all-state orchestra, and working four hours a week with residents of a nursing home near where she lived. "The work in the nursing home was probably the most interesting thing I've ever done," Susan says about working with the elderly. "I learned a lot from just listening to those folks—just asking questions about their lives."

What defines Susan most is her thirst for knowledge. "I'm an extremely curious person who loves seeking out information about the world," she says. "I'm constantly searching to understand myself, those around me, and my place in the universe. I'm someone who is always striving to be the person I want to be, whoever that is."

Susan's curiosity helped her accomplish an extraordinary feat: she got a perfect score on the SAT. She's now attending Harvard, where she continues to feed her curiosity and explore those interests that excite her most.

Two things stand out about Susan: how bright and multidimensional she is, and how similar she is to other students who scored 1600. Always searching. Always learning. This insatiable curiosity and engagement with the world—not just with academics—define Susan and the 540 other students who aced the SAT in 2000.

## CONDUCTING THE PERFECT SCORE STUDY

The most indispensable step in conducting the Perfect Score Study was obtaining the names and contact information for those students who scored a 1600 on the SAT. The first step was the College Board's agreement to forward my letter to all 541 students who achieved a perfect score on the SAT in 2000. Equally important, though, was their offer to forward a letter from me to 3,000 randomly selected students who scored between 1000 and 1200 on the SAT in 2000, which is average to slightly above average. These students would serve as the study's control group, and to provide a basis for comparison they would be asked the same questions as the perfect score group. They represent the "typical" students applying to four-year colleges.

After the letters were sent out, nearly one-third of the perfect score students—160 in total—contacted me and told me they wanted to participate in the Perfect Score Study. About 50 students from the control group also agreed to participate. These are not bad response rates, considering that these students had no incentive—I offered them no money or gift—for responding to my request.

I also requested all the quantitative data that the College Board collected in the survey that all students fill out when applying for the SAT. This survey asked students about the courses they took in high school, what extracurricular activities they engaged in, and what types of colleges they were planning to attend. The College Board provided data from all students who took the SAT that year and the prior three years, including those who scored a 1600. I cross-checked this information with the data I collected to ensure that I had a representative sample of perfect score students and of average-scoring students.

I found that the findings that I got within my sample mirrored the total population of perfect score students and all students who took the SAT. For example, the College Board data indicated that 90 percent of perfect score students maintained an A or A+ grade-point average, compared with 30 percent of the entire group of test takers. The Perfect Score Study measured similar percentages: 90 percent of perfect score students maintained at least an A average compared with 50 percent of the control group. (This higher percentage for the control group reflects the fact that this group was composed of average to above average students.)

The College Board data also verified that the Perfect Score Study included an adequate cross section of students who took the SAT in terms of gender, socioeconomic class, ethnicity, and locale. A sample that was overwhelmingly tilted toward, say, boys from the Northeast who went to private schools would have built a bias into the study.

The Perfect Score Study was conducted by doing phone interviews with both the perfect score students and the control group of students. A handful of perfect score students who lived in the Atlanta area were interviewed in person. The study participants were asked a fixed set of questions—both open-ended and yes/no type questions. None of the students was paid to participate, and all were assured privacy and confidentiality. To protect these students' identities, the names and residences of the students have been changed in this book. All quotes and other descriptions of the students, however, are real and taken directly from the interview notes.

About a dozen marketing researchers from Fortune 500 companies such as Coca-Cola and Kodak were consulted on the composition of the questionnaire and the research methodology. They also provided advice on how to phrase the questions to ensure that they would elicit truthful answers and not the answers the participants thought we were looking for.

Here's a sampling of some of the questions that were asked on the eight-page questionnaire:

1. How would you describe yourself in three sentences?
2. What kind of preparation did you do for the SAT, and how many times did you take the exam?
3. How important is the SAT to you?
4. What is your passion? What excites you to get up in the morning?
5. Who provides the greatest motivation? Parents, teachers, self? Who inspires you?
6. Are you involved in sports?
7. Are you involved in music? What instruments do you play, and how proficiently?
8. How popular are you on a scale of 1–7 (1 = very popular, 7 = very unpopular)?
9. How would you characterize yourself? (check all that apply): in-crowd, all-around, average, geek, loner, brain, athlete, social, artsy.
10. Do or did you have a girlfriend or boyfriend? How long did the relationship last?
11. What extracurricular activities did you participate in?
12. What do your parents do for a living?
13. If you have any siblings who took the SATs, what did they score?
14. What was your socioeconomic status growing up?
15. What do you do for fun?

In addition to interviewing perfect score students, we interviewed 50 students in the control group. We also spoke with about 35 parents of perfect score students, who were contacted at random, to corroborate the students' answers and to ascertain that the information from the students was accurate—from how much a student really studied and whether she was really first-chair violin in the state orchestra. The parents also added some depth to their child's answers about how self-motivated they were and what the family support system was like.

Overall, more than 500 hours of interviews were collected for the Perfect Score Study. After spending six months interviewing students and an additional six months analyzing the results from my interviews, I found certain differences beginning to emerge. I hired a marketing researcher to conduct a statistical analysis on all the Perfect Score data to determine which differences among the perfect score students and the control group were statistically significant. In some categories, the differences between the perfect score students and the average score students were slight or virtually indistinguishable—not statistically significant. In other areas, large differences existed between the responses of the perfect score group and the responses of their control group counterparts. Here are a few of the more surprising statistics that came from the study:

- Perfect score students on average spend 10 hours per week studying, which is no more than the control group of students.

- Not one perfect score student cited extensive test prep in junior high as a key factor in his or her success.

- The average class size of perfect score students is 23, which is close to the national average—not the 12 to 14-student size typically found in private schools.

- 80 percent of perfect score students went to public high school, compared with 92 percent of all U.S. high school students; one might expect an even higher percentage of perfect score students from small, elite prep schools.

- Only one percent of perfect score students are homeschooled, which is even less than the national average.

- 90 percent of perfect score students come from intact as opposed to divorced families, compared with 66 percent of all U.S. high school students who come from intact families.

But the Perfect Score Study is far more than a set of statistics. It's about real kids in the United States who have poignant stories that often belie their talented academic accomplishments. Most of these kids place far more value on their relationships with their family and friends than on the numbers on their transcript. Nearly all spent more time talking to me about their social life and school activities than about how they prepared for the SAT. In fact, I was told over and over that the SAT was just one stepping-stone on the path to their goals. It was the means, not the end.

Bob D. is just one example of a perfect score student who has a well-rounded view on life. Growing up in a small town in the Midwest, Bob is a National Merit Scholar who plays in five different bands and studies eight hours a week. With his perfect score and stellar grades, he got into all four of the colleges he applied to. His dream? To be an astronaut. Bob worked hard to do well on the SAT, but he keeps it in perspective. "I like to laugh," he told me. "I told myself I was going to have fun with the test. I think that's why I did so well."

Grace W., an immigrant from China, took the SAT five times before she aced it. But the SAT was certainly not the sum and substance of her high school life. She participated in fifteen different clubs, spent more time with friends than studying, and ended up class valedictorian. What's incredible is that both Grace and her parents learned English as a second language. "I guess I never took English for granted," she told me, chuckling. "I had to come at language from a fresh perspective."

## HOW THE SAT BECAME A NATIONAL OBSESSION

The SAT is the nation's oldest, most widely used college entrance exam. More than 60 million people in the United States have taken the SAT since its inception in 1926. Each year, another 2.3 million students take the test. Approximately 80 percent of colleges use the

SAT in college admissions. Other programs, such as the government-sponsored Presidential Scholars Program, also use the SAT to grant scholarships to applicants.

The idea of the SAT—which originally stood for "Scholastic Aptitude Test"—came from Army Mental Tests that were administered to test intelligence or IQ in soldiers. Only 8,040 students (nearly all of them white males) took the first SAT when it was first administered by the College Board. The number of test takers remained small for more than thirty years. Eventually, though, many top colleges began to rely on IQ tests for admission, as study after study showed that those with the lowest intelligence scores had the highest dropout rates from colleges.

The SAT slowly began to replace the IQ test as colleges looked for a nationwide standardized test that they could use to draw in students from a larger area of the country. As more institutions began requiring the exam for admission, the SAT grew in popularity. In 1959, more than half a million students took the exam.

The SAT was designed to measure not how much students knew from high school subject matter, but how effectively they learned. From the beginning, the College Board sidestepped the controversy of whether the SAT actually measured general intelligence. College Board administrators instead focused on the test's capacity to predict academic success.

Although the SAT has been accused of being biased against minorities and poorer students, it actually came into existence to try to wipe away these inequalities. Unlike college admissions officers, who can discriminate by race, religion, or class, the SAT is blind to these distinctions. It was instituted to expand educational access to those academically capable students who couldn't afford the right prep school or who were the first in their families to apply to college. Before the SAT, entrance to elite colleges had been based upon class, family status, and financial means. So the SAT was originally designed to increase, not limit, opportunity.

## INTRODUCING THE NEW SAT

Beginning in March 2005, for the high school graduating class of 2006, three major changes on the SAT will be instituted. The SAT will now be composed of three sections: critical reading (formerly called verbal), math, and a new section called writing. Each section will be scored on a 200- to 800-point scale. This means the maximum score of 1600 will now rise to 2400. Likewise, the minimum score will rise from 400 to 600.

Total testing time will increase from three hours to three hours and forty-five minutes; both the new and old testing times include the thirty-minute experimental section, which is not scored. The College Board contends that the new SAT will be different, though not necessarily harder. It will contain a few math questions from the Algebra II curriculum as well as a written essay. It will, however, still measure reasoning ability and problem-solving skills gained through activities and educational learning both in the classroom and outside of it.

The biggest change on the new SAT is the inclusion of the writing section. This section includes thirty-five minutes of multiple choice questions and twenty-five minutes for a written essay. The multiple choice questions will test students' knowledge of grammar, usage, and word choice. These questions, similar to those found on the SAT II, are designed to see how well students use standard written English. The essay will ask students to take a position on an issue and support it persuasively with examples from their studies and experience. It will be open-ended, so students can answer it correctly in many different ways.

The essay will be scored by high school and college teachers on a scale of 0 to 6. A perfect score of 6 (equivalent to 800 points) will be

## SUMMARY OF MAJOR CHANGES TO THE SATS FOR THE CLASS OF 2006

| Section | Current | Revised |
|---|---|---|
| Writing | None | • 25-minute essay<br>• 35-minute multiple-choice grammar questions<br>• Score Range: 200–800 |
| Mathematics | • 75-minute multiple-choice questions<br>• Number and Operations; Algebra I and Functions; Geometry; Statistics; Probability; Data Analysis<br>• Score Range: 200–800 | • 70-minute multiple-choice questions<br>• Same content as current test with addition of Algebra II questions<br>• Qualitative Comparisons dropped<br>• Score Range: 200–800 |
| Verbal | • 75-minute multiple-choice questions<br>• Sentence completion; Critical reading: long reading passages; Analogies<br>• Score Range: 200–800 | • 70-minute multiple-choice questions<br>• Sentence completion; Critical reading: short and long reading passages<br>• Analogies dropped<br>• Score Range: 200–800 |
| Test Length | 3 hours | 3 hours 45 minutes |
| Cost | $26 | $36-$38 |
| Top Score | 1600 | 2400 |
| Feedback | None | Feature to provide feedback on skills that need improvement |

given for an outstanding submission that demonstrates clear and consistent mastery of the topic and with few grammatical errors. A score of 0 will be given only for an essay that is not written on the assignment. Graders will be given a set of guidelines for scoring, but they may have to use their subjective judgment to differentiate, say, a 4 score (defined as "competent demonstrating adequate mastery") from a 5 score (defined as "effective demonstrating reasonably consistent mastery"). Some critics contend that this may compromise the objectivity of the SAT if one reader grades with more strictness than another.

Since the writing section is new, colleges may take some time before deciding how to weigh the writing score into their admissions decisions. Some schools may decide to weigh it as heavily as the math and critical reading (verbal) sections, while others may use the writing scores for research purposes only for the first few years. A college will be able to view the essay along with the rest of the SAT score.

The critical reading (verbal) section will include short reading passages along with the existing long reading passages. At least one passage from a work of fiction will be included. The analogy section will be eliminated, but sentence-completion questions will remain.

The new SAT will also include expanded math topics such as exponential growth, absolute value, and functional notation. It will span three years of high school math including Algebra I, Geometry, and Algebra II. The current test only includes Arithmetic, Algebra I, and Geometry. The new test will also place a greater emphasis on linear functions, manipulations with exponents, and properties of tangent lines. Quantitative comparison questions will be eliminated. Students will still be allowed to use calculators for the test.

In both the traditional and new versions of the SAT, the test is designed to be speeded, which means that many test takers won't be able to complete all the questions. The new test will continue to contain a thirty-minute experimental section. This is not scored, but students aren't told which section is the experimental one. The order of the math and English sections varies by testing date, and the experimental section may come from any of the sections. Because the "bugs" have not yet been worked out of the experimental section—test takers are used to identify these problems—it is often more difficult and confusing than the other sections.

SAT question writers gather each day at the Educational Testing Service near Princeton, New Jersey, to draft items that will determine the fate of college-bound students worldwide. This group is made up of teachers, school administrators, and other professionals. The 60 math and 78 verbal questions get progressively more difficult in each section. The questions are crafted to test aptitude, rather than the retention of rote facts.

Many topics are off limits for question writers, including abortion, divorce, drinking, drugs, date rape, terrorism, and parents dying of cancer. "Sometimes even topics that seem innocuous can cause problems. A narrative reflecting on the value of old trees was dropped after a complaint from a logger in Montana, who said that because he had recently received death threats from eco-terrorists, his daughter burst into tears upon reading the passage and could not complete the test," according to a 2002 article in the New York Times.

Given that the SAT is administered up to twenty times a year, a vast number of questions are needed—up to 1,500 per year. The development of this broad range of questions is a lengthy and complicated process. A single question may be reviewed as many as six to eight times by various committees and may take eighteen months to make its way to an actual SAT exam. A group of academics, nonacademics, and students from around the country review the questions to see if any are offensive. Mentions of Hitler and the Holocaust are two examples of forbidden topics that have been deemed to be too upsetting to the majority of people and even more so to specific groups. "Anything that stereotypes a certain race, religion, sex, or ethnic group is *verboten*. Birth control, abortion, evolution, gun control, and experimentation on animals are out as well—too controversial," according to a 2001 article in the Los Angeles Times.

Other items may be eliminated under a second fairness review that looks to see if a question might be inherently more difficult for a student of a particular gender, race, or ethnic background to answer. For instance, one test item used the word *obliterate*. Females who scored similarly to males on the SAT as a whole missed that item frequently, while the males did not. The item-making gurus determined that males are more accustomed to warlike and weapons-oriented words—perhaps because they're more inclined than females to play strategic video games. For this reason, males were predisposed to know what *obliterate* meant. *Obliterate* was, thus, obliterated from the SAT.

## WHAT DOES AN SAT SCORE REALLY MEAN?

The new SAT is more closely aligned with high school curricula. Scores don't reflect the exact number of right and wrong answers but are converted into a range from 200 to 800 points; total SAT scores range from 400 to 1600 points. They will soon range from 600 to 2400 points. This huge number of points, however, actually represents a much smaller range of correct or incorrect answers. For the current math and critical reading (verbal) sections, a difference of one correct or incorrect answer in the middle of the SAT range will generate about 10 points of difference in the SAT scale score. At the top of the range, two or three missed questions cost 50 points, resulting in a 750 rather than an 800.

The SAT scoring system was originally designed so that the median score would fall at or near the 500 mark for both math and verbal, to yield a combined average score of 1000—meaning that half of students got above 1000 and half got below that score. The College Board felt this would offer an easy benchmark to help measure which students were at or near the fiftieth percentile of students and which fell above and below that middle mark.

From the 1960s onward, SAT scores fell steadily, probably because a larger pool of average and below-average high school students were taking the SATs and applying to colleges. In 1994, the median SAT score was 910, with a 428 median score for verbal and a 482 median score for math.

The following year College Board administrators decided to shift

SAT scores back up to reflect 1000 as the middle mark. As a result of this new curve, most verbal scores were raised 60 to 80 points, while math scores were increased approximately 20 to 30 points. This new curve enables the College Board, researchers, and students to look at an SAT score and more easily determine where it falls in the spectrum of SAT scores.

Most high school seniors know their SAT scores off the top of their heads and know the test is a critical factor in determining which colleges to apply to and which ones will accept them. Even many years later, people still remember their SAT scores. For example, President George W. Bush recalled in a *Time* magazine news article that his score was 1206. Author Stephen King reported he got in the 1300s, while talk-show host and money wizard Ben Stein said his score was 1573. Our SAT scores are etched into our permanent psyche, forever associated with how bright we are and how well we did in school. This may be because the SAT has replaced the IQ test as a means to measure our intellectual abilities. It gives us a finite number that we can use to compare ourselves against our peers.

With all the hype over the importance of the SAT, we shouldn't be too surprised that there are some academic critics who have raised a rallying cry against the test. Some critics complain that the SAT is not a good measure of academic achievement. They contend that the SAT discriminates against African Americans, Hispanics, women, and poor people and is biased in favor of white males and Asians. These complaints are based on College Board statistics collected in 2001, which show that African Americans have an average combined SAT score of 859—almost 200 points lower than white males, who average 1060. Hispanics scored an average of between 908 to 925, depending on their ancestry. Women scored an average of 1000. Asians, on the other hand, had an average score of 1067.

Critics also claim the SAT is biased against poor people, since scores are correlated with income: the higher the income, the higher the score. According to 2001 data from the College Board, students from families earning less than $30,000 a year scored an average of

900. Those whose family income is between $30,000 and $70,000 averaged 1007, and those from families with incomes above $100,000 reported average scores of 1126.

Others assert that the SAT is limited in that it only assesses English and math skills. The test fails to measure other types of achievement, such as leadership, interpersonal skills, and musical talent, to name just a few. Fair Test, a grassroots organization that advocates for "fair and open testing," calls the SAT "this nation's oldest, most widely used—and misused—college entrance exam." This position had been given credence by the president of the University of California, Richard Atkinson, who recommended a few years ago that the University of California system (which has 138,000 students) stop requiring the SAT for admission. He said he favored a "comprehensive, holistic approach." In a speech delivered at the 2001 American Council on Education meeting in Washington, D.C., Atkinson said he favored the SAT II tests (formerly called Achievement Tests) over the SAT because the SAT II "focuses student attention on the mastery of subject matter rather than test preparation, and will help all students, especially low-income and minority students, determine their own educational destinies."

The new SAT clearly addresses Atkinson's concerns: It is designed to better align the SAT with high school curricula, nudging the SAT closer to achievement testing. The new test recognizes writing as a critical skill and eliminates reasoning sections on quantitative comparisons (math) and analogies (verbal), skills that generally are not taught in high school. The math section is more challenging but closer to the material taught to 97 percent of high school students who take the SAT.

Academic leaders have, by and large, reacted positively to these new changes. Atkinson stated that he was pleased that the revised test is better aligned with high school curricula. Linda Clement, vice president of the University of Maryland at College Park and chair of the College Board trustees, said that the addition of the writing test "will add great value [since] . . . it sends a loud and clear message that strong writing is essential to success in college and beyond." Admissions directors at Harvard and other institutions pointed out that the writing sample would allow colleges to evaluate writing samples that have not been edited or reviewed by others.

Despite these changes, there still is no one perfect test. I think the way to look at the SAT is similar to what Churchill said of democracy: "It has been said that democracy is the worst form of government except all those other forms that have been tried from time to time." The SAT may be the worst form of testing, but it is the best there is. Any admission test—no matter how well written— is inherently inadequate in some measure.

I believe that some form of standardized admission testing, however, is vital to smooth out the variability that exists in grading among various high schools. Less challenging classes may yield higher grades, and some schools may assign grades on a curve, where others grade solely on test results regardless of how many students get Cs.

The College Board contends that the SAT is an excellent predictor of future college performance, generally defined as a student's first-year college grade-point average. When used in conjunction with a student's high school grade-point average, it provides a more accurate prediction of how well a student will do in college, compared with using just the high school GPA. Most colleges agree with Michael McPherson, president of Macalester College, and Morton Shapiro, president of Williams College, who wrote in a column in the *Atlanta Journal-Constitution* on October 8, 2000: "[The SAT] does a reasonably good job of assessing students' capacities for mathematical and verbal reasoning. These capabilities are surely relevant to success in college and admissions judgments."

## HOW THE SAT REFLECTS ACADEMIC PERFORMANCE

Every so often, I hear about an average student with a 2.8 GPA who manages to score a 1500 or higher on the SAT. Perhaps you know such a student yourself. This raises a fundamental question: are SAT scores really indicative of academic performance? This, of course, leads to the follow-up question: do perfect score students excel academically in school, or are they just great standardized test takers?

Based on the statistics from my study and others, the mediocre student who aces the SAT is definitely the exception, not the norm. College Board data shows that SAT scores are highly correlated with grade-point average (GPA) and with class rank. A significant 72 percent of perfect score students rank in the top ten students of their class, and 98 percent have an A- average or above. You can see from the chart below how GPA and class rank rise with SAT scores.

## CORRELATION OF SAT SCORES WITH HIGH SCHOOL RANK AND GPA

| | 1999–2000 | |
|---|---|---|
| | Verbal Score | Mathematical Score |
| All Students | 505 | 514 |
| **High School Rank** | | |
| Top 10 percent | 589 | 608 |
| Second 10 percent | 528 | 543 |
| Second 20 percent | 493 | 500 |
| Third 20 percent | 455 | 453 |
| Fourth 20 percent | 425 | 419 |
| Bottom 20 percent | 408 | 401 |
| **High School Grade-Point Average** | | |
| A+ (97–100) | 610 | 628 |
| A (93–96) | 567 | 582 |
| A- (90–92) | 540 | 553 |
| B (80–89) | 482 | 486 |
| C (70–79) | 428 | 426 |
| D, E, or F (below 70) | 405 | 406 |

SOURCE: College Entrance Examination Board Report on College Bound Seniors 2000

Perfect score students are also recognized with academic honors. In the Perfect Score Study, these students reported winning an average four national or local honors or awards, including Presidential Scholar, regents scholar awards, National Merit Scholar, state debating championships, keys to their towns, and Bausch and Lomb Science award citations. Although scoring 1600 doesn't guarantee admission to a prestigious college, an impressive 34 percent of perfect score students went to Harvard, Yale, Princeton, or Stanford, according to the Perfect Score Study.

## BUILDING A BETTER STUDENT

In devoting the past three years to conducting the Perfect Score Study and chronicling the findings in this book, I wanted to share with you the insights I gleaned from students who achieved a perfect score on the SAT. I can't promise you that this book will enable you or your child to ace the SAT. But I do think that the secrets shared by perfect score students can help anyone become a better student by fulfilling his or her individual potential for learning.

Are the students who scored 1600 on the current version of the test just as likely to score 2400 on the new version when it is adopted in 2005? The answer is unequivocally yes. All of the perfect score students have good verbal reasoning skills. Nearly all are in the top 10 percent of their class, which reflects their performance in all subject areas. Since the new SAT test more closely approximates classroom instruction, and since perfect score students do extremely well in school, it would be hard to imagine that they would not achieve stellar results on the new version of the test.

Students can transform themselves by adopting an entirely new approach to learning—one that encompasses what I call the 7 Secrets of perfect score students. For instance, perfect score students approach their schoolwork, sports teams, and clubs with a sense of curiosity and anticipation. They maintain the philosophy of "live life to the fullest" and turn one or two interests into their life's passion.

Most of all, they have a sense of responsibility to themselves and the world at large. They want to give back to the world and know they need to excel in school in order to accomplish their vision.

And perfect score students don't live in a bubble. They have strong relationships with their family and friends and consider these relationships to be a high priority in their lives. They know how to rely on their parents for support without allowing them to dictate how and when they will study. And they spend time going to the movies and talking on the phone with friends, but not at the expense of their school assignments. In juggling their academics, extracurricular activities, and social lives, these high achievers have managed to strike a balance that works for them.

The best news is that the secrets that make perfect score students successful are easily attainable. *Any student can follow these 7 Secrets and use them to create success.*

I want to make clear that this book addresses larger issues of educational achievement, not specific SAT questions. The College Board, Kaplan, Princeton Review, Peterson, and others offer books filled with SAT questions and study tips. You will not see a single SAT question in this book. *SAT Perfect Score* offers more than a short-term solution to increase grades and SAT scores. It's a lifetime approach. Yes, this approach can be adopted at any point in a student's life. However, parents can expect to achieve the best results from the 7 Secrets if they incorporate them into their child's life earlier rather than later.

This book is really a tool for parents and students who want to see permanent results that will span the full range of academic and social accomplishments. If students can use the 7 Secrets to turn a C average into a B average, that would be quite an accomplishment— just as great as turning an A- average into an A. If students follow the examples of perfect score students and decide to give back to the world—by volunteering at a soup kitchen for instance—this would be another sign of success. The best parents can do is to help their children fulfill the potential they were born with.

One parent of a perfect score student summed it up wisely. She had this to say of her highly accomplished son, who also had an A+ average and scored perfect 5s on all his advanced placement exams: "What I like most about my son is that he is a concerned and caring individual. Sure, he does extraordinarily well academically, and yes, I am extremely proud of him for doing so well. But I am most proud of the humanistic values he embraces. Intelligence without compassion is meaningless. It is his humanism combined with his intelligence that will make him successful." This is at the core of what it takes to be an academic achiever.

## PORTRAIT OF A PERFECT SCORE STUDENT

From the time he could walk, Matthew S. loved taking things apart to see how they worked. In high school, he spent his free time on a website, e-how.com, taking things apart and putting them back together in cyberspace. "I'm very spatially oriented. I want to manipulate things, see how they work, what's going on. That fascinates me," he says.

Always looking for a challenge, Matthew took the hardest science and math classes his high school in Georgia had to offer, including AP courses in calculus, chemistry, and physics. Matthew approached the SAT in the same way—he saw it as a challenge, a puzzle to be solved. The first time he took the exam, he got a 1450. He thought he could do better. He decided to crack the SAT code to find out how the test worked. "I read articles and books about the test. I studied the questions, not the material, but rather the way the questions were phrased and the kinds of answers the College Board was looking for," he says. "I also took a lot of practice tests and began to distinguish between answers that were almost correct and those that were definitely correct." His approach worked: Matthew got a 1600 the second time he took the exam.

Like other perfect score students, however, Matthew is multifaceted. His explorations reach far beyond the realm of math and science. He's an avid reader who always searched around the house for whatever reading material he could get his hands on. "My dad got a subscription to *The New Yorker* and the *Economist,* so that's what I read in high school. I also read the newspaper and occasionally nabbed a book that my mom was reading."

Matthew also sought to make a mark on his high school. As one of only a handful of Jewish students in a private Christian high school, he found a humorous way to gather the Jewish students together for chat sessions. He started a group called the Nosh Club, which had the slogan "for the evangelically challenged." His group met regularly to talk, break bagels together, and keep their ethnic traditions alive. "We often had non-Jewish students come to our meetings, which was great because they could see what our religion was all about."

Other students in the school knew him by the plays he wrote for the drama club. Or they were his teammates on the Ultimate Frisbee team. "This sport is definitely catching on," says Matthew. "It's like Frisbee football, with an end zone and a goalpost, but without the tackling." Matthew has since joined the Ultimate Frisbee team at Brown University, where he's now a freshman. He's double majoring in engineering and humanities because he doesn't want to give up the pursuit of knowledge in either of his two loves. "I love science, but I also love writing and literature. I can get a dual degree in five years, which means an extra year of college, but it's worth it."

At first glance, Matthew might seem like a typical science whiz who prefers tinkering with machines or solving math equations to hanging out with his friends. Delving further, however, you can see that he's hard to sum up in a word or two. Yes, he loves science, but he also loves English. Yes, he likes to see how things are taken apart and put back together, but he also likes to write humorous plays. Yes, he studied a lot for the SAT, but he never missed an Ultimate Frisbee game.

Like other perfect score students, Matthew can't be defined simply. He's always searching, always exploring, always feeding his curiosity. He's always looking for answers to questions, even though he knows that the answers will lead to more questions. He doesn't mind, though, because he enjoys the journey far more than the destination.

Matthew is just one of the 160 students who participated in the Perfect Score Study. Each student has his or her own story to tell about achieving success in school and in life. Yet these students are also alike in many ways. The Perfect Score Study found that most had similar grade-point averages, activities that they enjoyed, and outlooks on life. This can be summed up in the prototypical male perfect score student, whom I call perfect score John, and the prototypical female student, called perfect score Jane.

## Perfect Score John

- ○ I took the SAT once or maybe twice and got a 1600. I didn't take a course to prepare, though I did prepare for the SAT and took practice exams.

- ○ I'm in the top 10 percent of my class. I have a 4.0 grade-point average. I applied to the top Ivy League schools. I didn't get into Princeton or Yale, but I did get accepted to Harvard. I'm going to Stanford.

- ○ I spend eight hours a week studying, and seven hours a week reading for school.

- ○ I have a strong relationship with my family. My parents encouraged me but didn't push. When I excelled in math, they sent me to a summer math camp. They knew I didn't work too hard in regular school and didn't study much for my tests. But as long as I kept my grades up, they didn't bother me.

- ○ I consume books. I read about a book a week for pleasure and read everything I'm assigned for school—plus extra material that the teacher recommends. I usually don't bother with best-sellers or thrillers. I prefer satire, science fiction, and fantasy as well as the classics. One of my favorite books is Joseph Heller's *Catch-22*.

- ○ I watch an hour of TV a night if I can squeeze it in. My favorite show is *The Simpsons*.

- ○ I love sports. I do cross-country in the fall and tennis in the spring. But team sports like baseball and football aren't my thing.

- ○ I have a particular passion that I devote an hour or more a day to. It might be a musical instrument, math or science research experiment, or a science fiction/fantasy game. I pursue whatever turns me on and feeds my curiosity.

○ I had a girlfriend during my junior year, but we broke up after a few months—nothing too intense.

○ I think it's important to do volunteer work. I spent last summer building houses for Habitat for Humanity.

○ Overall, I'm a happy person. I spend several hours a week hanging out with my friends. I have a pretty clear vision of what I want to get out of life. I may not have my profession completely mapped out, but I do know what I excel at and I want my career to focus in that area.

## Perfect Score Jane

○ I took the SAT one or two times until I got a 1600. I took a review course and several practice exams.

○ I go to a public high school and take a mixture of honors classes and regular classes.

○ I have a 4.0 grade-point average and am in the top 10 percent of my class. I won a few academic awards, including being named Presidential Scholar.

○ I applied to several top schools and got into Duke and MIT. I decided to go to Hampshire College because I wanted a small liberal arts school where I could design my own major.

○ I spend eleven hours a week studying and thirteen hours a week reading for school. I take advanced level math and science classes, despite the fact that most of the kids in my classes are guys.

○ I'm not in the in-crowd, but I do have a lot of friends. I would describe myself as popular and well liked.

○ I do one sport, track, but I'm captain of the team. I'm also captain of the debate club and am editor of the yearbook. I strive to be well rounded and always want to try new things.

○ My passion is the piano. I practice at least one hour a day, but I may practice two or three hours if I'm preparing for a competition. I love music, and I love to dance. My friends and I often get together on a Saturday night to blast our favorite CDs and dance in my basement.

○ I make it a point to give back to my community. I spend four hours a week as a volunteer tutoring poor kids from troubled homes.

○ I enjoy reading for pleasure. My favorite books are *Anna Karenina* by Leo Tolstoy and *A Separate Peace* by John Knowles.

○ I love my parents. I consider them my role models. My mother doesn't work, but I always felt she was there for me to guide me academically. My father taught me to play chess and challenged me but didn't push. We took family vacations to exotic places and went to local museums and the theater once or twice a month.

As you can see from these two composite students, perfect score students aren't set off in a class by themselves. They share a lot of qualities with other high school students who pursue academic excellence. They put in a considerable amount of time studying, and most do prepare for the SAT by taking practice exams, an SAT prep course, or both.

They also place a lot of stock in their relationships with their family and friends, just like other high school students. And they seek out the fun pleasures of high school life: going to the movies, attending football games, and hanging out at the mall with friends.

But perfect score students have distinct differences as well. The Perfect Score Study found these students take life seriously and strive to make an impact on the world. They understand that their life should have deep meaning and that they're responsible for determining what that meaning is. They also look upon their academic talents as a gift, one that needs to be shared with others who are less fortunate. Just as these high achievers find ways to balance study time with sports and clubs, they also embrace the other duality in their lives—the party spirit with the sense of social responsibility.

So, who are these perfect score students? Are they geeks who hang out with other geeks? Are they good at anything besides math and English? Do they have an educational advantage, like going to an elite private school? Are they happy, or are they stressed out about schoolwork most of the time? Do they join anything besides the chess club and the math team? Do they all get into Harvard? These are some of the questions I was often asked by my friends and colleagues when I told them about the Perfect Score Study. Let's address each of these questions one by one.

## ARE PERFECT SCORE STUDENTS GEEKS WHO HANG OUT WITH OTHER GEEKS?

When Katie Couric, host of NBC's *Today* show, interviewed one perfect score student recently, she called him a "brainiac." She's not alone in assuming that those who ace the SAT fall into the geek or "brain" category. Even friends of my own son Ted, who all scored very well on the SAT, told me that those who get a perfect score are nerds who study all the time. (I raised my eyebrows about the twisted sense of logic that led them to think there was a huge divide between those who got a 1500 and those who got a perfect score on the SAT.) When I discussed the Perfect Score Study with parents and educators around the country, I kept hearing over and over again, "Aren't those kids nerds? Do you really want a kid who is so smart that he has no friends?"

The fact is, parents and students alike have always had an uneasy relationship with the idea of "brainiac" kids. Young parents today may remember watching movies like *Revenge of the Nerds* when they were teenagers—and even today, some perfect score students say they're careful not to discuss their perfect SAT scores in public, lest other students treat them harshly or accuse them of bragging. But in many ways, kids today are far more worldly than their parents were. They may not read more, but they take in an enormous amount of information from a far wider array of sources, from cable TV to the Internet. As a result, they usually have a lot of respect for the true achievers among them, those smart kids who are socially adept, leaders in their class, and are confident without being arrogant.

The cultural messages they encounter from popular TV shows are far more complex and sophisticated than those in the past. Sensitive, attractive Malcolm, from the hit TV show *Malcolm in the Middle,* has replaced nerdy, funny-looking Steve Urkel from the early 1990s TV show *Family Matters.* Both characters are bright and at the top of their class, but while Urkel speaks in a high-pitched, squeaky voice and wears flood pants with suspenders, Malcolm dresses, looks, and sounds like a typical fourteen-year-old kid.

*Malcolm in the Middle* is based on the premise that Malcolm, a perfectly ordinary kid who was happy, well adjusted, and good at skateboarding, is suddenly discovered to be a genius when he scores 165 on his IQ test. He is moved into an elite class full of gifted (and weird) kids, and people suddenly start treating him differently—especially his family. All he wants to do is return to being an average kid.

Conscious that his high intelligence has landed him squarely in the nerd category, Malcolm makes an effort to shed this image. In one episode, he starts his first day of high school and tries to distance himself from his brainy friends in the gifted class. He does everything he can to ignore them, looking away when they call out his name. He even considers smashing up his mother's car in an effort to create a bad-boy image.

Yes, TV shows still often portray bright kids as social outcasts, but smart lead characters, like Malcolm, have been crafted into complex individuals that viewers can relate to rather than one-dimensional caricatures. Kids watching these shows can sympathize with Malcolm because his problems are common to any kid who is labeled smart in high school.

On the long-running animated show *The Simpsons,* Lisa, the supersmart daughter of superdumb Homer, is the only character on the show who makes sense most of the time. Words of wisdom pour from Lisa's mouth as she corrects the misguided notions of her family and friends. In one episode, eight-year-old Lisa and her friends are planning a school dance, and Lisa is having second thoughts about whether she's old enough to be interested in dancing with boys. One of her friends tells Lisa to buy a short, black revealing dress and lip gloss for the dance—and that she should probably drop five pounds. "You want to look nice for your date," says her friend Janey. "I don't want a date!" screams Lisa. "And I don't want to wear perfume and cocktail dresses. Am I the only one who just wants to play hopscotch and bake cookies and watch *The McLaughlin Group*? Hello?"

Recent movies have also challenged our notions of what smart kids are supposed to look like and be. In *Finding Forrester,* Jamal Wallace is an academically underachieving basketball player from the Bronx whose high standardized test scores give him the chance to attend an exclusive private school, although everyone presumes he's there just to win basketball games. Jamal encounters a reclusive writer named Forrester whose first and only novel won the Pulitzer Prize, and the writer determines that Jamal has a gift for creative writing. When Jamal writes a masterpiece short story, no one believes he wrote it until Forrester himself comes to class to vouch for him. The movie illustrates that society has a hard time believing that a poor young black man—a basketball star no less—could possibly be a literary genius. But although the idea of smart yet hip kids is starting to take root in today's society, we're still far from there. Many of us would be surprised by the following findings from the Perfect Score Study.

When perfect score students were asked about popularity, a striking 67 percent said they were popular, while only 4 percent described themselves as unpopular. This is slightly higher than the 56 percent of average students in the control group who described themselves as popular. Those who described themselves as popular also tended to be more active in sports and school clubs and hold leadership positions in these activities.

Another indication that perfect score students have a healthy social life: 54 percent of them said they dated and had a boyfriend or girlfriend sometime during the previous year. Although this percentage is lower than the 76 percent of students in the study control group who said they had a boyfriend or girlfriend, it's still a healthy number—and a telling indication that academics don't completely take over the lives of perfect score students.

"I dated a lot in high school," says perfect score student Cindy B., who graduated from a public high school in Cincinnati, Ohio. "I did a ton of activities with my friends. One of my closest friends was into rock climbing, so I took up that hobby for two years. I was really into traveling and learning foreign languages. I had a passion for French and became president of the French club. I also speak Spanish and Italian." Cindy and a group of friends headed off to Europe the summer after they graduated high school to make use of their language skills.

Lucy Z. says that although she was raised in a traditional Chinese-American household, she never limited her friendships to smart Chinese students like herself. "I have friends who are white, Indian, African American, and Hispanic, as well as Chinese," she says. "My friends are culturally diverse because I'm interested in getting to know all sorts of people." Lucy even went on an exchange program to Switzerland, where she lived with a family for a month.

It's apparent from their choice of friends that perfect score students don't want to box themselves into a simple stereotype of smart kids who can't get along socially in the world. They seek out friends who will widen their experiences and introduce them to new ideas and adventures.

## ARE PERFECT SCORE STUDENTS GOOD ONLY IN ENGLISH AND MATH?

You might think so, especially if you listen to some education experts who are critical of the SAT. These critics postulate in books and articles that the SAT is an inaccurate measure of intelligence and can't measure creativity or predict success in life. They imply that students who ace the SAT have superior math and verbal skills but little else going for them academically. Some even question whether these students are truly intelligent or are just fabulous test takers.

The Perfect Score Study suggests that these contentions are completely false. Those who ace the SAT perform extremely well in all areas of academics. About 97 percent of these students maintain at least an A average (above 92 percent), while 88 percent maintain an A+ average (97 percent–100 percent). This high GPA, of course, translates into a high class rank: 97 percent of perfect score students ranked in the top 10 percent of their class, and 72 percent were ranked among the top ten students. An impressive 40 percent of perfect score students were valedictorians.

Okay, so perfect score students are smart and do well in classes. But how do they get along in the real world? Do they measure up outside the world of standardized tests and term papers?

In his book *Multiple Intelligences,* Harvard professor Howard Gardner argues that "we should get away altogether from tests and correlation among tests and look at more naturalistic sources of information about how people around the world develop skills important to their way of life." Psychologist and best-selling author Daniel Goleman, Ph.D., takes this one step further, suggesting that life success depends more on emotional, rather than academic, intelligence. "One of psychology's open secrets is the relative inability of grades, IQ, or SAT scores, despite their popular mystique, to predict unerringly who will succeed in life," Goleman writes in his landmark book *Emotional Intelligence.* He defines emotional intelligence "as being able to motivate oneself and persist in the face of frustrations; to control impulse and delay gratification; to regulate one's moods and keep distress from swamping the ability to think; to empathize and to hope."

Every person has a mixture of both academic and emotional intelligence, but given a choice, it is emotional intelligence that "adds far more of the qualities that make us fully human," Goleman says. He goes on to say that having a high IQ has nothing whatsoever to do with how happy, successful, or satisfied people are with their lives. He cites the example of a fellow he knew at Amherst College who had perfect scores on his SATs and Achievement Tests in high school but who cut classes, blew off studying in college, and took ten years to graduate.

Results from the Perfect Score Study, however, fly in the face of the theory that academic success doesn't predict success in life. On the contrary, this research finds that in order to ace the SAT, students must also possess high emotional intelligence. Yes, there are always exceptions to the rule, but in general perfect score students meet several criteria that indicate high emotional intelligence. They are socially adept. They are outgoing. They are committed to people and causes, and volunteer regularly. Above all, these students are engaged in deep, caring relationships with their family and friends. In fact, perfect score students are more adept at these areas in their life than those whose SAT scores were between 1000 and 1200.

John T. is a perfect illustration of a perfect score student with high emotional intelligence. "I am able to connect with people one on one. I am someone people can count on to help as a friend. People trust me." John said his social life in high school was good because he got involved in a lot of activities, from which he made a lot of new friends. He even met his girlfriend while the two were acting together in the school play. Regardless of the fact that he aced the SAT and got into Harvard, John sums himself up like this: "I'm a pretty simple kind of guy. I love to learn. I love good music."

I don't think it's happenstance that high academic achievers also possess high emotional intelligence. High emotional intelligence contributes to academic success, including high SAT scores. This will become even more important on the new SAT, which requires writing and other skills. Perfect score students create their own luck by finding ways to overcome roadblocks that stand in the way of academic success.

## DO PERFECT SCORE STUDENTS HAVE AN EDUCATIONAL ADVANTAGE?

If you think an elite private school education or costly SAT tutor is what it takes to ace the SAT, think again. For the most part, perfect score students didn't get a personalized, elite education to propel them to academic stardom. About 80 percent of perfect score students went to a public high school, while only 20 percent attended a private or parochial school. Although this is higher than the national average of 8 percent of students who attend private schools, it's still fairly low.

Of those perfect score students who went to public high schools, half said their school was upper middle class, while the other half said it was either a middle- or lower-middle-class public school. Interestingly, only one perfect score student who participated in the study was homeschooled. The 7 Secrets will reveal that homeschooling doesn't offer an advantage—and may even be a disadvantage when it comes to doing well on the SAT.

In terms of class size, the vast majority of perfect score students attended classes that averaged 23 students. The small classes that are typically found in private schools may give more personalized attention, but the Perfect Score Study found that this doesn't translate into higher SAT scores.

Regardless of their choice of high schools, perfect score students make the most of the educational resources around them. About 33 percent take only honors-level classes, while 61 percent take a mixture of honors and regular classes. Just 6 percent are in regular classes. Even more impressive, they take an average of six advanced placement (AP) college-level courses while in high school (enough to earn them a semester or more of college credit). A number of perfect score students also reported that they took more advanced courses at a local college during the school year or at a high-achiever program during the summer.

Academics, though, don't tell the whole story. Students who earn a perfect score know that school is about much more than course work. Tom M., a perfect score student from a suburb of Boston, made the most of the public high school he attended. Tom's parents briefly considered sending him to a private high school to enhance his education, but Tom insisted on staying in the public school system.

"I'm getting a good education," Tom told me. "My classes are great. I'm in all APs and honor classes. I play tennis and play clarinet in the school orchestra, and I'm the editor of the local section of the *Daily Record,* our school paper. But most of all, this is where my friends go. I might be able to get a slightly better education elsewhere, but I know my close buddies would definitely not be at another school. My grades, no problem. If school were only about grades and classes, my education and certainly my achievement would be good. But school means so much more than that."

The lesson here is that parents don't need to invest their life's savings in a private school in order to get their child a top-notch education. Perfect score students manage to find what they need by seeking out the best their school has to offer. The vast majority of them don't sit perched in oak-paneled classrooms in a prep school that's been around since the days of Lincoln. You'd be more likely to find perfect score students roaming a locker-filled hallway in jeans and sweats, carrying MP-3 players blaring Eminem.

## ARE PERFECT SCORE STUDENTS HAPPY, OR CONSTANTLY STRESSED OUT ABOUT SCHOOLWORK?

Actually, they're about as happy as those who get average SAT scores. The Perfect Score Study measured overall happiness by having students rate their state of mind on a 7-point scale (1 being not happy and 7 being extremely happy) and found that perfect score students, on average, rated their lives as 5.6, or "very happy," in high school and in their first year of college. Average-scoring students had about the same level of happiness as perfect score students in both high school and college. You might think that high academic achievers put more pressure on themselves to succeed and thus would be miserable. But this doesn't bear out in the research.

Perfect score student Brian M. grew up in Montana in a middle-class family with a mother who worked as an administrator for a local insurance company and a father who worked at a canning factory. Brian attended a lower-middle-class high school and did extremely well, graduating third in his class of 435 students.

Although Brian studied eight hours a week, he spent far more time hanging out with his friends, watching TV, and tuning in to sports events. He was cocaptain of his school's football team, which took up the rest of his spare time.

"My philosophy on life is simple: you have to make yourself happy while treating others fairly," says Brian. But his pursuit of happiness doesn't mean the abandonment of self-discipline. "Make no mistake about it," says Brian. "I am a person who is highly motivated and who loves athletics and academics."

Yes, perfect score students are more driven and more internally motivated to do well in school than their average-scoring peers. They are, however, just as happy, possibly because their family, friends, and activities all help them create a fulfilling life for themselves. Although academic achievements do play a role in these students' happiness, it's more of a supporting rather than a leading one. Students told me that when their perfect SAT scores came in the mail, they were ecstatic and proud of their accomplishment, but that the excitement wore off after a few weeks. Upcoming finals, term papers, and college applications quickly pushed aside the SAT perfect score afterglow in these students' minds.

Close friendships and family relationships were a far greater contributor to happiness than academic achievements. Perfect score students put these relationships at the top of the list of what's most important to them in life. Most would describe their social lives the way perfect score student Tom M. does: "I have good friends. We hang out together. We talk constantly." Most listed their mother or father as their number one role model in life, the person who has had the most influence in shaping who they will become as adults.

Brian T. summed this up nicely when asked if he was happy. He smiled and said, "I am extremely happy. Why? Because I get a great deal of support from people I love." Brian wasn't happy because he's a star football player or he scored 1600 on the SAT, but rather because of the people who loved him.

Interestingly, family size doesn't appear to play a role in students' happiness or whether they're more likely to achieve a perfect SAT score. About two-thirds of perfect score students were firstborn or only children, about the same percentage as their lower-scoring peers. When I analyzed the SAT scores among the siblings of perfect score students, I found that birth order or family size wasn't a factor in predicting which sibling would achieve a 1600. In fact, some of the perfect score students who participated in the study said they pushed themselves to get a 1600 because their older sibling had achieved a perfect score.

Although perfect score students place a high value on family and friendships, most didn't spend as much time socializing with their friends in high school as their average-scoring counterparts. According to the Perfect Score Study, perfect score students spend an average of 8 hours a week hanging out or talking on the phone with their friends, compared with 14 hours a week spent by average students. This is a pretty big difference and may suggest that too much partying with friends isn't a good thing. Yes, perfect score students know how to have fun and see their friends as the ticket to good times. But they also exercise discipline over themselves. *Study first, party later* is a motto they live by.

## WHAT'S A TYPICAL DAY IN THE LIFE OF A PERFECT SCORE STUDENT?

First of all, the study found that the lives of perfect score students aren't all that different from those of typical high school students. Both groups spend about the same amount of time each week studying. Both spend about the same amount of time reading for pleasure and watching TV. They even both spend the same amount of time engaged in sports and clubs. There were, however, a few telling differences in how perfect score students spent their time compared with average score students. These differences are shown in bold on the following chart.

## HOW PERFECT SCORE STUDENTS AND AVERAGE SCORE STUDENTS SPEND THEIR TIME (HOURS/WEEK)

| Activity | Perfect Score Students | Average Students |
|---|---|---|
| Studying | 10 | 9 |
| **School Reading** | **9** | **4** |
| Pleasure Reading | 5 | 4 |
| TV Watching | 4 | 5 |
| Computer | 6 | 8 |
| Sports | 7 | 9 |
| **Socializing** | **8** | **14** |
| Clubs | 6 | 7 |
| **Work** | **9*** | **20** |
| Total (excluding work) | 55 | 60 |

\* LIMITED SAMPLE BASED ON 25% OF STUDENTS WHO SAID THEY WORKED

NOTE: Statistical tests were employed to identify whether the differences between samples could be attributed to sampling error. These tests identified whether one could be 90% certain that the observed difference was not due to chance. That is to say, if the study was repeated 100 times, the same result would occur at least 90 times. Results in bold are those identified to be statistically significant differences.

According to a statistical analysis of these measurements, perfect score students spend more time reading for school and less time socializing with friends or working at an after-school job. Clearly, students have to make time trade-offs. The fact that perfect score students spend far less time working means that they have more time to read material and books that are assigned for school. And they don't let their social lives interfere with their schoolwork responsibilities, whereas other students might skip the assigned textbook reading to chat on the phone at night. Looking at the time allocations on the chart for various activities, it appears that perfect score students have found a better way to balance school with socializing.

Work is a trickier issue. Just 25 percent of perfect score students worked, and those who did worked few hours. This is dramatically less than the 62 percent of average students who worked. What's more, average score students put in more than twice the number of hours working than perfect score students. While it's true that perfect score students come from households with somewhat higher family incomes than average students, the vast majority of perfect score students are from middle-class homes. Yes, some students, for financial reasons, do have to work to save for college or have some spending money, but the Perfect Score Study suggests that working 10 or more hours a week takes time away from academic studies and SAT preparation.

## DO THEY JOIN ANYTHING BESIDES THE MATH CLUB OR THE CHESS TEAM?

Yes, yes, yes. The Perfect Score Study found that perfect score students devote about as much time to extracurricular activities as typical high school students, spending an average of 13 hours a week on sports and clubs, compared with 16 hours a week spent by average-scoring students. While it's true that perfect score students are more involved in academic clubs—72 percent of them join an activity like debate club, National Honor Society, math club, or Science Olympiad—they also engage in other activities that span the spectrum. Several students I spoke with played in rock bands. Others worked on the school yearbook or edited their school newspapers. Some students were actors or wrote plays for the high school drama club. More than 80 percent of perfect score students took part in a social after-school activity like French club, yearbook, or marching band.

Even more interesting is the finding that Perfect Score Students are just as athletic as other high school students. The Perfect Score Study found that 65 percent of perfect score students participate in school sports, compared with 66 percent of average students. There is, though, one major difference, which is in the types of sports these students tend to choose. Perfect score students tend to play individual sports, such as cross-country, swimming, and tennis, rather than team sports, such as baseball, basketball, football, and soccer.

For perfect score student Patrick B., tennis was his life throughout his high school years. He won state tournaments and was ranked 105th in the nation for players under eighteen. "I really enjoyed the competition, but often I felt I was just competing against myself." Several perfect score students told me they enjoyed the solitary endeavor of their sport, whether it was running through the fall leaves on a cross-country trail or swimming laps in the quiet hush of the water. They used the quiet time to take a moment out of their hectic schedules to reflect on the meaning of their lives.

Although perfect score students aren't limited in the variety of activities they choose to pursue, they do limit themselves to one or two activities at a time. They prefer to delve into a special interest with a passion, rather than dabbling in many things. This is one of the 7 secrets that set perfect score students apart from the rest. More than 90 percent of perfect score students reported having a particular talent that they pursued with a passion, whether it was practicing cello or electric guitar; putting together a novel science experiment or the latest issue of the school newspaper; or playing water polo or street hockey. These naturally curious students are able to follow whatever piques their interest with a singular determination. They develop passions not to be the best at what they do (though some of them are), but to soak up and experience every last bit of excitement in what they do.

## DO ALL PERFECT SCORE STUDENTS GET INTO HARVARD?

The short answer is: no, they don't *all* get in. Harvard, Yale, and Princeton certainly don't accept all perfect score students who apply, although they do accept a significant percentage of them. And most of these high achievers do get in to one of the top ten colleges in the nation.

So where do these perfect score students apply to college? Where do they get in? And where do they wind up going? How do perfect score students select which college to attend?

With regard to college applications, those who ace the SAT apply to three or four colleges on average. Their six most popular choices are listed below.

## Top College Choices of Perfect Score Students

| College | Percent of Perfect Score Students Who Apply |
|---------|:---:|
| Harvard | 47 |
| Princeton | 33 |
| Stanford | 31 |
| Yale | 23 |
| Duke | 22 |
| MIT | 22 |

MIT is the sole technical school in the top six, which is surprising, given that more than two-thirds of perfect score students say that math (35 percent) or science (33 percent) is their favorite subject. Let's look at the breakdown of acceptances and rejections from these top six schools, and the percentage of perfect score students who wind up attending these schools, entering their freshman year in the fall of 2000.

### COLLEGE ADMISSIONS FOR PERFECT SCORE STUDENTS (PERCENTAGES)

| Colleges | Acceptances %* | Rejections % | Attending % |
|----------|:---:|:---:|:---:|
| Harvard | 53 | 30 | 16 |
| Princeton | 36 | 55 | 2 |
| Stanford | 66 | 28 | 12 |
| Yale | 39 | 48 | 5 |
| Duke | 100 | 0 | 4 |
| MIT | 68 | 29 | 3 |

* PERCENTAGES OF ACCEPTANCES AND REJECTIONS DON'T ADD UP TO 100% BECAUSE STATISTICS DO NOT INCLUDE STUDENTS WAIT-LISTED OR APPLICATIONS WITHDRAWN.

Despite scoring 1600, perfect score students do indeed get rejected from top colleges. In fact, in the year 2000, admission rates ranged from a low of 36 percent for Princeton to a high of 100 percent for Duke. Harvard accepts about half its 1600 applicants, while Princeton is the only school to reject more than half of those who apply. Harvard and Stanford are by far the most popular choices of perfect score students, with 28 percent of them choosing to attend one of the two schools. Other schools that are popular with 1600 students include: Cal Tech, University of Pennsylvania, Columbia University, and the University of North Carolina.

Overall, 1600 students usually get into several of their top choice schools, even if they get rejected from one or two schools. They then must make the difficult decision about which college to attend. (Though it's hard to feel bad for students who have to choose between Penn and Dartmouth!) The Perfect Score Study sheds some insight into how 1600 students make this selection.

## Top Four Reasons Perfect Score Students Choose a College (Percentages)

| Reasons | Percent |
| --- | --- |
| Academics | 18 |
| Money/Financial Aid | 18 |
| Reputation | 8 |
| Location | 8 |

Like all high school students considering which college to attend, perfect score students have to balance academics with finances. Both play an equally important role in their decision. These students weigh the particular academic qualities and majors that a college offers against the cost of tuition and room and board and whether they'll get scholarships to help defray these costs. With the soaring costs of private colleges, and the fact that more than half of perfect score students have household incomes of less than $100,000, it's no wonder that these students consider financing to be as important as academics when choosing a college. After these two issues are factored in, a school's location and reputation are considered. Less common reasons perfect score students picked a college were: size, makeup of the student body, flexibility, and gut feel.

The vast majority of perfect score students said they were very happy with their choice of college. In general, they liked the academics, the students, the professors, and the freedom. Many said they worked harder, were challenged more intellectually, and enjoyed the course work more than in high school, and none said they wished they were back in high school. Overall, perfect score students were very satisfied and stimulated by the college experience. "College is amazing," says perfect score student Matthew S., who is a freshman at Brown University. "I keep a journal of everything that happens so I can remember these intense days long after I've graduated."

## THE 7 SECRETS OF PERFECT SCORE STUDENTS

I have to admit that I was surprised by many of the findings of the Perfect Score Study. As a professional educator and a high-level executive recruiter, I have studied the best and the brightest for twenty years. When I looked at the information I had gathered in the Perfect Score Study and shared the results with knowledgeable professionals in the education field, we all agreed that we were amazed by the common trends that exist among perfect score students.

The brightest of the bright students have common personality traits and lifestyle habits that made it possible for them to score a 1600. I call these the 7 Secrets of Perfect Score Students. I call them "secrets" because I don't think any of us really understood until now what tools were necessary to achieve the astonishing potential that lies in every student. These 7 Secrets are:

**1.** **They're self-confident,** self-effacing, and self-motivated.

**2. They are intellectually curious** and excited about learning new and different things.

**3. They read** quickly and voraciously, following their interests wherever they lead.

**4. They develop a core group of passions,** pursue them eagerly, and excel within them.

**5. They're proactive;** they create their own luck.

**6. They develop a social network** of friends and family that gives them critical support.

**7. Their real goal isn't to ace the SATs**—but to succeed in life.

What do these 7 Secrets add up to? Not necessarily a perfect SAT score, though for some students it might. But students don't have to be brilliant or academically gifted to benefit from these 7 Secrets. I think we all know there are probably some untapped academic talents that lay hidden within every child. Students can achieve more than they ever thought possible once their full potential is realized.

Even a brief glimpse into the lives of perfect score students reveals that these students have been able to find a balance in life that works for them. They're happy and have strong family support and parents they can count on. They also found a way to achieve their academic potential while still maintaining solid friendships and participating in school activities.

The benefits of the 7 Secrets extend beyond SAT scores and even beyond academics. Understanding them will ultimately lead students to a stronger sense of self-awareness. Perfect score students all have this awareness: They know who they are and how they want to live their lives. They may not know exactly what they want to do after college graduation or what kind of person they'd like to marry. But they do have a sense of what drives them to get up in the morning.

"I'm an incorrigible optimist," says Maria G., a typical perfect score student. "Life is what we make of it. I believe we should help other people. Life is beautiful." Assured and inquisitive, these perfect score students have the social safety nets they need to reach out fearlessly to try new things. "I am driven by a sense of curiosity and adventure," says Joe R.

Perhaps most significantly, the SAT is not the be-all and end-all for these students. Most of the perfect score students realize that their perfect score has opened some doors for them and probably will in the future. But they also appreciate the fact that life and success are defined in terms of family, friends, and school—not the test. (No one ever regrets on his deathbed not getting a higher SAT score.) "I like to learn. I try to have fun. I don't work too hard," says Susan K. That's a philosophy of life we can all live by.

# PART II

## The 7 Secrets

# Secret 1:
# They're Self-Confident, Self-Effacing, and Self-Motivated

Perfect score student John J. has a combination of traits that are rarely found in high school students: he's self-confident, self-effacing, and self-motivated. When I was working to set up an interview with John, I ended up talking at length with his father, David, a middle manager for a local company in Phoenix, where the family lives. I told David I was interested in how he had raised John and why he thought his son had done so well on the SAT. David waxed eloquent about his son, but with a tone of puzzled awe. It was as if he wasn't quite sure how his smart son had gotten that way. But he was quick to explain how curious and creative his son had been at an early age—motivated to learn anything he could about everything.

"It wasn't like he was an Einstein or anything," David explained. "But from a very early age he did things differently and thought differently." Even in elementary and junior high school, whenever he encountered a seemingly unsolvable math problem, he immediately accepted the challenge, analyzed the problem, and solved it. Later, in high school, John was captain of the math team, a star athlete, and a straight-A student. "He was always quick, always eager," John's father said. "Sometimes I think he was just motivated by the urge not to be bored, ever."

When I later interviewed John, he seemed embarrassed by the accolades that his father had bestowed about him. I could hear a kind of shrug in his voice. "I'm just a person who tries to do his best," he said. He paused, figuring out how he could explain himself accurately. "I'm someone who likes to be spiritually, mentally, and physically fit." He admitted that the SAT was challenging and said he was surprised he had aced the test. John said his early motivation to do well in school came from his parents, although once he got to high school he pushed himself to perform because he knew he could.

John J. is an all-around nice guy. You'd never know he was academically brilliant unless someone else told you. He is, however, confident in his own abilities and never wants to put forth less than his best effort. Yes, John's parents played a major role in shaping his approach to learning early on, but by the time he was in high school, he was clearly capable of following his own lead.

John's win-win combination of confidence, humility, and motivation has no doubt contributed to his academic success. It's a combination found in most perfect score students and is the first of the 7 Secrets.

While interviewing students for the Perfect Score Study, I was struck by how at ease these perfect score students were with themselves. They spoke quietly and earnestly about their hopes and dreams. They showed a certain self-confidence, knowing that if they put forth their best effort, they could accomplish whatever task was before them.

When asked to name their biggest challenge in high school, these high academic achievers barely mentioned tests or course work. One perfect score student mentioned that running on the cross-country team was a personal challenge for him. Another told me that preparing a difficult piece for a piano competition was her toughest challenge. Though they admitted the SAT was challenging, very few students mentioned the SAT as their toughest challenge.

You might figure that these students are extremely bright, so of course they wouldn't find academics to be challenging. And yes, those perfect score students who earned high grades and SAT scores with very little studying would be expected to say that high school classes were a piece of cake. However, I got the same sense even from those perfect score students who had to earn their academic achievements through a lot of hard work and discipline. Across the board, perfect score students exhibit self-assurance in their ability to achieve in school and on the SAT.

Yet this self-assurance doesn't mean perfect score students have all the answers. When I asked them to describe themselves in three sentences, they usually paused and took a minute or two to formulate their response. They were thoughtful, not pat, in their replies. They knew it would be hard to describe themselves in just three sentences in an authentic, not artificial, way.

Nor does this self-assurance mean these students are arrogant. I believe this is because they have an innate ability to balance self-confidence with self-effacement. Perfect score student Amy C. clearly has found this balance. She describes herself as "an intelligent person who is ambitious and knows what I want, but I also have my faults and limits." Unlike the 40 percent of perfect score students who got 1600 on their first attempt, Amy had to work hard for her perfect score. She took the SAT four times, including twice in her senior year. And she put in a considerable amount of time studying for it, taking a lot of practice tests and memorizing vocabulary words. "I would tape the vocabulary cards around my room, and that's how I learned them." Amy is realistic about life and the potential difficulties she might encounter, but she says, "Life is never as hard as you think it is, and it will always get better in the end."

## AVOIDING SAT BRAGGING RIGHTS

What's apparent from the Perfect Score Study is that perfect score students are motivated to do well on the SAT and are confident they can do well if they prepare adequately—though very few actually thought they'd get a perfect score. What's interesting, however, is that once they accomplish the goal of acing the SAT, these students downplay their achievement.

When I asked the perfect score students how important their SAT scores were to them, 46 percent said they were "somewhat important." Just 29 percent said they were "very important," and 6 percent said they were "extremely important." With their curiosity and drive to learn, perfect score students can put the SAT in perspective. Yes, it's certainly important, but it's not the sum and substance of life. This realistic view of the SAT is one of the secrets behind why these perfect score students were able to ace the test. They were able to relax and focus on the test itself, rather than on their fears that they might blow their shot at getting into Harvard.

Perhaps these perfect score students just don't want to brag about their academic accomplishments. Or perhaps these students just see the SAT for the test that it is, another measure of how well they learn. Perfect score student John C. expressed the sentiments of many perfect score students when he told me, "Getting a good score on the SAT is a means to an end. The end is to get into a good college and then have a career you like that makes a difference in the world. Bragging about SAT scores is pretty pointless, if you think about it."

Friends, family, and teachers often made a bigger deal out of a perfect SAT score than the student who actually earned it—much to the embarrassment of the perfect score student. One mother proudly told me that her son, Victor M., had scored 1600 on the SAT, a perfect 36 on the ACT, and a perfect 5 on all eight AP exams. Victor didn't tell me this when I interviewed him. He just said, "I did well in school." His mother, however, was happy to broadcast his scores even before I asked.

Sometimes an entire town likes to revel in a perfect SAT score. When word spread in Sheboygan, Wisconsin, that one of its young residents, Tom H., had aced the SAT, small-town pride was so strong that the mayor named a day after him and presented Tom with a key to the city. "It was like I was a returning war hero," explains Tom. "While this was an honor, other students in my class were jealous and felt I was bragging. In truth, I had nothing to do with it." Tom says he had to spend a lot of time repairing friendships that were hurt by the local fame that came with his perfect score.

Shannon B. says she had to put up with her friends calling her "1600" for a year after she earned her perfect SAT score. "It was a little embarrassing," she says. "They got a kick out of telling their parents that they were friends with a 1600 girl. I knew they were just joking, but still, I really didn't want my SAT score to define me."

The primary reason that perfect score students are humble concerns their values and attitudes. The test is not the most important thing in their life, and therefore getting 1600 is not their crowning achievement. They recognize the importance of the SAT in gaining admission to the college of their choice. But scoring 1600, being valedictorian or salutatorian, or winning prestigious national awards is not the essence of who they are or how they define themselves. In fact, one perfect score student almost forgot to mention that she was a Presidential Scholar when I asked her if she had won any academic awards in high school. This award, given to only two high achievers in each state, entitles the winner to meet the president and influential members of Congress. It was only when I asked the Oklahoma native if she traveled to any interesting places that she remembered she had gone to Washington, D.C., to accept this prestigious award.

Although self-effacement wasn't an item that the Perfect Score Study could measure statistically, responses from students in the control group seemed to indicate that they didn't have the same humility as perfect score students. When asked to describe themselves, average scoring students typically replied that they were great at school or exceptional in sports. Poring through these responses, I got the nagging sense that these students were trying to build themselves up to prove that they were smart and successful in high school.

Since I work as an executive job recruiter, I know when I'm getting a sales pitch from someone trying to impress me. One student in this control group even reported that he had been accepted to New York University and was going to play football for their team. "I think he must be mistaken," I told my colleague who conducted the interview. "NYU doesn't have a football team." I went to NYU for my master's degree and would have been happy to attend football games—if any were actually played there. (I wound up disqualifying this particular student from the study for his dishonesty.)

The perfect score student's combination of confidence and humility may help boost academic performance and even success in life. These students make great team players because they're smart and capable but also recognize their limitations. They're happy to consult others in areas where they don't excel. After all, no one wants to do a project with a know-it-all who completely takes over. And teachers may be less likely to provide support and guidance to students who think they know everything, even if these students are at the top of their class.

In general, perfect score students manage to be both smart and likeable, and this wins them the friendship of their peers and the respect of their teachers. Despite their high intelligence, these students want to belong and fit in, and they make a concerted effort to be part of the crowd. They don't want to stand out for their brains or SAT scores. They just want to be accepted and liked.

After all, that's not so much different from what every other high school student wants. At the end of the day, kids who get along socially are more likely to achieve academically. Studies have shown that those kids who feel isolated or depressed are more likely to receive failing grades in school. In other words, to get along, you really do have to get along.

## MOTIVATION IS KEY

Perhaps the humility shown by perfect score students stems from the fact that they set very high standards for themselves. They're rarely satisfied that they've accomplished enough, and they see their education as a path of discovery as opposed to a destination. For this reason, these students don't sit back and coast during the last semester of their senior year. Even after they send off the last of their college applications, they continue to take the most challenging classes their high school has to offer.

Perfect score students have a certain yearning, not just for knowledge but also for meaning in their lives and for achieving the best within themselves. Nearly all of them have been academic superstars from elementary school on and have had to live up to high expectations—often their own, but also shaped by friends, family, and teachers. When perfect score students don't get all As, their parents might say, "What happened?" When average kids don't, their parents might say, "Well, at least you tried."

So, which came first, the expectations or the achievement? The Perfect Score Study couldn't answer this question, but it did find that, almost without exception, perfect score students are incredibly motivated to succeed—not just in academics but also in life. Motivation is the key to high academic achievement and a perfect SAT score. It's the spark that drives students through their high school years, college, and beyond. It's the dividing line that separates successful people from those who aren't.

I think steel magnate Andrew Carnegie was right on the mark when he said, "People who are unable to motivate themselves must be content with mediocrity, no matter how impressive their other talents." Without motivation, we can never fulfill our true potential—no matter how substantial our intelligence, athletic abilities, or musical talents. We've all seen students who have a lot of potential yet never seem to go anywhere. Many parents blame it on burnout or laziness, but the missing $x$ factor is really motivation.

Motivation stems from a variety of sources. Perfect score students are incredibly self-motivated, but they also have parents who expected them to achieve from the start. By believing in their children, these parents infused their kids with a belief in themselves, which led to strong self-esteem. This self-esteem enabled perfect score students to become their own motivators in high school and beyond.

When perfect score students were asked to name a person who motivated them academically, 90 percent said they motivated themselves. This compares with 69 percent of the average students who said they motivated themselves. And even though perfect score students cared about meeting the expectations of their parents and teachers, they didn't cite them as the major reason that they pushed themselves in high school. One perfect score student explains, "I'm a self-motivated person. I understand that I determine my own future. I enjoy finding out new things and learning." Another states, "I've always admired people who are industrious, intelligent, and successful. Therefore, I try to be like them." A third responds, "I just approach every class with the desire to do my best. I have high standards and am driven."

Many parents of perfect score students told me their children not only fulfilled but also completely exceeded their expectations for academics and the SAT. These parents found themselves providing words of comfort when their child was deeply disappointed by a B+ test grade. They usually didn't need to criticize or cajole their child to try harder next time.

Because these perfect score parents planted the seeds for self-sufficiency when their child was younger, they were able to sit back and serve as a support system during their child's high school years. And, yes, some children may be born more internally driven than others, but all of us have the potential to be self-starters. We all want to seek out the best possible lives for ourselves, and we learn how to do this from our youngest days.

Scott Adams, the creator of *Dilbert*, the popular comic strip about life in an office cubicle, says, "I'm slowly becoming a convert to the principle that you can't motivate people to do things, you can only *de*motivate them. The primary job of the manager is not to empower but to remove obstacles." Replace the word *manager* with *parent*, and you've got a formula for helping children become self-motivated. Just as Dilbert's boss is incredibly successful at throwing roadblocks in the way of Dilbert's progress, many parents unwittingly throw their own roadblocks in the way of their child's success—by doing their children's homework for them, for example, or rewarding them with money for good grades.

Perfect score students learned to become self-motivated by watching their parents giving the right amount of assistance, enough but not too much—during their grade school years. These students said they relied strongly on their parents to motivate them in elementary school and junior high, but that their parents stepped back from this role when their children entered high school and became self-reliant. These students relied on their parents instead for emotional guidance and support during their high school years.

Two-thirds of the perfect score students said their parents placed a high priority on providing academic support and guidance when they were in high school. An even higher percentage—77 percent—said their parents continued to provide intellectual stimulation, and 80 percent said their parents continued to provide some motivation, even though most of their motivation to excel came from within. Teachers were somewhat less of a motivating factor but still played a meaningful role in these students' lives. A significant 75 percent of perfect score students said their teachers provided some motivation for them to achieve.

## PERCENT OF PERFECT SCORE STUDENTS WHO SAID PARENTS OR TEACHERS GAVE THEM STRONG SUPPORT

|  | Parents | Teachers |
|---|---|---|
| Academic guidance and support | 67% | 56% |
| Stimulation to explore ideas, events, and larger environment | 77% | 60% |
| Academic expectations and motivation | 80% | 76% |

Findings weren't that different for average SAT score students. In this group 62 percent said their parents gave them academic guidance, 70 percent said their parents provided stimulation, and 88 percent said their parents gave them motivation. The one big difference appeared in those who received academic guidance from their teachers. A full 78 percent of average students received academic guidance from their teachers, compared with only 56 percent of perfect score students.

This indicates an interesting trend: parents have more of an academic impact on the best performing students, and teachers have more of an impact on children who fall into the middle of the class. The question is: Are schools better able to serve the average kids in the middle than those at the top? Or are the parents of high-achieving children more directly involved with their education? If the latter is the case, does this mean that parental involvement leads to higher achievement—and possibly a perfect SAT score—or do these parents make themselves more involved because they realize that schools can't accommodate the needs of superbright kids? Which came first, the perfect score student or the perfect score parent?

I don't know if we can really answer these questions. Certainly, perfect score students do rely more on their parents than on teachers for input and guidance in their schoolwork. A full 75 percent of perfect score students list either Mom or Dad or both parents as the most influential person in their lives.

Maria G. has the internal drive typical of many perfect score students. She took six AP courses, maintained an A average in high school, and was accepted by all four elite colleges to which she applied. She scored 1600 the second time she took the SAT, after buying a Princeton Review book and taking a dozen practice tests. Maria, though, comes from a different world than most perfect score students. She grew up in low-income housing, and her parents are both immigrants who speak little English. Her mother is a housewife, and her father is a laborer. Her yearly family income is below the cost of a single year of tuition at Harvard.

Maria worked eight hours a week in high school to help her family make ends meet. But she still had time for Hispanic club, math team, and classical guitar lessons. She was also captain of the swim team.

So what motivated Maria? She is quick to acknowledge that her parents were her greatest inspiration. Her mother scraped together money to get Maria dance and guitar lessons. "She took me to these lessons, spent time with me, but most of all, respected and encouraged me as a person," Maria says. "And my father, an immigrant who spoke little English, still managed to support the family, not only financially, but emotionally." Boosted by love from her devoted parents, Maria drove herself to succeed. "My parents were supportive," she said, "but I was told it would by okay if I got lower grades. It was my own wish to push my limits and see what I could accomplish."

What's apparent from Maria's story is that perfect score students don't operate in a vacuum. They can't tap into their inner motivation without first having high self-esteem. They need to believe they can succeed before they develop the drive to succeed. Parents, of course, can build or tear down their children's self-esteem. Starting at the youngest age, children get cues from their parents about how high their expectations are. If children know that their parents expect great things that are realistically achievable, then they will be motivated to achieve those things.

Students who ace the SAT display one outward sign of their motivation: they're self-confident and feel good about their academic abilities. When asked about strengths and weaknesses, John S., a perfect score student, put it succinctly: "I'm intelligent, pretty well rounded, do things well, and work hard when I put my mind to it. When I want something, I go for it." When perfect score students were asked to list their strengths, intelligence, determination, and hard work were the three qualities that came up the most frequently.

This self-confidence comes from a feeling of self-control. Perfect score students say their decisions about which colleges to apply to or what to major in largely came from their own preferences, not the preferences of their parents. Although their parents offered advice

## PROFILE: MOTIVATED BY THE CHALLENGE
## OF A NEW COUNTRY

Imagine moving as a young child to a foreign country where no one speaks English. You have to learn a completely new alphabet and master a new language—with little help from your parents, who don't know the language themselves. Now imagine that you take a college-entrance exam in your second language and score in the top one percent of students who have been speaking the language their entire lives. Sounds pretty incredible, but it can happen. At least several dozen students a year who ace the SAT aren't native English speakers. Many immigrated to the United States from an Asian country like China, South Korea, or Thailand. In fact, a significant 24 percent of perfect score students are Asian Americans—even though this minority group makes up only 4 percent of the U.S. population. Most of these students either immigrated to the United States or have parents who aren't fluent English speakers.

Qian L. embodies the experience shared by many perfect score students who grew up in Asian households. She has the kind of drive and ambition that enabled her to face life's challenges head-on. "I am definitely a very hardworking, committed, persistent person. I'm very loyal to family and friends. I'm constantly looking to improve myself," she says in describing herself. Pretty, with straight black hair and a warm smile, Qian grew up in New York City in a lower-middle-class neighborhood in Queens, where her mom was a research technician and her dad was a computer scientist.

English was a second language for both Qian and her parents. The family emigrated from China when Qian was six years old. Barely speaking a word of English when she came to the United States, Qian mastered the language and was able to ace the SAT and maintain an A+ average. She graduated valedictorian and got into ten of the eleven colleges to which she applied. Like other Asian American perfect score students, Qian studied about fourteen hours a week and spent thirteen hours a week reading for school. This is far more than typical perfect score students, who spend an average of ten hours a week studying and nine hours a week reading for school. But Qian wasn't satisfied with excelling only in the world of academics. She jumped headfirst into extracurricular activities, participating in more than a dozen during her high school years. She joined everything from the debate club to track. She was elected to the executive council in the student government and participated in the Interact Service Club, where she volunteered to baby-sit the young children of poor working mothers. And she was editor of the newspaper, treasurer of the art club, and captain of the Science Bowl.

"So what *didn't* you do?" I asked her. She smiled and said, "I didn't get a lot of sleep, and I really had to make the most of my limited social time with friends. Really, school clubs were my personal social life." When I asked Qian what drove her to fill her days with constant activity, she said she wanted to make her family proud. She knows how important her achievements are to her parents, who are trying to etch out a new life for themselves. She also knows, though, that she wants to succeed for herself.

With an air of maturity that is beyond her years, Qian told me, "I control my own destiny. I know how much it means to my future to have a good academic background. My philosophy is do the best you possibly can, but never leave without having made a difference." Qian's determination and confidence are apparent in her tone. You get the sense that she will do well at anything she tries because she won't allow herself to fail. Now a junior at Yale University, Qian will do whatever it takes to get where she wants to go, and her family, friends, and teachers all respect her for that.

and guidance on these decisions, they tried not to push their own dreams on their children. This encouraged their kids to be more internally motivated than externally motivated. Internally motivated students are able to maintain their motivation beyond the promise of a tangible reward like a good grade, academic award, or parental approval.

Externally motivated students are motivated to learn primarily to earn a good grade, approval from parents, or some other tangible reward. Kids who get paid $10 for every A they make on their report card may be able to buy themselves the latest Nintendo game, but they'll never obtain the right source of motivation. Their parents are telling them that money is the motivation for learning. Without the external motivation of money, will their children simply keep their books closed and their minds shut? After all, they've got their Nintendo—what else could they possibly need?

## WHAT ABOUT INSPIRING TEACHERS?

You may be surprised: only 6 percent of perfect score students cited a teacher as being the most influential person in their lives. This means we can't point to good teachers and say, "Aha! *This* is why this student aced the SAT and became the brilliant mathematician he is today." The portrayal of inspiring teachers in popular movies leads us to believe that teachers are the true motivation behind a student's success. In *Stand and Deliver,* based on the true story of math teacher Jaime Escalante, a group of lackluster students from poor, broken families were inspired by their teacher to pass the AP calculus exam. In *Dead Poets Society,* Robin Williams encouraged students to think and develop their creative potential by following his carpe diem (seize the day!) philosophy. Yes, these are truly inspiring teachers, and they do have their counterparts in the real world.

However, these teachers are few and far between. And they often have the least impact on perfect score students, who have already found ways to navigate the academic terrain of high school on their own. Perfect score students did occasionally mention that they found a particular teacher to be inspiring. Some opted to major in astronomy in college after being turned on by their physics teacher, while others entered literary competitions at the suggestion and guidance of an engaging English teacher. They didn't, however, suggest that their entire life was turned around by a teacher. These high achievers were already on the path to academic and life success.

## GETTING THE RIGHT MIXTURE OF CONFIDENCE, HUMILITY, AND MOTIVATION

Confidence alone won't raise SAT scores. Nor, of course, will self-effacement, or even self-motivation. A perfect mixture of these three traits, however, will help students boost their SAT scores and achieve academic feats they never thought possible. Perfect score students use these qualities to set goals, to recognize any possible roadblocks in meeting these goals, and then to drive themselves to achieve these goals. Any student, regardless of his or her academic potential, can follow the same path if they have these tools.

Motivation to excel in all areas springs from both confidence and self-effacement. Students who are confident and have healthy self-esteem will be motivated to do well because they think they are entitled to succeed. On the flip side, those who have a good dose of humility will understand that they will need to work hard to maintain a high grade-point average or become a starter on the basketball team. They'll be motivated to put in the effort because they know they won't be able to accomplish their goals if they don't.

Parents can help their kids maintain a balance of confidence and self-effacement. Most parents today think they know how to boost their children's confidence. They lavish praise for a job well done and reward their children for goals accomplished. In fact, some would argue that we've gone too far in boosting children's confidence, handing out trophies to every Little League player regardless of whether the team won or not. Too much praise for too little accomplishment can give children an inflated sense of their own abilities, which can ultimately cause them to fail if they wrongly believe they don't need to expend a lot of energy to succeed. Children who have a keen understanding of their limitations, however, can counterbalance their confidence with self-effacement. Perfect score students tend to carry within them an ideal balance of these two opposing forces. As a result, they have a healthy dose of self-motivation.

All of us are motivated to do things by a mixture of sources both external and internal. We might want to advance professionally for our own self-respect or to earn the approbation of our parents or spouse. We might want to drive a fancy car because it feels good to be behind the wheel or because we can't wait to see our friends' looks of envy. A student's motivation to succeed academically also stems from factors both within their own psyche and outside themselves, in the expectations of parents, friends, and teachers.

Perfect score students are no exception, but they do depend largely on their own inner motivation to drive them to success. For example, these students report that they were motivated to do well on the SAT for the sake of meeting a challenge. They knew they could do well—some even thought they could ace it—and they wanted to see if they could meet the challenge. Did they enjoy receiving the academic awards that came with their perfect score, and did they bask in the kudos given to them by their parents and teachers? Yes, of course, but this wasn't the main source of their motivation.

Perfect score students would probably never have been able to develop their strong drive to succeed if their parents never took the giant leap of letting their kids have some control over their academic lives. They avoided the mistake that a lot of parents make when they decide to push their kids to the extreme. This misguided strategy usually backfires, and the child achieves less instead of more. Some parents view their child's success as their own and make it known that they won't be satisfied unless their child is at or near the top of the class. To stack the odds in their child's favor, they "help out" extensively with homework assignments and even rewrite college application essays. The message these parents are sending is loud and clear: "My child can't do it on his own, so I must step in." As a result, their child becomes even less motivated.

When I spoke with perfect score parents, I was struck by how little most of them had thought about what they expected in terms of their child's success. They didn't push their high achiever to take all AP classes or to practice a musical instrument several hours a day. They didn't tell their kid to go premed in college or handpick an Ivy League school. And they certainly never said the words *perfect score* and *SAT* in the same sentence. Over and over again, I heard from perfect score students, "My parents didn't push me. I think they were as surprised as I was by my 1600 score."

Parents who feel that they need to set expectations and goals for their children can often damage both themselves and their children. First of all, their children become dependent on them for motivation. This means homework won't get done until a parent is there to supervise, which puts a huge burden on the parent. It also means that once these children are finally on their own in college, they may not have a clue how to motivate themselves without a parent to organize their time and prod them along.

Perfect score parents certainly don't ignore their child's academic life. They do apply pressure when their child isn't meeting his or her potential. They also provide a lot of positive feedback when their child nails a big exam or oral speech. Their constructive criticism helped foster modesty and humility in their child, while the compliments helped boost their child's self-confidence. Both of these tactics helped create the self-motivated child, one capable of doing what it takes to earn a perfect SAT score.

Perfect score student Cindy B. admits that she blew off studying at the beginning of high school. "I was lazy. I really didn't need to do much in school to get good grades." Although happy with her grades, her parents were worried that she had no motivation to learn because everything came too easy. They encouraged Cindy to apply to a magnet public high school in her area for gifted and talented students. Cindy took the exam and gained admission to the high school. She says her new school taught her that learning could be challenging and was encouraged to put in more effort.

Other perfect score students faced similar challenges in high school. Perfect score student Yuan P. admits that he wasn't very social in high school. He says he was limited by his high school's small size—fewer than 450 students—and the small-town, provincial atmosphere. He found that "there weren't many people I could associate with either socially or intellectually." He knew, though, that he had strengths in other areas, so he decided to pursue them. He became editor in chief of the school newspaper because he was a good writer. He also served as cocaptain of the math team and science club because these were two areas he excelled at academically.

"It's important to do things you really enjoy," Yuan reflected. "I spend a lot of time thinking about everything, including why I think the way I do." Yuan relishes his time alone. "I spend a couple of hours a day reading everything from the classics to science fiction."

Yuan's strong sense of who he is and what he wants to do with his life helped him make the most of the small high school he attended. He wasn't able to click with a group of peers until he went to college, but this didn't hold him back. Yuan simply shrugged off the social limitations of his high school and went about fulfilling the goals he set for himself. He was able to do this because he has that inner drive to succeed, a gift that's universal in all those who achieve.

# Secret 2:
# They Are Intellectually Curious, and Excited About Learning New and Different Things

John Nash, the brilliant mathematician whose life was the subject of the Oscar-winning film *A Beautiful Mind,* wanted more than anything to be creative—to think up a completely original idea. When he first began his graduate work at Princeton, he embarked on a search for an extraordinary solution to an ordinary problem. He was interested in how people competed in different situations, and who achieved success and who didn't. He graphed everything from touch football games to board games to dating.

According to the movie, Nash's breakthrough came when he was in a bar, and he and his classmates were trying to pick up some girls. One girl was gorgeous and stood out from the rest. Nash had an epiphany. He explained to his friends that if they wanted to score with the women, they should do the opposite of what they'd normally do. If they all made a play for the prettiest girl, which is the most likely scenario, then none would succeed, or possibly one at most. However, if they all ignored the pretty girl and each went for a different girl in the group, then all the girls would be flattered and more likely to accept dates from them. This was the best way to maximize the chance that all the guys would win and get a girl. In the movie, this became the basis for Nash's thesis on game theory for which he later won the Nobel Prize.

Nash succeeded in coming up with a truly creative idea. He had a drive to produce something original, and he managed to accomplish a feat that changed the way we think about the world. Perfect score students also have this yearning to tap into their own creativity. Many engage in creative pursuits like painting, composing music, and writing poetry. Some simply spend their time dreaming up creative ideas like new ways to solve math problems or an interesting twist on a scientific theory.

Like John Nash, perfect score students continually engage in this search for new ways to look at the world. According to the Perfect Score Study, natural curiosity is one of their defining characteristics. Almost without exception, perfect score students actively seek answers to the probing questions they have about the way the world works.

"What are you curious about?" I asked Ari S. "This may sound strange," he answered, "but I've always wondered about moths and light. Several years ago, I saw moths flying up against the windows at night. What attracts moths to light? If moths are nocturnal, why should they be attracted to light? I've searched biology books, textbooks, and science books. Interestingly, I've found that no one really knows why. There is no explanation in the books, so I'll keep searching. For some reason, I'm really curious about this." Ari told me that he planned to pursue research on moths and their attraction to light during his college years. He said his curiosity will keep driving him until he finds the answer.

For Alex H., theoretical physics was the wellspring of his curiosity: "I've read everything I could get my hands on, including all of Stephen

Hawking's works and Brian Greene's book *The Elegant Universe.* I even tried to get Brian Greene to speak on my college campus."

Perfect score students pursue their curiosity in varying ways. Some read every book they can on a given topic that entices them. Others haunt their local museums or take summer classes to quench their thirst for knowledge. If they're taking a high school course to advance their level of understanding, they'll read all the supplemental materials in addition to the assigned coursework. They told me they are compelled not by the pursuit of a high grade, but by their interest in the subject matter.

Jane C., a perfect score student, talked about her advanced calculus class, in which she spent fifteen hours over three days trying to find the answer to one particular problem. She met with the professor twice, worked with kids in her study group (who thought she was a little crazy), but she eventually solved it. She never mentioned the grade she got in the course because the grade wasn't important to her. Jane's problem-solving quest was typical of those perfect score students who were focused on science and math.

This innate curiosity crosses over into all areas and subjects, both academic and nonacademic. Like all students, perfect score students are curious about whatever interests them most and whatever they excel at. They may be Civil War buffs or computer whizzes. Or they might have an encyclopedic knowledge of sports. Regardless of what drives them, perfect score students nearly always take the next step, which is to turn their curiosity into creativity.

## THE BENEFITS OF BEING CREATIVE

From curiosity springs creativity, and perfect score students find ways to express their own unique creativity. This creativity enables them to reach the highest echelons of academic success. It gives them a broader range of knowledge and exposure to a lot of different topics.

Paul C. explores and gains knowledge through firsthand experience. Though fascinated by physics and artificial intelligence, he says he's a mathematician at heart. And he finds that the books he reads just don't give him enough of what he's seeking. He doesn't get truly excited until he's actually exploring on his own. "I think a lot about what I want to do," explains Paul. "With all the things I'm interested in, I try to find focus. I tend to be very logical and analytical, always asking the *how* questions rather than the *why*, whether I'm thinking about school, science, myself, or whatever."

Paul works on differential math equations for fun, but he also pursues his mathematical curiosity by manipulating 3-D graphics on the computer or creating animation from a mathematical formula he's dreamed up. And in the manner of other mathematicians who dissect the works of Bach to study mathematical principles, Paul composes his own music on the computer, attempting to insert his own mathematical patterns to see how this alters the composition—the work of a truly creative individual.

You might wonder why creativity is so important for doing well on a standardized test like the SAT. After all, aren't standardized tests the antithesis of creativity? Answering questions on a bubble sheet that will be scored by a computer may seem as far as you can get from producing something creative and original. And yet, those who do the best on the SAT are often the most creative.

Remember, the SAT isn't a test of knowledge but rather a test of the way students think. The easy questions require straightforward thinking. The more difficult questions require students to think in a more roundabout way, to consider novel approaches to a problem. This is a sign of a creative thinker.

While most students see things only once, the creative student looks at math, English, and other subjects from a whole series of different perspectives. Algebra isn't just a course, it's something that may spark an interest in string theory to explain how the universe works. English may be a gateway into classical writers like Shakespeare or Socrates and their use of language, character development, and themes that transcend time.

Being a creative thinker also sparks a desire to seek solutions to intriguing problems. One perfect score student went to a challenging mathematics competition and was able to solve half the problems that were presented to him, earning him a ranking of 14 out of the 167 students competing. Although he was proud of his accomplishment, he went home and immediately began looking at the questions he missed to find out how they worked, and to devise different ways of doing them. He wanted to find the quickest, most streamlined solutions to these problems. This student's creative mind never stops working, even after the competition is finished and the judges are gone.

Perfect score students continuously seek to learn more and do more until they're satisfied they've exhausted all the avenues that interest them. They're always encountering new areas, which helps them figure out how to approach different problems with different solutions. In essence, they are conceptual thinkers, which means they learn how to apply their understanding and thinking from one area to another. This allows them to take more risks intellectually. When confronted with a challenge, these students consider and reject obvious solutions that appear right on the surface but aren't ultimately the best answer. This trait can help them enormously on the SAT. The SAT contains a variety of tricky questions, usually near the end of each section, designed specifically to trip up students. To answer these questions correctly, students must find creative ways to approach them. Ultimately, this challenge is what separates the perfect score student from the above-average student.

## TURNING CURIOSITY INTO CREATIVITY

According to the Perfect Score Study, these students display a wide variety of types of creativity. Steve S. told me his passion was computers. At first, I took this to mean that he loved spending time surfing the Internet—far from a creative pursuit. But then Steve elaborated on what his passion was really all about. "I really like programming computer games. It's exciting to be able to stretch the limits of what I am able to do on the computer."

Daniel B. is also a computer whiz, but he broke the mold with his creative pursuits. While a senior in high school, he served as vice president of Interact, a club that developed Internet websites and won freelance contracts from local manufacturers to develop their websites. He worked with a student from Argentina to develop a 160-page bilingual website, with text in both English and Spanish, that explored psychology and the emotional complexities of being a teenager. He also worked with a friend to redesign his high school's website and won a national contest for this creative design. He and his friend were sent on a paid trip to Geneva, Switzerland, to compete in a worldwide competition. Now attending Stanford University, Daniel is continuing with his website work. "He recently got to meet Bill Gates at a leadership conference," says his father, Gary. "That was really exciting for him, since Bill is one of his heroes."

What exactly is creativity? In his book *Creativity: Flow and the Psychology of Discovery and Invention*, Mihaly Csikszentmihalyi defines creativity as a process by which major changes are made in our culture —from new ideas to new songs to new machines. To find out how the creative process works, Csikszentmihalyi studied 91 exceptional individuals, such as Nobel Prize chemist Linus Pauling and sculptor Leonard Baskin, who made a broad impact on our culture.

Csikszentmihalyi found that the major attribute that distinguishes creative individuals from noncreative ones is complexity. By this he means that creative people often exhibit contradictory extremes to bring together an entire range of human possibilities within themselves. We all have dual qualities within ourselves, but usually we favor one and repress the other. For instance, we might grow up cultivating the aggressive, competitive side of our nature, and disdain or repress the nurturing, cooperative side. A creative individual is more likely to be both aggressive and cooperative—either at the same time or at different times, depending on the situation. Having a complex personality means being able to express the full range of human traits with a full spectrum of human emotions. In his work with creative individuals, Csikszentmihalyi found that certain conflicting traits are more likely to be present.

Creative people are more likely to be both smart and naive, both responsible and irresponsible, both extroverted and introverted.

I noticed many of the same paradoxes and conflicting traits in the perfect score students whom I interviewed for the study. I found that perfect score students are very serious academically, yet they still crave fun and spend a lot of time unwinding with friends. They are firmly planted in reality in terms of doing what it takes to succeed in high school and get into a good college. Yet, they also live in a bit of a dreamworld, making plans for how they're going to change the world and searching for metaphysical answers to how the universe works. Some are even a little flaky. Shannon B. recalls that she almost got to the testing center too late to take the SAT. "I'm really absentminded and got lost on the way driving to my friend's house to pick her up. We literally got there with less than a minute to spare." And yet Shannon was then able to pull together her mental focus and answer every question correctly.

Creativity can also be defined as the generating of novel and valuable ideas that may be viewed by others, at first, as counterintuitive or counterproductive. The creative person defies the crowd and persists in pursuing these ideas. Eventually, these ideas are embraced by society as valid and often as a superior alternative to the typical way of thinking. Psychologist Robert Sternberg, author of *Successful Intelligence,* sums it up perfectly when he writes: "Creatively smart people are like good investors. They buy low and sell high. They defy the crowd and, eventually, come to lead it."

Perfect score students cherish those who think outside the box and try to emulate these role models. Cindy B., a perfect score student from Cincinnati, Ohio, knew she wanted to do something creative in high school, so she entered a national robotics competition. She worked with a team of students to build a robot, and she wrote and designed a book about designing and testing the robot that she presented to the committee of judges. "I enjoyed being part of this process, being around people who could truly create something out of nothing," Cindy said.

In high school, Cindy found that most of her creative talents took the form of putting images on the page, whether it was doing design work and layout for a gifted and talented newsletter that her mother edited or taking photographs on her trips abroad. "I took my camera everywhere I went and took photography classes. The subjects I found most interesting were photographing people in urban environments."

During her second year in college, Cindy decided to study abroad for a semester. Since she was nearly fluent in French, she chose the French-speaking country of Senegal in Africa. "I took some interesting photos of the people there," Cindy said. "I'm planning on entering them in a photography competition."

Other perfect score students look for creative solutions to the world's problems. Some joined a mock economics team where they pretended to be members of the Federal Reserve deciding whether and when to change interest rates. Some participated in a Model UN, where they took on roles as delegates from foreign nations voting on international policy. By and large, these students were always searching for ways to develop and express new ideas.

Michelle W. describes herself as "a curious person who enjoys learning about all different subjects. I have a wide range of interests and eclectic tastes. I've never liked trying to describe or categorize myself." This perfect score student said she joined a mock trial in order to explore a lot of contemporary issues, from women's rights to gun control. She says the purpose of her life is to "experience as much as I can," which is why she plays both piano in a small chamber ensemble and clarinet in a jazz band.

Michelle chose to go to a small liberal arts college for the specific purpose of designing her own major. "I've created a major in sustainable technology," she told me. "This major will allow me to explore which technologies are going to predominate in the future and why some technologies succeed while others, like the Bowmar Brain and eight-track tapes, fail." It's the kind of major that only a creative person could design.

Most would agree, however, that creativity isn't just the ability to come up with new ideas. It's the balance of the analytical, creative, and practical that makes a creative idea applicable in the real world.

Emily D., a perfect score student from Atlanta who is now attending Princeton, is a creative writer. She describes herself as a poet and says she often writes to express her emotions, but her writing is grounded in reality. "I never write about fantasy. My poems deal with real-life problems and my plan for solving them. The way I think is more analytical. That's when my writing is at its best," she explains.

We don't normally think of creativity as a form of scientific thinking, but that's precisely what it is. In fact, the same analytical thinking that fuels creativity is the type of thinking needed to figure out SAT questions. Some perfect score students say they aced the SAT because they were able to get inside the heads of the question writers. "After taking practice tests and analyzing the questions I got wrong, I figured out the correct way to answer the questions," says Matthew S. "We're always taught in school to look at things from different angles, but there's a certain logic to the SAT questions. I learned it and gave the answers I knew the College Board was looking for. The second time I took the SAT, when I got a perfect score, I knew which section was experimental just by the types of questions that were asked. I was so certain of it that I left this section completely blank."

What's interesting is that Matthew used his creative skills to crack the code of the SAT. Most of us wouldn't think of this as an act of creativity, but that's exactly what it was. Matthew employed his analytical way of thinking and meshed it with a practical approach to the test. When he thought his answer seemed too obvious for a difficult question at the end, he applied a fresh creative approach to the question and took another stab at it. I would argue that Matthew is a case in point that the SAT can, indeed, test a student's creative thought processes. In fact, the essay portion of the new SAT will give students a chance to actually express their creative thoughts.

## DEVELOPING CREATIVITY

Most parents want their children to break new ground, to venture out where no others have gone before. But can creativity really be learned, or is it simply a natural gift that we inherit along with freckles and an outgoing disposition? The answer is the former. Creativity, like all abilities, can be developed. Still, creative people do have certain characteristics that can be emulated by high school students or anyone else interested in tapping into their creativity.

1. **Creative people seek out, and later become, role models.** Parents who want their kids to be creative need to be creative themselves. If a daughter sees her mother's passion for writing poetry, she may be inclined to write down her own thoughts and impressions of the world in a unique way. If a son helps his father build a wood dining room table from lumber they cut down and sanded together, he might appreciate the creative gifts of building something by hand. Creativity springs from children when they are shown—not told—how to be creative. One perfect score student told me she and her mother took an origami class together, which helped them to bond, be creative, and learn about their Japanese roots all at the same time.

2. **Creative people question so-called facts/and want others to do so.** Even scientists' leading theories can be wrong, and creative people know this. They know how to discern absolute truths from opinion, and they don't shy away from questioning opinions. For example, the recent destruction of the space shuttle *Columbia* had NASA managers frantically trying to determine the cause of the disaster. Upon reviewing E-mails written by lower-level engineers before the shuttle crashed, they found that some creative thinkers had predicted that the shuttle might malfunction upon reentry due to a piece of insulation that flew off when the shuttle left Earth. We can't help but wonder if the circumstances would have turned out any differently if these high-level managers heeded the warnings of these intuitive engineers instead of listening to reassurances from the broader group of experts.

   Parents should encourage children to question assumptions that many of us believe to be valid. Many of these, of course, are valid, but creative children need to understand why we think and act the way we do. Creative children will always ask "why?" And they may not give up until they find the answer.

3. **Creative people take smart risks and admire others who do so.** In order to produce an original work that others will ultimately appreciate and accept, some amount of risk is involved. It's important to understand, however, that these are smart or sensible risks. It's not the kind of risk involved in, say, investing in a snow-removal business in Florida. It's the kind of risk that comes from being unusual or unique.

Schools often discourage risk taking in favor of conformity. Teachers emphasize rules and structure, with the idea that deviation only leads to chaos. This may make it easier for the teachers to teach according to their lesson plans, but it shortchanges the student.

Students who ace the SAT mentioned fairly often that they took risks. Stephanie W. says she had the idea of helping immigrants learn English as a second language. She decided to volunteer at a program, exposed herself to a roomful of strangers, and expanded the program into a language appreciation class. She emphasized not only English but also all the native languages that the immigrants spoke. She wanted to help the immigrants learn English and appreciate one another's languages and see America in a different light. She knew she was taking a risk in expanding the way this program was taught, but it was a chance she was willing to take.

4. **Creative people seek out tasks that enable them to express their creativity.** Creative people, of course, do creative things. What's interesting, however, is that they place a premium on their creative works. Lucy Z. told me that writing is one of her passions. "Whenever I get the chance, I write. I've written short stories, poems, even a column in my local newspaper in Atlanta on the cultural differences between Chinese Americans and Americans."

Lucy says her writing is largely autobiographical, detailing her life growing up as the daughter of Chinese immigrants. She says even when she wrote essays for her high school classes, she drew on her creativity and put her life experiences into her analytical writing. "It helped make my academics less tedious," she explains. She says she's prouder of her writing than of her 1600 SAT score. "It felt good to get a perfect score, but then the excitement wore off after a little while. But with my creative writing, the excitement doesn't wear off."

5. **Creative people allow themselves time to think creatively.** Perfect score students take the time to keep journals. They take the time to practice an instrument, sometimes two or three hours a day if it's a passion. They take the time to figure out complicated math equations, sometimes staying up all night if they're driven by a particular challenge.

Contrary to what many of us think, creative ideas don't just pop into people's heads. We mull them over and take the time to develop them and rework them again and again. Einstein didn't figure out his theory of relativity on a paper napkin. It took him several years to develop. And although Einstein came up with theories on quantum mechanics, he spent a lifetime trying to figure out exactly how the behavior of subatomic particles could mesh with the laws of nature.

Unfortunately, heavy demands are placed on high school students in the United States to the extent that most have little free time to engage in creative pursuits. Very few students cherish their time alone and use it to express themselves as individuals. Perhaps if high school teachers placed more emphasis on individual creativity, more students would see the value of setting time aside for producing something original.

6. **Creative people recognize the best environment in which to grow.** Creativity can only flourish in an optimal environment. Michelle W. recognized that the creative major she wanted to design wouldn't be appreciated at the three Ivy League colleges where she'd been accepted. So she turned down the prestigious

colleges for a less prestigious school that would allow her to put together her own major with courses that she chose.

Creative people look for places that will encourage their talents, not force them to conform to a set of standards that will hamper their creativity. Research shows that people do the most creative work when they're doing what they love. They need to be in an environment that makes them happy.

All students should be encouraged to develop their creativity in areas where they are most talented. Whether it's designing clothes or creating new traffic patterns to reduce congestion, creativity comes in all shapes and forms. But the most important spark for creativity is an individual's passion.

This passion, though, should be mingled with objectivity. Most creative people who are passionate about their work can also be extremely objective about it. They can view their work with an air of detachment in order to evaluate both its strengths and weaknesses. This conflict or contradiction illustrates the complexity that is the hallmark of Csikszentmihalyi's theories on creativity. It's this complexity that is at the central core of most students who ace the SAT. And I believe this complexity lies within all students, regardless of their academic accomplishments. This complexity carries the creative potential. The question is: what amount of time and effort are students willing to spend to see their own creative talents flourish?

Curiosity is the driving force behind learning. It forms the questions in our mind and triggers our explorations into the unknown. As the Perfect Score Study suggests, the students who are the thirstiest for knowledge are the ones who reach the greatest intellectual heights. While exploring whatever piques their interest, perfect score students often allow their imaginations to expand into new and different ideas. They get a buzz from creating something original that has their own unique mark. These curious and creative pursuits enhance the world of perfect score students and ultimately enable them to enhance the world.

# *Secret 3:*
# They Read Quickly and Voraciously, Following Their Interests Wherever They Lead

With their heavy course loads and packed schedule of after-school activities, perfect score students have little free time. When they do find an hour or two to spare, what are they most likely to do? Curl up on the couch with a good book. "I absolutely love to read just for fun," says Emily D. "I used to read all the time. In second grade, I won a contest for reading the most chapter books in my grade during the school year. I would breeze through one Agatha Christie book a week in junior high."

In high school, Emily found, to her dismay, that her assigned reading for school left her with less free time to indulge in novels of her choosing. But she still read for fun whenever she could. "Once in a while, I read the best-seller paperbacks that my parents had lying around the house, but I usually went for more challenging books. In my junior year, I got into philosophical books about existentialism. I also fell in love with southern writers like Faulkner," says Emily, who grew up in Atlanta.

Emily is convinced that her avid reading habits increased her vocabulary for the SAT. She says she never made a single vocabulary flash card and actually recognized several challenging words on the test that she had seen in books she recently read. "Reading gave me such a leg up in high school and on the SAT. It improved my writing and helped with word usage and sentence construction, which are both on the test," she explains.

Most important, Emily found that reading enabled her to become, well, a better reader. "I learned to quickly read through passages and determine what's most important or relevant. This definitely helped me speed through the reading comprehension section on the SAT."

What's more, the new reading section of the SAT will feature, for the first time, at least one fiction passage on every test. These passages will come from challenging works often assigned in good English classes. Coincidentally, many of the titles being considered by the College Board are also among the list of favorite books read by Perfect Score students (see pages 94 and 95). Students who have already read these passages—especially in the context of the whole book—will have a clear advantage over those who haven't.

The Perfect Score Study found that reading is integral to achievement, not only on the SAT and in school, but also in all aspects of life. Perfect score students gain much of their knowledge about the world through books, newspapers, and other materials that they read. Reading opens up worlds into the unknown and enables them to feed their curiosity while at the same time leaving them hungry for more.

## THE AMOUNT OF TIME SPENT READING IS CRUCIAL

So how much reading do students need to do to be academically successful? That's a difficult question to answer. According to data from the Perfect Score Study, students who ace the SAT read an average of fourteen hours a week. Average score students, on the other hand, read only eight hours a week—an immense drop-off. The biggest difference, however, was found in the amount of time students spent reading for school. Average score students spent four hours a week reading literature, textbooks, and other assigned reading for school. Perfect score students put in nine hours a week for school-assigned reading, more than double the amount of time.

## TIME SPENT READING (HOURS PER WEEK)

| Activity | Perfect Score Students | Average Students |
|---|---|---|
| School Reading | 9 | 4 |
| Pleasure Reading | 5 | 4 |
| Total | 14 | 8 |

Does extra time spent reading translate into a higher SAT score? The Perfect Score Study can't conclude that with certainty, but it certainly suggests that this is the case. Like Emily, perfect score students breeze through the reading comprehension portion of the SAT with time to spare. The sheer volume of reading they've done over the years has made it easier for them to digest reading material and zone in on what's most important in a given passage.

Reading also naturally increases vocabulary, which is important for the word analogy and sentence completion sections on the SAT. While many perfect score students confessed to making vocabulary flash cards to review for the SAT, nearly all of them said that their vocabulary skills were strong to begin with. Cindy B. says that her knowledge of French helped her snag a few vocabulary questions that she might otherwise have gotten wrong. In her last two years of high school, she took advanced French and read novels in French like *Le Petit Prince* by Antoine de Saint-Exupéry. "I remember looking at a few unknown words and thinking that they looked like they were derived from French words that I knew," Cindy recalls. She was able to make a good educated guess about what these words meant, and apparently her guesses were correct.

## FAVORITE READING CHOICES OF PERFECT SCORE STUDENTS

What do perfect score students read for fun? What do they read for school? The Perfect Score Study didn't identify one book that stood out from the rest as a must-read for all superbright students, although there were one or two books that were mentioned as favorites by as many as ten students. The book most frequently mentioned—by a total of 6 percent of perfect score students—was *Catch-22* by Joseph Heller. Overall, however, the books spanned a vast range from classical literature to contemporary novels; from science theory to science fiction; from satire to philosophy.

The top book choices of perfect score students, selected from books they were assigned to read in school, look like a typical list of great books that many top high school students across the nation are reading.

## Perfect Score Students' Favorite Books Assigned for School

*Anna Karenina* by Leo Tolstoy

*1984* by George Orwell

*Catch-22* by Joseph Heller

*Brave New World* by Aldous Huxley

*Heart of Darkness* by Joseph Conrad

*The Grapes of Wrath* by John Steinbeck

*The Great Gatsby* by F. Scott Fitzgerald

*The Awakening* by Kate Chopin

*A Separate Peace* by John Knowles

*To Kill a Mockingbird* by Harper Lee

*Hamlet* by William Shakespeare

*Great Expectations* by Charles Dickens

*Huckleberry Finn* by Mark Twain

The favorite books that perfect score students choose to read for pleasure also span the spectrum and include a mixture of classical and modern works. *Catch-22* again came up as a favorite reading choice, along with these wide-ranging selections:

## Perfect Score Students' Favorite Books Read for Pleasure

*The Right Stuff* by Tom Wolfe

*The Day of the Jackal* by Frederick Forsyth

*Gone with the Wind* by Margaret Mitchell

*The Hunt for Red October* by Tom Clancy

*The World According to Garp* by John Irving

*Pride and Prejudice* by Jane Austen

*Animal Farm* by George Orwell

*The Little Prince* by Antoine de Saint-Exupéry

*Les Miserables* by Victor Hugo

Other works appearing on both the favorite lists for school and pleasure included Hermann Hesse's *Siddhartha,* Ayn Rand's *The Fountainhead,* Fyodor Dostoyevsky's *Crime and Punishment,* J. D. Salinger's *The Catcher in the Rye,* and William Golding's *Lord of the Flies.* Novels appear to rate over nonfiction books as the reading choices preferred by perfect score students. Although some students mentioned that they read popular science books by such authors as Stephen Hawking and Carl Sagan, nearly all students named a work of fiction as their *favorite* among books they read for fun.

The fact that *Catch-22* came up as a favorite on both lists is telling. A classic work of antiwar satire, Heller's novel most likely appeals to these sophisticated high school students because it challenges authority figures and embraces rebelliousness. We all know that teenagers often go through a tough time during the years when they're not children anymore but not quite adults. Parents and teachers still dictate the rules, and teenagers resent being told what to do. They learn to challenge and question these rules as they become their own individuals and separate from their parents.

Other students look for entertaining novels with exciting plot twists that will take them on mental adventures. Some students listed the best-selling Harry Potter books by J. K. Rowling as their favorites (and, remember, these students were interviewed some time ago—by the time this book is published Harry Potter will doubtless have won over even more perfect score students); others named *The Firm* by John Grisham. Many students mentioned science fiction as their favorite genre. Leslie V., now in her junior year at Harvard, says she was an avid reader of science fiction and fantasy books. She read the Harry Potter books in high school, as well as *The Lion, the Witch and the Wardrobe* and the other *Chronicles of Narnia* books by C. S. Lewis. "I really like the escapism of these books, with their adventure plots and interesting story lines," Leslie says. "Journey books appeal to me far more than nonfiction, realistic books. What can I say? I like being entertained. I watched a lot of fantasy and sci-fi shows on TV in high school and read these books. My everyday life in high school didn't involve crazy adventures. I didn't take too many physical risks. I found my books were a good break from my studying and the humdrum life I led."

By and large, perfect score students chose to spend their time reading challenging books. One student named *The Satanic Verses* by Salman Rushdie as his favorite book. Another said she loves Amy Tan's generational novel *The Joy Luck Club* because it reflects the relationship she has with her mother and grandmother. Other students listed Toni Morrison, Ernest Hemingway, and Henrik Ibsen as their favorite authors.

As you can see, no one book or author stands out among perfect score students. The common denominator is that perfect score students simply read and read—whatever they can get their hands on. They read newspapers and magazines that their parents subscribe to. They read books their teachers recommend. They read a variety of authors and don't limit themselves to Dickens and Shakespeare.

One student even confessed that she devoured comic books. Jane S. embodies the complexity typical in perfect score students. The reading material that had the most impact on her during high school was comic books and *Gödel, Escher, Bach* by Douglas Hofstadter, a highly sophisticated nonfiction book linking the mathematical theories of Gödel with the patterns in Escher's art and Bach's music. "It was a real mental trip," she says with a tinkle of laughter in her voice. "My math teacher recommended it, though at the time I didn't fully grasp the integrated process of math, art, and music that the book was trying to prove." Attending a magnet math and science school in downtown Chicago, Jane says most of her friends read and discussed Hofstadter's book and other books on scientific theory. "I was really into math and passionate about music—I played the cello and bassoon in the orchestra—but I really didn't think about art until I got into comic books. Visual arts really weren't discussed much in my school. Our teachers pretty much assumed that we were heading for careers in computer science, math, or physics."

It wasn't until Jane discovered comic books that she began to think about drawing as a career. "My favorite comic book was called *Love and Rockets,* which deals with the punk scene in California. I was into stuff that blended literary concepts with real-world issues. This book goes far beyond generic superheroes." Jane always enjoyed doodling in high school and spent her free time sketching pictures of her friends eating lunch, studying, or chatting with one another. "I found it to be a great stress reliever, a great emotional outlet," she says.

When Jane got accepted to Yale, her teachers and parents assumed she would major in computer science, a continuation of the course work she focused on in high school. But Jane couldn't get those comic books out of her mind. "I always liked to draw and was always interested in art, but it wasn't until college that I actually made the bold move of considering art as a profession," she explains. Jane decided to declare herself a visual arts major with a focus in painting and drawing. After she graduates from Yale, her dream is to become a comic book illustrator and writer. "I grew up in an Asian community, and my parents' friends think I'm crazy to be going to

Yale for art. But drawing feels good. It feels right, and now I finally have enough guts to pursue it."

## INCREASED READING AND INCREASED SPEED

The typical perfect score student reported reading a book or two a month for pleasure in addition to the books they read for school. The results also show they read faster than average students. Reading quickly is definitely a vital skill to have when taking standardized tests like the SAT. It also helps students manage the prodigious amounts of reading material that they'll encounter in college. Far too many college freshmen are unprepared for the amount of reading they're assigned. Just as physical fitness is improved by working out, students can improve their reading fitness by spending more time reading.

The major difference between the reading habits of perfect score students and those of their average-scoring counterparts is the amount of time spent reading for school. The Perfect Score Study found that both groups spend about the same amount of time reading for pleasure and studying for class exams, but perfect score students trounce the average students when it comes to completing school reading assignments. They spend more than twice as much time reading for school, and this appears to make a difference in their academic outcomes.

This extra time devoted to reading may help to increase the reading speed of perfect score students. Consider the experience of John D. When I interviewed John for the Perfect Score Study, he told me reading was a passion of his and that his favorite book was Tolstoy's voluminous *War and Peace*. He said he spends twenty hours a week reading, which was more than the average perfect score student. He added that he was turned on to reading by his parents, who read to him extensively as a child. But John also has the mystery *x* factor that fosters his love of reading. "I read very quickly," he revealed. "This enables me to do not only the required reading for school, but also some supplemental reading. In addition, I can indulge my eclectic reading tastes."

John enjoys reading, at least in part because he's a fast reader, and the same holds true for the majority of perfect score students. A significant 54 percent of perfect score students said they read fast; 38 percent reported their speed is moderate, and only 8 percent said they are slow readers. When the same question was put to the average academic achievers, only 42 percent said they read fast, 48 percent reported a moderate speed, and 10 percent said they are slow.

Many perfect score students believe their reading speed gives them an academic edge. Given the fact that perfect score students are fast readers, you might assume that they spend less time reading for school than average students. Actually, it's the opposite. These high achievers actually spend *more* time reading. The only conclusion that can be made is that perfect score students simply read more material for their school assignments. In fact, many of them, like John, told me that they not only thoroughly read all the assigned books they get for class, but for extra credit or just personal interest they also frequently read additional books that their teachers recommend.

Somewhere along the line, average-scoring students may be cutting corners academically. We've all seen students who skim novels and read just the plot summaries of Shakespeare's plays instead of sitting down and reading a book cover to cover. When students read for pleasure, they usually savor every page. Reading for school is another story. Cliff Notes and other materials that coach students on the book's central themes may be partly to blame. If students are given an easy out, many choose to take it. This is unfortunate because really these students are cheating. They're cheating themselves out of a good book. And they're cheating themselves out of improved verbal skills that would naturally raise their SAT scores. Now who would knowingly choose to rip themselves off?

I realize that some parents—and probably far more students—worry that reading too much will take time away from activities that are, well, active. No one wants the pale pasty look of someone who sits in a quiet room reading all day. The good news is that the Perfect Score Study lays that fear to rest.

While perfect score students do spend fourteen hours a week reading, they spend far more time engaged in other activities. Perfect score students spent over thirty hours a week, almost three times as much time, playing on the computer, watching TV, playing sports, socializing, and participating in clubs. The exact breakdown is given below.

### TIME SPENT BY ACTIVITY FOR PERFECT SCORE STUDENTS (HOURS/WEEK)

| School Reading | 9 | reading—14 |
|---|---|---|
| Pleasure Reading | 5 | |
| Computer | 6 | |
| TV | 4 | |
| Sports | 7 | other activities—31 |
| Socializing | 8 | |
| Clubs | 6 | |

Average students, in contrast, spend eight hours a week reading and nine studying. They spend a total of forty-three hours a week on other activities like TV watching, socializing, and participating in sports and clubs. So, yes, the amount of time that perfect score students spend reading does take away time from other activities but not to such a significant extent.

What's more, watching TV and playing on the computer are just as physically inactive as reading, and both groups of students had plenty of time a week to devote to those. Average score students spent five hours a week watching TV and eight hours a week on the computer; this is a total of three extra hours spent on these activities, compared with their perfect score counterparts. I'd hazard a guess that these three hours probably replace time that could have been spent reading for school.

Other research has found that dismal reading skills are an epidemic nationwide. According to a survey published by the Yankelovich polling firm, 77 percent of all young adults between the ages of sixteen and twenty-two watch more than ten hours of television per week, and 27 percent of the respondents reported watching more than thirty hours per week. At the same time, almost 70 percent of the participants said they read four books or fewer a year. A startling 45 percent said they read nothing at all.

These reading rates are even more dismal than what I found among the control group of students in my study who scored average to slightly above average on the SAT. The reason for this difference probably lies in the fact that my control group is composed of higher academic achievers than the typical young adults surveyed by Yankelovich, who may or may not be bound for college.

There is a lesson to be learned here, even if it's an obvious one. The highest academic achievers spend the most time reading and the least time watching TV. The more students read, the more they will excel—in school, in academic activities, in life.

## READING FROM THE MOMENT OF BIRTH

Almost universally, perfect score students had parents who read to them from the moment of birth. These parents instinctively knew that even before their children understood language, they could glean insights from the colorful pictures in *Goodnight Moon* or *The Very Hungry Caterpillar*.

Science backs up these instincts. The latest discoveries in neuroscience show that reading aloud to babies actually stimulates the growth of their brains. In fact, according to research from the University of Chicago, an infant's brain structure is not genetically predetermined. Quite clearly, early experiences have a decisive impact on the architecture of a baby's brain.

A report from the 2001 Conference on Brain Development titled "Rethinking the Brain: New Insights into Early Development" states: "A child care provider reads to a toddler. And in a matter of seconds, thousands of cells in these children's growing brains respond. Some brain cells are 'turned on,' triggered by this particular experience. Many existing connections among brain cells are strengthened. At the same time, new brain cells are formed, adding a bit more definition and complexity to the intricate circuitry that will remain largely in place for the rest of these children's lives."

Despite these benefits, only 53 percent of women and 42 percent of men reported in a *USA Today* poll that their parents read to them in childhood. This differs significantly from the experiences of perfect score students. They reported that reading was an integral part of their lives, starting from their earliest memories. After sports, reading was the second most frequently mentioned activity that they engaged in from preschool onward. Moreover, reading at a young age carried over to high school, since a significant percentage of perfect score students listed reading as one of the most common activities they did for fun. Reading remained pretty high on the list of favorites despite the fact that it had to compete with "cooler" teen activities.

### ACTIVITIES PERFECT SCORE STUDENTS DO FOR FUN IN HIGH SCHOOL (PERCENTAGES)

| Activity | % |
| --- | --- |
| Socializing | 72 |
| Movies/TV | 36 |
| Sports | 26 |
| Reading | 22 |
| Music | 20 |
| Computer | 14 |

## TURNING YOUR CHILD INTO A PERFECT SCORE READER

It's clear from the Perfect Score Study that parents of perfect score students made a dramatic impact in fostering their child's reading habits. By the time these students entered high school, they had a solid reading foundation and intrinsically continued a habit that was instilled in them since the earliest days of their memory.

So what did these parents do to turn their kids on to reading? First of all, they looked for signals that their child was ready to read, regardless of their child's age. One mother of a perfect score student said she saw signs that her four-year-old son, Jonathan, was ready to begin reading. He knew all his letters and the sounds they made and was beginning to recognize words by sight. She went to the principal of Jonathan's preschool and asked her to evaluate her son. The principal said she would test the boy but later reported back that the child was not ready to read. Since the principal was a "professional," the mother accepted the finding. One week later, the mother recalled, "I found my son in a little corner of his bedroom reading a book aloud." After that, she took it upon herself to teach her son to read. Jonathan was reading fluently before he entered kindergarten.

Reading is one of the first skills children learn when they enter school. Some, like Jonathan, even teach themselves to read before entering kindergarten. Educational experts, developmental psychologists, and even First Ladies make it a point to tell parents to read to their children. We all know that reading is fundamental. It's been drummed into our heads over and over again.

And still, some kids hear this message louder than others. Some kids are drawn to books and read everything they can get their hands on. Others have to be prodded to turn off the TV and pick up a book. I've heard far too many parents complain, "My child just doesn't like to read." But this is a cop-out for both the parent and child. Both need to spend time together figuring out what kinds of things the child would like to read about. I can't tell you how many nine-year-olds were turned on to reading by the Harry Potter books.

Fostering a love of reading in your child takes more than just sitting down and reading books together (though that is an important factor). America Reads, a panel of education experts convened by the U.S. government to study the literacy issue, issued five recommendations to parents for encouraging reading development in their children:

1. **Place value on literacy.** Parents who have a positive attitude toward reading can help their children become more successful readers. If you read, your child will too. Children, especially young ones, use their parents as role models and will be excited by activities that excite their mother or father. Parents can read in front of their child and, if the books are age appropriate, discuss them with the child. Children who learn from parents that reading is fun may be more likely to sustain efforts to learn to read when the going gets tough.

2. **Press for achievement.** Let your child know that you expect her to achieve. There is, though, a fine line between pressing and pushing. If your child retreats from books after your urging, you've probably pushed too hard and should take a step back, letting your child gravitate to books naturally.

3. **Make reading material accessible.** Homes full of books and writing materials for children create more opportunities to develop literacy. You should have at least twenty-five books at your child's disposal. And make sure to have a set of encyclopedias in book form or on CD-ROM, child-friendly magazines, and newspapers on hand for your child to peruse. Keeping writing utensils and paper accessible will encourage your budding writer to create stories, poems, or a journal. Take your child to the public library at least once a month. And give books or magazine subscriptions as a present or recognition of a special achievement.

4. **Read with your child.** Parents who read to preschoolers and listen as older children read aloud will help their children become

readers. Reading challenging books a grade or two above your child's level can improve your child's vocabulary, grammar, and spelling and will probably improve writing skills as well. Parents can play an active role in fostering reading even after their child reaches high school. Parents can read the same books alongside their teenagers and discuss the book afterward—a type of informal family book club. This can help advance their child's comprehension skills and may help boost SAT scores.

5. **Take any opportunity for verbal interaction.** Don't dumb down your conversations with your child. Use complex words and phrasings, and take the time to answer your child's questions. If you think your child is curious about something that he heard on the news or saw in the world, then provide information about this issue. Let your child's questions guide you as to how much information to provide.

For perfect score parents, involvement in their child's literacy often went far beyond these five steps. David T. recalled what steps he took with his son, Peter: "We live in a small town. Peter went to a public school, which was good, but not great. Since school was not challenging to Peter, we encouraged his musical talent. He started to play the cello when he was four, and he practiced several hours a day. We also read to Peter all the time. And he liked strategy board games, which I ended up playing with him, since they were too complicated for his friends."

Peter's parents invested time and effort in him, which gave him a love of music and reading. As a result, Peter loves performing, and he reads a lot, at least a book a week, "science fiction, the classics, and popular novels." When asked what he does for fun, Peter replied "read." Clearly, Peter's parents did something right.

If perfect score students share one gift, it's that they're good readers. But this gift, unlike other kinds of intellectual talents, is not inborn. It is a gift that their parents gave them by sitting patiently with them while they sounded out words or by filling their house with appealing books and keeping the TV turned off as much as possible. It is a gift that they give themselves every time they pick up a book or read through course materials that their teacher hands out.

They don't limit themselves to books in only those subjects that interest them. The perfect score math whiz is happy to sink her teeth into *Gone With the Wind*. English literature buffs take time out to read sci-fi cyper-punk novels. Reading isn't a chore or a self-improvement technique. Perfect score students read because they want to and because they like to. They choose a book because they're curious about it and want to find out why it's considered a classic, or why it sold a million copies, or why it was awarded a Pulitzer Prize.

These students know that reading is the fundamental way to satisfy their curiosity about the world and how things work in the universe. They know that reading exercises their mind and makes them sharper, faster thinkers. They understand intuitively that reading is the pathway to knowledge and ultimately the pathway to success.

But above all, perfect score students embrace reading because it is pleasurable and offers them an enticing escape from the real world. If only for a few hours—or even a few minutes in between classes—perfect score students take a small mental vacation in the books they read. No, they're not turning their brains off but are turning themselves in to a world of fantasy. And they savor every moment of this time well spent.

*Secret 4:*

# They Develop a Core Group of Passions, Pursue Them Eagerly, and Excel Within Them

○ "French is my biggest passion. The language comes easily to me, and I enjoy speaking it. I've been lucky enough to travel to several French-speaking countries, and I try to read as many books written in French as I can."—*Jennifer F.*

○ "I feel very strongly about my religion. I attend church once a week and teach Sunday school to preschoolers in our community. I also belong to a national Christian organization, and my social life revolves around it. I've met a lot of friends from this group who share the same values as me."—*Nancy C.*

○ "I'm really serious about the piano. I took lessons for ten years and played in numerous recitals. But what I most enjoy is playing by ear. I can pick up almost any song on the radio and sound it out on the piano. I'm now starting to get into a little bit of composing—I'm writing some music for my school's upcoming talent show."—*Harold B.*

If you look at the way the three perfect score students above describe themselves, you might think they didn't have much in common beyond their perfect scores. Yet they're a lot more alike than they seem. They all have a passion that they pursue to the fullest. They put their heart and soul into these passions and excel at them as a result.

More than 90 percent of these exceptional academic achievers have a particular talent that they pursue with a passion. Instead of dabbling in dozens of different extracurricular activities, they focus on one or two interests at a time and develop their talent in these areas. They aim for mastery over one thing rather than a taste here and there of passing fads. The passions they engage in span from contemplating challenging math problems to pitching on the varsity baseball team to performing in a community orchestra. Usually a passion grows from an activity that a student is particularly adept at and enjoys. A passion may start out as a natural talent, but it will develop into a refined skill as the student puts forth more and more effort.

I define *passion* as any activity to which a student devotes more than five hours a week. Taking a half-hour flute lesson once a week and never practicing does not make the flute a passion. Playing the flute two hours a day, for practice or pleasure, does. Signing up for debate club and going to an occasional meeting doesn't make debate a passion. Becoming captain of the debate club and entering local and statewide competitions does.

The Perfect Score Study found that about 75 percent of perfect score students who participate in a social club (for example, student council, yearbook, school newspaper, drama, art) hold a leadership position and spend more than nine hours per week on this activity. This is about the same as the 69 percent of average-scoring students who hold leadership positions in social clubs—one more piece of evidence that perfect score students are as well rounded as their peers.

Even in sports, perfect score students strive toward leadership. About 65 percent of perfect score students play on a sports team, and 43 percent are either captain or cocaptain. They spend an average of eleven hours per week participating in sports, usually in daily practices with their team. One perfect score student I spoke with was ranked nationally as a tennis player. Another served as cocaptain of his football team. "I live for soccer," says Dina P. "It takes my mind off upcoming exams and papers that are due." Clearly, achieving a perfect SAT score doesn't limit one's athletic abilities. As a group, perfect score students put the same passion into sports as their other interests and activities. (Average score students, however, typically devote more time to sports, putting in twenty hours a week on their teams.)

Participation rates in extracurricular activities don't differ significantly between perfect score students and their average score student counterparts, except when it comes to academic clubs. About 70 percent of perfect score students participate in academic clubs, and 67 percent of them hold leadership positions. This compares with a 46 percent participation rate of average-scoring students, with only 30 percent holding leadership positions.

## PARTICIPATION IN EXTRACURRICULAR ACTIVITIES

|  | Participation Rate (%) | | Hold Leadership Position (%) | | Hours/Week (Average) | |
|---|---|---|---|---|---|---|
|  | Perfect Score Student | Average Student | Perfect Score Student | Average Student | Perfect Score Student | Average Student |
| Academic | **70** | **46** | **67** | **30** | 5 | 7 |
| Sports | 65 | 66 | 43 | 45 | 11 | 20 |
| Social | 87 | 84 | 75 | 69 | 9 | 15 |
| Religious/ service organization | 32 | 32 | 56 | 58 | 3 | 5 |

BOLDFACED NUMBERS REPRESENT STATISTICALLY SIGNIFICANT DIFFERENCES. FIGURES IN THIS CHART ARE DERIVED FROM DATA DIFFERENT FROM OTHER CHARTS IN THE BOOK, SO FIGURES MAY VARY.

But the stories that perfect score students tell about their lives reveal far more than the statistics about the way these students pursue their passions. They have a sense of earnestness and drive in all their activities. Some perfect score students have one particular passion. Others have two or three. Perfect score students use their passions to define themselves. One student told me, "I'm a musician who loves the cello." Another described himself as "intensely curious about science and how things work."

Interestingly, many of the perfect score students define their passions by their volunteer work. About 80 percent said they contribute time every week to volunteer work. Some tutor kids in lower-income areas, and others work in nursing homes and hospitals. Some students also mentioned building homes for Habitat for Humanity. Most perfect score students saw their talents as a gift that should be given back to others.

The kind of volunteer work these students gravitate toward also says a lot about them. Perfect score students seek out work that requires personal contact and physical labor, such as meeting poor people while dishing out meals in soup kitchens. These students aren't sitting in an office soliciting phone pledges for a charity organization. They want to touch someone personally, to feel that they're directly making a difference.

Perfect score students volunteer an average of two hours per week. Some, who have made volunteer work their passion, volunteer more time, and some, who have other passions, volunteer only on occasion. Overall, though, a sense of civic responsibility is definitely ingrained in the minds of these students. In thinking about the future, most perfect score students said they feel an obligation to use their intelligence and skills to try to have a major impact on the world. For instance, some said they would strive to make a breakthrough scientific discovery or medical advance to help humankind.

Charity work is also a priority among average students, who volunteer at about the same rate and for the same amount of time as perfect score students. What's interesting, though, is that few consider giving back to society as a lifelong goal they should pursue. When asked to list their top hopes, only 6 percent of average students said they want to make an impact on the world or do something worthwhile. In contrast, 19 percent of perfect score students listed this as one of their top hopes.

Some interesting insights can also be gained from a nationwide survey conducted by Yankelovich. This survey found that almost 60 percent of young adults (ages sixteen to twenty-two) agree with the statement "I feel I have an obligation to make a contribution to the community I live in," and 74 percent agree with the statement "Everyone should donate some of their time for volunteer work." In practice, though, only 35 percent said they actually "contributed time to a charity or organization in the past year."

## PASSIONS VERSUS HOBBIES

I've counseled countless high school students in the preparation of their college application essays. Frequently, they fill in long lists of their various activities. They're so proud of the number of activities they've participated in, but they look at me quizzically when I ask them, "What's your passion?"

Perfect score students can answer this question without hesitation. They identify themselves by their passions and would never consider them to be hobbies. Their passions take center stage in their lives, rather than existing on the periphery. Part of the reason they have such a strong sense of who they are and where they want to go in life can be attributed to these passions.

When colleges say they want a well-rounded student body, they don't mean that every student has to be well rounded in all areas. They mean they want a student body composed of champion gymnasts, prodigy piano players, chess tournament winners, all-state debaters, and star basketball players. Admissions officers want to know how students define themselves—and usually this is by knowing their passions.

Education experts agree that passions are an important predictor of success in life. Our passions are ingrained in our self-identity and tell us where we have the most aptitude. They tell us how we are unique and possibly what we should pursue as a career choice. Howard Gardner, a well-respected educator at the Harvard Graduate School of Education, coined the concept of multiple intelligences to describe our natural talents or passions. In his book *Multiple Intelligences* he identifies seven types of intelligences, including logical mathematical intelligence and linguistic intelligence—both of which are necessary to achieve a perfect SAT score. He also identifies some intriguing forms of intelligence, like spatial intelligence (good sense of direction/adept at visual arts), musical intelligence, and bodily kinesthetic intelligence (good at sports or dance/handy around the house). Gardner extends this concept further to include interpersonal intelligence (knowing how to read and understand other people) and intrapersonal intelligence (knowing oneself) as part of the group of multiple intelligences.

Whether you agree with all of the categories that Gardner defines as intelligence, his point—that intelligence is far more complex than the sum of our grades and SAT scores—is a valid one. Engaging in passions allows perfect score students to stretch their intelligence beyond the world of academics. They hone their hand-eye coordination skills by mastering the game of tennis. They refine their interpersonal skills by volunteering with the elderly or learning to read body language during a debate tournament. Countless perfect score students are passionate about their music, and some practice their instrument more than they study.

Without a doubt, passions that help develop one form of intelligence will also benefit other kinds of intelligence as well. Musical abilities and math talents are often intermingled. Engaging in a team sport or club can help broaden a student's ideas about the world. Whether or not these benefits are linked to improved grades and SAT scores is impossible to say, but the larger benefits from pursuing passions are immeasurable.

Perfect score students use their passions to express themselves as creative, unique individuals. They use them as a launchpad toward becoming the person they'd like to be. Most of all, they use these passions to tell themselves and the world that they can make an impact, that their time on this planet is being well spent.

### Jennifer L.—A Passion for Shakespeare

Perfect score student Jennifer L. embraced her love of language and discovered a passion for Shakespeare. She grew up in a household where her parents read to her a lot and started taking her to plays when she was three years old. Her mother, a first-grade teacher, and father, a speech therapist (not every smart parent is a university professor), put a strong emphasis on written and spoken language, and they saw, even before Jennifer started to read, that she had a love of words and a love of learning.

Jennifer always excelled in English and spent an equal amount of time reading for school and for pleasure—up to twenty-five hours a week. She joined the literature club in high school and worked to indulge her passion for English. She read Jane Austen's *Pride and Prejudice* for pleasure, and her favorite book for school was James Joyce's *The Dubliners*. She watched no TV, she says, because she preferred to spend her time reading.

In eighth grade, Jennifer discovered her love of Shakespeare. "I saw the movie *Much Ado About Nothing*, and a light was switched on," she reveals. "It was logical. It was beautiful. I had to learn more. So I decided to read the entire works of Shakespeare, and this wasn't for school. I read everything from *All's Well That Ends Well* to *Twelfth Night.*" When probed further, Jennifer says she was compelled to master Shakespeare completely, including what his critics had to say over the last four hundred years.

Jennifer also told me that she realized that she couldn't fully understand Shakespeare without understanding history, so she became a history buff. "I wanted to see how accurate the plays really were. For example, was Richard III actually a murderer? I ended up studying the whole historical debate. I realize most kids have trouble getting through *Hamlet, Macbeth,* and *Romeo and Juliet* in high school, but for me it's different."

Clearly Jennifer has strong linguistic abilities. This is apparent from her perfect verbal SAT score. Jennifer has, however, a true passion for the English language and is happy to devote most of her time and energy to studying it, not for a better English grade but for the sheer love of it. Few students list Shakespeare, Joyce, and Austen as their favorite authors. And how many of us have read more than three or four plays by Shakespeare?

Interestingly, Jennifer L. also sees and uses her linguistic abilities to enhance her communication skills. She says, "The quality I value most about myself is the kindness with which I interact with other people." She is very active in school clubs, has a lot of friends, and also volunteers at a senior citizen center. So while Jennifer is happy to be alone with her Shakespeare, she's passionate about her personal connections with the living as well.

### Grant H.—A Passion for Cello

Grant H. is musically gifted. "I practice the cello three hours a day, which gives me an ability to explore the musical sounds of the instrument." When asked if everything comes easily, Grant replies, "Some things are easy, but other things are difficult. Even the easy things are easy only up to a point." He points out that he creates challenges for himself if his schoolwork or the pieces he's working on ever get too easy. One challenge he took on was to enter a national math competition, which he says was the most difficult thing he's ever done.

Grant says that his musical passion also requires a lot of blood, sweat, and tears. "I practice to get better and to reach a higher plateau. This enables me to better understand music and the cello. When you play music you are channeling emotion through an artistic medium. You can express your emotions in art. The best cellists are able to evoke emotions in the audience. I am curious about how this happens. That is my ultimate goal."

To Grant, playing the cello is a way of inspiring and communicating with others. Still, he doesn't practice cello to the exclusion of all else. He makes a point to go out every weekend with his friends.

Music is Grant's first love. Like the other perfect score students, though, Grant has a high facility for math and also engages in this passion. It's interesting to see how Grant blends these two talents to help him excel academically and to nurture his passions.

### Eli B.—A Passion for Fractals and Number Theory

Most students struggle through trigonometry and calculus and certainly wouldn't do them for fun. Advanced math can be incredibly difficult to comprehend, even for the brightest students. For a certain subgroup of students, however, calculus is as easy as riding a bike. It is logical. It is challenging. And it makes sense the minute they are taught new material. These students may think nothing of spending hours a night solving complex problems. They read math books for fun. They enter competitions and relish finding the answer to particularly difficult problem sets.

Eli B. is one of these students. He has a passion for math and feeds it by attending a public high school for the gifted in the math and sciences. He has a straight-A average and belongs to a math team. He describes himself as "a mathematician who likes logic and reason."

Math is the center of Eli's world. "I read a lot of popular science books that relate to math, especially complexity theory and fractals. Once in high school, when I got bored in class, I decided to program fractals into my calculator. (A fractal is something that self-replicates at many levels of magnification, like crystal.) I had read about fractals and wanted to see whether I could make them myself. It took a while, but I did it."

But math, to Eli, is more than just programming a code into a calculator. Eli did a summer program his junior year at Boston University called PROMYS (Program in Math for Young Scientists). "We studied number theory for six weeks. It was very intense. We spent four hours a day in class and four to six hours a night doing problems. But, unlike school, they would give you the problem to work on the night before class. The next day they would teach you how to solve it, if you hadn't figured it out by then. We all sat around at night and worked together, suffering as we tried to find the right answer. It was long. It was extremely difficult, but it was definitely enjoyable."

Eli clearly has a gift for math, but he certainly doesn't consider it to be his only passion. He plays in a rock band and is a jazz DJ at the local college radio station. He also acts and got a part in a musical comedy at his college. And he's passionate about socializing with his friends. In his college dorm room, he posted Eli's Rule, which says there can be no schoolwork after dinner Saturday night. And as Eli points out, the rule often applies to Thursday and Friday nights as well. But it doesn't apply to his math passion. Eli sets no limits on how much he can pursue whatever he loves and is passionate about.

### Jerome R.—A Passion for People

In order to be successful in life, we've got to get along and work well with other people. Interpersonal skills are often seen as even more important than technical skills. After all, what's the point of coming up with a new idea if we're incapable of communicating it to others? Einstein was a great communicator, and he's one of the few scientists that most people know by name.

This raises the question: Do perfect score students have these savvy social skills? Can they put aside their academic techno-speak when relating to others who aren't as bright? Actually, the Perfect Score Study found that the majority of perfect score students rank their relationships with friends and family as the most important priorities in their lives. And 67 percent of them described themselves as popular. Some students were even passionate about their social adeptness.

Meet Jerome R. He is your quintessential perfect score student: valedictorian of his high school class, 4.0 GPA, National Merit finalist, a Presidential Scholar finalist, and winner of numerous national awards. When asked to describe himself, Jerome said he was "a curious learner dedicated to achievement," which is consistent with his academic record. But then he added, "I'm devoted to my family and friends."

Jerome didn't use the words *like* or *enjoy* to describe his relationships. He purposely called himself "devoted." He then continued along the lines of the typical high school student. "I have a fantastic group of friends who are a lot of fun. We go out often." He characterized his social life and interactions with others as excellent and quipped, "Never let education interfere with your social life."

Jerome is definitely a people person. He organized and ran the freshmen orientation week at his high school. "We worked on it all summer. It was a lot of work, all volunteer, but it was important figuring out how to help new students orient themselves and feel comfortable," he explains. "It was a great success. A month into the school year, I was eating at a restaurant when the grandfather of one of those freshmen came up to me. He personally thanked me for looking out for and showing attention to his grandson. It meant a lot to the kid, but more important it meant everything to the grandfather. It meant the same to me."

Jerome continues his social activity in college by mentoring freshmen and providing advice and counsel to thirty first-year students. His philosophy on life is: "Do the best I can." And he says his Catholic upbringing helps him feel connected to his faith and God, and it helps him rely on the people he loves. Thus Jerome incorporates his interpersonal intelligence into his entire outlook on life.

Jerome has a knack for winning the trust and confidence of others, even strangers he meets for the first time on the street. He understands other people and goes to extraordinary lengths to work with them. He spends twenty hours a week in club activities and has held numerous leadership positions, including editor of the newspaper, vice president of the National Honor Society, and president of the Community Service Club. People, clubs, and social activities are not just a part of his life. They *are* his life.

### James C.—A Passion for Crew

We don't usually think of a smart kid and a jock embodied in the same person, but plenty of perfect score students are serious athletes. The majority of them participate in some form of sports, and for some, sports is a passion that even weighs into their choice of colleges.

Smart professional athletes do exist. There's Bill Bradley, who was a star basketball player at Princeton and played a couple of years for the New York Knicks before going on to become a U.S. senator. And today, one of the best pitchers in baseball, Tom Glavine, combines brains and athletic ability and has been described in news articles as "the ultimate thinking man's pitcher." Glavine, a future Hall of Famer, said in an interview with the *New York Times,* "I have been given the ability to put the ball where I want to. It's been a lot of hard work to refine that. That's part of what is and always has been fun for me: go out there on the mound and try to outthink or out-execute the guy you're facing." Glavine exercises daily, practices pitching, and watches videotapes of opponents. He also has won more than 240 games.

James C. also has supreme athletic talents. He describes himself as "an athlete who rows crew." In fact, he picked one Ivy League college over another because they had a better crew team. Although James participated in other extracurricular activities, crew was his real love. He participated in crew during all four years at his private high school. "I rowed fifteen hours a week. I got up at six-thirty in the morning to exercise and then practiced three hours each afternoon. My teammates were my closest friends. I eventually became captain of the team."

James told me that he had such strong passion for crew because of what he got out of it. "It is something I can throw myself into, practice, work hard, and improve." He says he wins most of his races but really enjoys the thrill of the competition and seeing if his team can beat their own best time.

James's parents steered him in other directions as well. His father, a university professor, sparked his interest in philosophy, and his mother, a music teacher, encouraged him to learn the cello, which is his second love. James's two passions make him the Perfect Score Study's answer to those who say that perfect score students are only focused on grades and standardized test scores. James, as well as the other students described above, proves this is not the case.

## DEVELOPING A PASSION

All students, regardless of their academic potential, can benefit from developing a passion. They can actively explore whatever intrigues them and piques their curiosity through these passions. This will foster their love of learning and may spur them to explore other areas, perhaps even those in the academic realm. Those who are passionate about their ballet dancing may want to read books about famous ballerinas, a way to foster linguistic skills—or listen to ballet music from classical composers, a way to develop musical intelligence. Baseball fanatics may be interested in calculating batting averages—a way to sharpen math skills.

The most important thing parents can do is let their child discover this passion naturally. Perfect score parents told me again and again that their children developed strong interests largely on their own. They allowed their child to lead the way. Yes, these parents encouraged them by sending their budding scientist to a summer science camp or buying books on subjects that interested their kids. But they didn't push their kids into an activity just because they thought it might strengthen their high school transcript. Kids who are forced into certain activities often wind up developing an aversion rather than a passion for it.

This doesn't mean, though, that parents should completely disengage. Children may be able to express their wishes of the moment, but that doesn't mean they know how to go about fulfilling them. Nurturing a budding passion may require a fair amount of effort from both parents and children. Perfect score parents said they had an open line of communication with their children. Their children trusted them enough to be open about their true desires, rather than trying to fulfill those that their parents set for them. Of course, finding a true passion may take a bit of trial and error. As we all know, kids sometimes like the idea of something in theory—until they actually try it.

Yes, helping a child develop a passion can require a level of time commitment, which can be difficult if both parents work. However, those children who put all their energies into one activity, rather than into three or four, often have easier, rather than harder schedules. Parents don't need to spend as much time in the car shuttling them back and forth between activities. Economic factors can also come into play. Private ballet lessons and gymnastics can get pretty expensive compared to the theater, softball, or soccer that is offered through the school.

Despite these potential hurdles, students who find their passion and throw their all into it will find they experience a tremendous payoff: a strong sense of identity and improved self-esteem. Students who ace the SAT spoke avidly about their passions and defined themselves by what they pursued, not by their grades or SAT scores. As a result, they were much happier and saw their high school years as a fulfilling experience—not merely a stepping-stone for getting into college. The cost of a high school experience like this? Priceless.

## Secret 5:
# They're Proactive;
# They Create Their Own Luck

Many of us think that students who get great grades and perfect SAT scores have it easy. They learn everything in a snap and have photographic memories. They have an air of moral superiority because they're smart. And we resent the hell out of them for it.

One episode of *The Simpsons* illustrates best what our society thinks of high academic achievers. Homer, the father, who is a simpleton, has a crayon removed from his brain that somehow got in there when he was a child. This increases his IQ by 50 points, and he becomes academically gifted. Homer abandons his usual T-shirt and sloppy pants for a "spiffy new outfit" that includes a sweater and tie. He goes around asking his family arcane questions like, "What is the capital of North Dakota?" Then he answers himself smugly, "Bismarck!" He lectures his kids that "it's cool to be smart," but he also develops a self-righteousness that leads him to try to correct code violations at the nuclear power plant where he works by alerting the federal government to safety problems. Unfortunately the nuclear plant has to close down to correct the violations, which puts his friends out of work. But Homer tells them, "You can't hate me—I'm your better."

But his friends do hate him. He's no longer welcome at the local bar. He gets kicked out of the movies because he doesn't appreciate lowbrow humor. He then wanders the streets in search of contentment and happiness. His precociously bright daughter, Lisa, the only one he has really bonded with, observes that as intelligence goes up, happiness goes down.

In the end, Homer is so miserable he goes back to the doctor and has the crayon inserted back up his nose into his brain. This returns Homer to his subnormal intelligence and his blissful, carefree life. He abandons his life as a high academic achiever and his proselytizing. Yes, *The Simpsons* takes the intellectual Homer to an extreme, but it's so funny because we all buy into this stereotype—at least a little.

All too often, academically superior high school students are stigmatized for being bright. No one wants to be labeled the smartest kid in the class. Far too many straight-A students allow their grades to fall after they gain admission to the cool crowd or became a jock or a cheerleader. They don't want to be resented for being smart.

If only we knew the truth about the best and brightest students, we'd take all these resentments and stereotypes, crumple them into a ball, and toss them into the wastebasket of ignorance. Students who have an A+ average or who ace the SAT aren't born to succeed no matter what. They don't have some magical set of test genes that enables them to breeze through any exam. These students are proactive. They create their own luck and their own success. Yes, they have natural abilities and probably higher IQs than the average student. But it's what they do with these abilities that brings about their success. They certainly don't sit back and coast through life.

Let's consider how they prepare for the SAT. According to the Perfect Score Study, far more average score students found the SAT to be difficult compared with perfect score students, yet *the average score students studied far less for the SATs than their perfect score counterparts.* More than 75 percent of perfect score students put in some preparation for the SAT, compared with only 42 percent of students who scored 1000 to 1200. Of the perfect score students 29 percent took practice tests before taking the exam, while only 2 percent of average score students took a practice exam. Both groups of students viewed the SATs as a "somewhat important" exam in terms of getting into a good college, but perfect score students took the task of SAT preparation far more seriously.

As I mentioned earlier, perfect score students work harder than their peers in all academic areas. They spend more hours reading for school and a bit more time studying. Overall, perfect score students spend nineteen hours a week on their schoolwork compared with thirteen hours a week spent by average score students. They also tend to take more honors classes and AP courses.

But the real difference shows up in attitudes. Perfect score students define themselves as self-motivated individuals. They say their parents rarely had to force them to study and rarely nudged them about taking SAT practice exams. They did what they needed to do to succeed on the test. They were driven to excel all on their own. Succeeding academically and in extracurricular activities is central to who perfect score students are as individuals. They define themselves by their efforts and always strive to better themselves.

I think the hard work put in by professional athletes best illustrates this point. We hear about the natural talents of basketball star Michael Jordan (and yes, some perfect score students are born intellectually gifted), but far more athletes put in the daily grind to make it in the pros. Take the case of football player Eric Johnson, whose story was recently reported in the *New York Times*. Eric was a wide receiver at Yale who had a great college career in which he broke numerous football records. Yet while Yale is a top school academically, it is not a prime recruiting source for professional football. Moreover, Eric was extremely slow by pro-football standards. Nevertheless, Eric was determined to play professionally. So he hired a personal trainer who developed a plan of action to prepare him for the football draft. The trainer identified what Eric needed: namely, to put bulk on his six foot three, 226-pound frame and to dramatically increase his speed in the forty-yard dash.

The trainer put Eric through a rigorous six-day-a-week training program for two months, which included strength, flexibility, and speed drills. In the end, Johnson added 22 pounds of muscle, decreased his body fat, and increased his vertical leaping ability. He also shaved time off his forty-yard dash, decreasing to 4.74 seconds from 5.0 seconds. As a result, Eric was drafted in the seventh round and currently starts for the San Francisco 49ers.

Many would say that Eric was lucky to be drafted to the 49ers from a second-rate football team like Yale's. Perhaps he was lucky, but he had to create his own luck. He had to be proactive and use his natural talents to the fullest, while overcoming his natural limitations. Perfect score students do the same thing. They create their own luck by working with what they've got and working on what they don't. For instance, some of the math whizzes barely needed to review any questions on the math portion of the SAT in order to get a perfect 800, but they studied the verbal portion for months to sharpen their skills. The proactive approach these students take goes far beyond academics. It extends to extracurricular activities, to making friends, and to achieving success and happiness in life.

## CREATING LUCK BY MAXIMIZING LEARNING

Perfect score students aren't all born brilliant, and they don't all learn things the same way. For some, academics come effortlessly. They barely need to study, are lightning-fast readers, and can hammer out an insightful essay in thirty minutes. For others, academics require a great deal of effort. They might be B+ students if they didn't try, but they push themselves hard to maintain an A average. They took the SAT once and might have gotten a 1350, but they studied hard and took it three or four times to get a perfect score. Regardless of how they learn, perfect score students have an innate understanding of what they need to do to succeed and fulfill the goals they've set for themselves. They know their strengths and their limitations.

I refer to these variations in learning as learning styles. In fact, the Perfect Score Study identified four distinct learning styles that were most common in 1600 perfect score students. These styles are those of the Natural, the Driver, the All-around, and the Different Drummer. About 77 percent of perfect score students fall into one of these four groupings. The rest blend two or three of these styles. And I think most parents will find their own child probably falls into one or two of the four learning styles.

Perfect score students employ their own learning style to achieve their best academic performance. They might adjust their learning style over time if they find it's not working for them. (Often this happens in college, as workloads become more demanding.) Ultimately, they know they're in the driver's seat. They know best what they need to do to get where they want to go.

Sam R. is a natural learner who barely studies an hour a night to keep a 4.0 GPA. His mother says she kept vague track of when his exams were and asked him periodically if he was prepared. She never, though, pushed him to review the material on the night before the test. She understood that he just didn't need to put in the same amount of study time as his peers. (Lucky him!)

While it's true that Sam's natural gifts enable him to achieve academically without much effort, he's an exception, not the rule. Only 14 percent of perfect score students are natural learners. The other 86 percent have to work hard for their perfect score. The same likely holds true for average and above average students who don't get perfect SAT scores. For some, learning comes easier and requires less study time. For others, schoolwork is a struggle that requires time and dedication to master. In fact, average students who are natural learners might well be able to raise their grades and SAT scores significantly by adopting a different kind of learning style. Like perfect score students, they can take a proactive approach to academics and create their own luck. Here's a brief description of the four different learning styles.

## The Four Learning Styles

1. **Naturals.** Everything comes easy for these students. They study only a limited amount of time—just five to eight hours a week. Schoolwork for them is a breeze, but so are other activities. Naturals tend to have an easier time learning musical instruments and are equally adept at new sports. Their attitude is that life comes easy, and, for them, it does.

2. **Drivers.** For these students, doing well entails hard work. Drivers put in a lot of time and effort to do well academically. They generally study twenty or more hours a week. If they don't score 1600 on the SAT on the first try, they study math problems, memorize vocabulary words, and then take the test again. And again. And again, until they get a perfect score. Some drivers become so focused on their schoolwork that they end up working on academics to the exclusion of their social activities. Others are driven to excel in both their schoolwork and their extracurricular activities. (Some of these kids wind up exhausted by the time they graduate!)

3. **All-arounds.** These kids never met a club or activity they didn't want to join. Their primary distinguishing characteristic is their level of involvement and participation in school and extracurricular activities. They generally spend twenty or more hours per week in school clubs, sports, music, or organizations outside of school. They love to hang out with their friends, at the movies, the pizza place, or a rock concert. The perfect score all-arounds put in an additional ten to fifteen hours a week studying or completing their course work—usually in the most difficult courses.

4. **Different Drummers.** These are kids who go their own way, who have a different outlook on life. They aren't part of the in-crowd, or even the average crowd. They are more individualistic, with a few close friends like them. They engage in eclectic or alternative activities—dressing in goth style, joining a rock band, or hanging with

fellow Dungeons and Dragons fanatics. Different drummers usually have a particular passion that they pursue pretty much to the exclusion of other activities. They become fascinated with and engrossed in a single pursuit and often follow it to what many of us might consider an extreme.

Of course, not all perfect score students fit neatly into these four learning categories. Many fall into a combination of categories. For instance, some students are a combination of drivers and naturals—the typical bright kids who excel by working as hard as the average student but don't drive themselves to perfection. These students study about eight to twelve hours a week, hang out with friends, play sports, and typically do what other kids their age do. They won't spend all night studying calculus or reading Shakespeare, but they work hard to rank in the top 10 percent of their class.

The secret to creating luck is to first identify your or your child's own learning style and then to see how perfect score students use their style to their best advantage. I phrased these questions for parents, but students can also use them to evaluate themselves.

## Naturals

1. Do you find your child barely needs to crack a book to get good grades?

2. Does your child have a talent for sports or music, making the activity seem effortless?

3. Does your child seem laid-back when it comes to school, even the night before a final exam? If so, does your child do well on the test?

4. Do you find that you have no clue about what projects or essays your child is working on?

5. Does your child complain about boredom in class and frequently read ahead in the textbook?

6. Does your child learn skills (math, reading, musical instruments, and so on) on his or her own?

7. Does your child need just one to two hours a night to complete high school homework?

If you answered yes to three or more questions, your child is a Natural.

Perfect score students who are natural learners are straight-A students with Type B personalities. They don't stress out about life because they don't need to. Everything comes so easily. Naturals in the Perfect Score Study spent less than half the time studying than do those with other learning styles.

Having a child who is a Natural may seem like a dream come true, but it does come with its downside. Naturals sometimes aren't challenged enough by their course work in high school, and never really learn how to organize their time to complete a project. Many of these students find their first year as a college freshman requires a huge adjustment in their learning style. Suddenly, they have to study hard for the first time in their lives.

Ethan J. is a typical Natural. The tall, good-looking, red-haired Oregonian has a slow, wide smile that immediately puts you at ease when you talk to him. But you can tell he's always thinking two steps ahead of you. Ethan earned straight As in high school, played drums in the band, and swam competitively. He even coauthored a book on getting into a good college that was published during his senior year.

Ethan describes himself as a "fairly outgoing person who likes music, reading, science, and math." He plans to be an aerospace engineer and possibly an astronaut. For fun in high school, he pursued his passion for the tympani drums playing in the school orchestra and band, and marching band. He said he was able to master these drums with very little practice.

"In high school, it came real easy," Ethan explains. "I didn't have to work hard at all. I took two years of physics, didn't do most of the homework, but still got one of the highest grades in my class. I spent far more time surfing the net and hanging out with friends than studying."

Even though he studied only about six hours a week, Ethan scored a 1600 on the SAT the first time he took it. He was president of the quiz bowl and captain of the Science Olympiad team. And he was accepted to all four colleges he applied to, including two of the most selective in the country.

Now attending M.I.T., Ethan is finding that his Natural learning style is no longer working for him. He finds himself glued to his dorm-room desk up to seven hours a day studying—particularly for his freshman math class. "Even though the course is pass/fail, it takes eight hours to do three to four problems. It's a course designed for math majors with the purpose of weeding out future majors," Ethan says. "I've met my challenge in college. I work really hard there."

Like other perfect score students, Ethan was able to switch gears and adapt to his new challenges. Being self-motivated, he took charge of his new situation and found himself creating the luck that he had naturally in high school. Though Ethan learned to take on the learning style of a Driver, he's still a natural learner in his heart. His philosophy on life is the essence of a Natural: "Get the most out of life you can. Do your best and don't think anything is impossible."

## Drivers

1. Would you describe your child as a perfectionist?

2. Does your child spend more than three hours a night on homework?

3. Is your child very self-motivated?

4. Does your child get stressed out over routine assignments and exams?

5. Does your child have a strong work ethic, feeling upset or guilty if he or she fails to complete an assignment on time?

6. Does your child approach school and extracurricular activities (sports, music, clubs) with a serious—rather than laissez-faire—attitude?

If you answered yes to three or more questions, your child is a Driver.

Drivers don't need much parental encouragement to accomplish their academic goals. Their motivation comes from within. Most parents of perfect score drivers are amazed by their child's single-mindedness when it comes to doing homework or studying for exams. They never have to ask twice if assignments have been completed. Drivers don't procrastinate. They worry too much that their tasks won't get done.

Students who are drivers are much more likely to have an easy time adjusting to the rigorous demands of college. They're used to hard work, and college is just more of the same. On the downside, they're more likely to feel stressed by the schoolwork and often have to be reminded that learning should be fun as well as challenging.

Drivers are constantly striving for perfection, which means not only acing an exam but acing an exam in the most difficult class. They often question whether they are really "good enough" or "smart enough" to achieve the goals they've set for themselves. In other words, Drivers may have a lot of angst on their pathway to success.

Drivers need reassurance that they're capable of fulfilling the challenges they've set for themselves, and they rely on loving words and support from their parents and friends if they fall short of their own demands. Sometimes they may need their parents to help set realistic expectations. Parents who set goals that they know their child can fulfill may relieve any stress their child may be feeling and help enhance the joy of learning.

Kara A. is a quintessential driver. She puts extraordinary effort into everything she does and everything she accomplishes. Kara, the daughter of Asian immigrants, is instilled with a strong work ethic and a belief that hard work pays off. She describes herself as a "meticulous, detailed-oriented person, someone who makes deep commitments." Her most important commitments, she says, are to her family and her education.

Kara first took the SAT in seventh grade and got a 1200, which earned her admission to a summer program for gifted students. She took the SAT again in tenth grade and received a 1400, but she was determined to get a 1600. "I took two prep courses, one given by my school district and one by an after-school program," she recalls. "I took about twenty practice tests, each of which lasted three hours. I even took some practice tests twice. It paid off. I got 1600 in the fall of my junior year."

Even with all this SAT preparation, Kara still studied thirty hours a week for her high school classes. She completed her homework plus any extra credit assignments that were given. She also devoted one to two hours a day to practicing the piano. "Music is my passion," she explains. "I love playing the piano, but I have really small hands. So, I have to practice a lot just to keep them stretched out to play some of the more complicated pieces. Once I entered a competition where I had to play Debussy, who legend has it had six fingers because his music is so difficult to play. I practiced three hours a day on this one piece for two months." She didn't win the competition—or even make the finals—but she said she was thrilled just to have been able to play the piece competently. "It didn't matter that I didn't win," she says. "It was good to know I could play Debussy if I worked hard enough."

Kara's proudest accomplishment? Not her SAT score, nor her piano playing. "It's an after-school program in Chinatown that I'm involved in," she says. "It's an enrichment program for kids in grades one through six, held three afternoons a week. We meet with the kids and work on projects and talk with them about any issues. One student I worked with wasn't doing well in school, not because he wasn't bright, but because he didn't understand the assignments and his parents didn't speak English well enough to help him. I helped him understand the assignment and then do the homework. I made a difference in his life. It's great working with kids and watching them grow."

All of Kara's hard work paid off. She got accepted to the University of Pennsylvania, which she now attends. She stands by the philosophy that anything worth doing requires time and energy. While Ethan, the Natural, is easygoing about his work load, Kara, the Driver, takes her responsibilities very seriously. Although Kara managed to juggle all of her responsibilities in high school, I wonder whether she didn't cheat herself a little out of her childhood. Some of us may wonder, "Well, she got a 1600, but at what price?"

The truth is, Drivers are extremely self-motivated and make their own decisions on how to pursue their lofty goals. Kara may learn in time that there's a value in just sitting back and taking a moment to reflect on life once in a while. In fact, she probably has that realization already. When asked what she would do if she had an extra hour built into every day, she said without hesitation, "Just relax."

## All-arounds

1. Does your child excel in a broad range of academic subjects, doing as well in literature as in physics?
2. Does your child participate in three or more after-school activities?
3. Is your child adept in a lot of different activities (from sports to art to music to public speaking, for example)?
4. Is your child always on the go—to the library, to the movies, to a friend's house or to one of many extracurricular activities?
5. Does your child have a lot of friends from various social groups or cliques?
6. Is your child a natural leader (for example, president of a club, captain of a team, editor of the yearbook)?

If you answered yes to three or more questions, your child is an All-around.

All-arounds have a variety of interests both academically and socially and have a hard time pinning down their favorite subject or extracurricular activity. "I like everything" is a frequent refrain you might hear from an All-around. This type of student has a zest for life and a yearning to try new and appealing things.

All-arounds tend not to devote their attention to a particular area, which means they may not realize their full potential in all—or even any—of the activities they participate in. They usually aren't the fastest runner on the track team, though they may come in second or third. They may not be the concertmaster of the orchestra, though they may be third or fourth chair. They may be treasurer of the honor society instead of president.

But that's okay with the All-arounds. For them, variety is the spice of life, and not worth giving up for a shot at being the best at one thing. And usually All-arounds find one or two things that they're most passionate about, where they really concentrate the bulk of their time. They excel at these things and dabble in the three or four other activities that pique their interest.

"I'm a very busy person. I enjoy everything from reading to writing papers to sports. I'm a hyper-achiever." These are the words of Denise W., a classic All-around. Denise doesn't have enough fingers on one hand to list all the high school activities she was involved in: student government, National Honor Society, debate club, French club, school newspaper, drama, tennis, and the cross-country team. But she focused most of her energy on the debate club, which she captained, and on the cross-county team, which she cocaptained.

"These activities are my life. I enjoy participating. I enjoy competing. I enjoy succeeding. I guess part of the reason I'm involved in so many is that I have a lot of different interests," explains Denise. She admits that sometimes she spreads herself too thin. "Balancing time commitments is always difficult. Unfortunately, the state debate championship occurred the week before our biggest cross-country meet. I got so caught up in debate that I didn't have time to run for a week. So after the debate tournament was over, I got home at 10:30 at night. I then ran from 11:00 P.M. to 12:30 A.M. just to get back in shape."

In high school, Denise spent about twelve to fifteen hours a week studying, which is typical of the All-arounds who participated in the Perfect Score Study. She graduated in the top 10 percent of her class, with a 4.0 average.

Now attending college at Stanford, Denise has had to amend her All-around ways. She's cut back on the number of activities she's involved in to focus on her one or two passions. One semester she worked hard to get into a course called U.S. Foreign Policy for the Future, which accepted only 12 out of 193 students who applied. She was required to read 150 pages a night and had two assignments, which required all-night preparation. This course took almost all her free time and left little room for other activities.

"The final was a real killer," Denise recalls. "For thirty straight hours we played a simulation game in which each student was assigned a role as a member of the president's cabinet. We had to respond to a terrorist threat against the United States. We had thirty hours to decide if we should negotiate with terrorists or suffer the consequences. As we made our decisions, we got new information and news updates. By the end of the course, we were all stressed out. We were yelling and screaming at one another. We were crying and laughing at the same time. Our college friends thought we were crazy." Denise happily reported that she got an A in this course because her team worked hard and made a well-reasoned decision. "This was my favorite course. I liked it because, like all my other activities, I got out of it exactly what I put in."

## Different Drummers

1. Is your child an introvert—happy to sit for hours engaging in a solitary activity for pleasure?

2. Would you describe your child as "unconventional"?

3. Do you find your child only puts effort into activities or school subjects that he or she likes?

4. Is your child engaged in creative pursuits (for example, creative writing, painting, music composition, computer programming, scientific or mathematical research)?

5. Does your child have just two or three close friends instead of a dozen acquaintances?

6. Do you find your child doesn't care that much about what other people think (including parents and peers)?

7. Is your child single-minded in his or her interests? (Has one or two favorite pursuits instead of half a dozen.)

If you answer yes to three or more questions, your child is a Different Drummer.

Different Drummers truly march to their own beat. They think outside the box, and this can be unnerving for parents—especially those who are not Different Drummers themselves.

Different Drummers tend to be creative thinkers: they compose music, write poetry, and program computers. Different Drummers may set fire to the kitchen while trying to conduct a chemistry experiment using household cleaners. They may challenge a teacher on the outdated ideas expressed in the class textbook. They're refreshing and exasperating at the same time.

You might be surprised to hear that we found a fair percentage—12 percent to be exact—of Different Drummers among the Perfect Score students. Yes, even unconventional learners can ace a conventional standardized test. Different Drummers can, indeed, have stellar academic achievements. They may be nationally recognized for their scientific or artistic achievements. But they usually go about their studies in a unique way. They don't feel the need to be involved in everything or be good at everything. They may invest all their time in the science lab trying to carry out an experiment for the Intel Science Competition. Or they may be volunteering thirty hours a week at Greenpeace to pursue their passion for the environment.

Curt J. would agree that he falls into the Different Drummer category. Yes, he did well in school, earning a 95 average and getting into six of the seven colleges he applied to. But he wasn't involved in a lot of organized activities, nor did he want to be most popular or active in his class. In fact, his favorite extracurricular activity was tae kwon do, followed by his work on the school yearbook. Curt grew up in suburban Chicago and went to a prestigious elite school in the city. His outlook on life and his unusual interests make him fascinating to talk with. I think I'll let his interview transcript speak for itself:

Q. Curt, describe yourself.
A. I do very well in things I'm interested in. And I'm interested in some weird things: science fiction and fantasy games like Dungeons and Dragons. What I'm good at is being good at things. What I'm not good at, I don't do.

Q. So, what are you good at and not good at?
A. I'm good at many things at school, especially standardized tests and introductory material. I'm not that interested in art or sports, especially football. And I'm not particularly good at foreign languages. Relationships can be difficult, but I do have a few close friends.

Q. What are you really interested in at school?
A. Learning new things in science fascinates me. I'm always looking for an explanation of how things work. In high school, you learn a very imprecise version of equations or how to solve them. In college, they give you a more precise and better understanding. For example, in high school you learn to calculate motion using the equation: velocity × time = distance. In college, you use calculus and derivatives to more precisely measure the mathematical reason that things behave the way they do.

Q. How do you spend your time outside of class?
A. I tend not to spend much time at mainstream activities such as school parties. There is a subculture of people like me who do gaming, strategy, and foam-sword fighting. I spent a weekend in the woods of New England with sixty other people, dressed in period garb, slaying dragons, searching for treasure, and rescuing maidens. Think Venetian politics. The plot was complicated. One family won.

**Q.** What about friends?

**A.** I did go out [in high school], but I also stayed home a lot because I just didn't feel like going out. I also had a girlfriend. We went out for about four months.

**Q.** So how did you prepare for the SAT?

**A.** I ate a big breakfast.

**Q.** Did you do any studying?

**A.** No. I got 1470 as a sophomore, so I thought I would do pretty well the second time.

**Q.** Who had the greatest influence in your life?

**A.** No question. Walt Disney.

**Q.** Any final thoughts?

**A.** I really like dynamic events and spontaneity. I feel my strength is my raw potential, but that can always be done in by indifference.

Curt spends ten hours a week studying, but twenty hours a week reading for pleasure (his favorite book is Robert Heinlein's science fiction classic *Stranger in a Strange Land*) and twenty hours a week programming on the computer. He excels in math and science and took first place in a national math competition.

But Curt's thinking and his activities clearly distinguish him from other students, including those who score 1600. He didn't really care that much about acing the SAT or getting a high GPA. His motivation is the sheer desire to learn, rather than grades, admission to a good college, or some other end point. Curt does well academically because he likes the subjects he's learning about. If he doesn't like a class, he'll probably tune it out and not read the material.

Some perfect score students focus solely on academics, to the exclusion of all else. But this is a small minority. About 4 percent of perfect score students fell into the "Intellectual Giant" category—a subgroup learning style that's part of the Different Drummers. These 4 percent probably have a genius-level intelligence and find it more rewarding to bury themselves in scientific journals than to participate in extracurricular activities. Yes, these brains do exist (and will probably wind up as head of a research lab), but they don't represent the vast majority of perfect score students.

Different Drummers tend to be more introspective and to live by their ideals. They know how they want to live their life, and they live it—regardless of what others think.

## MIX-AND-MATCHES

As we all know, dividing people into categories has its limitations. This holds true for learning styles as well. A student may fit neatly into one learning style or another, or may follow a blending of two— or even three—learning styles. About 77 percent of perfect score students fit into one of the four distinct learning styles. The other 23 percent have a Mix-and-Match learning style. They do a little of this, a little of that, and find what works best for them to achieve high grades and social success. What's more, the majority of perfect score students find that they have to adjust their learning style from time to time in order to reach their goals. They may lean a little more toward being a Driver during finals week and adopt more of a Natural attitude during the last semester of their senior year.

Some of the perfect score students who fit the Mix-and-Match learning style describe themselves as "just regular" students. Their peers would be shocked to hear that these "regular" students aced the SAT. Steve F. is one such perfect score student. He says, "I'm an average kid with a talent for test taking. I'm outgoing, not a nerd who studies textbooks for hours. I do, though, like reading books, specifically on government and computer science."

Steve F. employs a variety of learning styles, falling somewhere between a Natural and a Driver. He studies about five hours a week, reads another eight hours for pleasure (usually a serious book, such as Ayn Rand's capitalist philosophy novel *The Fountainhead*). He also socializes with his friends about ten hours each week. Steve chose to attend a state university and admits he's bright, but isn't a Type A, superstressed kind of student.

"I like math because it's challenging to solve complex problems," he says but adds that math certainly isn't his life. "I enjoy my friends, and I'm in an entertainment club. I'm also in Latin club and debate club. I do well in school and have a 92 average. But my friends and social life are more important."

Steve's philosophy in life is to "try to have fun." He admits that he doesn't work as hard as he could and would probably do better if he spent more time studying. "But that's not what's important to me. Friends and family mean more to me than school. Fun for me is hanging out with my friends and going to the latest movie."

Steve says he's fascinated by the way things work, though he doesn't have much propensity for fixing things. "When I was younger, I had the bad habit of taking things apart and then not being able to put them back together again," he says. "I had this portable CD player that wasn't working well. After I attempted to fix it, it never worked again." Good grades, good college, good friends, and a good balance to life define those with a mixture of learning styles. They may achieve greatness one day or they may not, but they'll accomplish respectable feats and have fun doing them.

## HOW COMMON IS EACH LEARNING STYLE?

Perfect score students were pretty evenly scattered across the spectrum when it came to their learning styles. What sets perfect score students apart is that they have a conscious awareness about the ways in which they learn best and what they need to do to reach their fullest potential. Perfect score parents have a fairly good idea about how their children went about achieving academic goals. They may not have known their child's specific learning style, but they could tell me if grades came easily for their child or if they came through a lot of intense study sessions. These parents could say, without hesitation, what their child was passionate about and whether some extracurricular activities were a higher priority than others.

## BREAKDOWN OF THE LEARNING STYLES OF PERFECT SCORE STUDENTS

| | |
|---|---|
| All-arounds | 30% |
| Mix-and-matches | 23% |
| Drivers | 21% |
| Naturals | 14% |
| Different Drummers | 12% |

## CREATING LUCK FROM LEARNING STYLES

With all these differences in learning styles, you might think that perfect score students operate on completely different tracks, depending on their innate ability to learn. But these high achievers are far more sophisticated than these rough categories suggest. They all share common threads that carry them through and help them achieve success in academics and in life. These qualities enable them to create their own luck, to be proactive in shaping their abilities, and to ultimately head down the pathway of their dreams.

○ *Academics are not their entire lives.*

Schoolwork is to the lives of perfect score students as the heart is to the body: central and critical, but not sufficient to exist by itself. Almost without exception, perfect score students are actively involved in multiple activities, their passions running from music to sports to computers. Few spend all their waking hours on schoolwork. Even the Intellectual Giants have passions that lie outside of the classroom, even if they're brainy pursuits like working on their chess game or a mind-bending puzzle.

○ *They seek out challenges.*

Perfect score students take the most challenging courses and usually go above what's expected of them on class assignments. They read extra material and books recommended by their teacher. Or they'll head off to a museum to get more information on a topic that interests them. Above all, they have a passion for learning and really understanding the subject, and they constantly evaluate themselves to see if they're accomplishing the goals they've set. If they find their life is too easy, they'll add more challenges. If they find their luck has turned, they make changes to shift the winds back in their favor.

○ *They have good social lives, however they define them.*

Perfect score students create luck in their social lives just as much as in academics. They aren't set off into a social class by themselves. They seek out friendships, join clubs, play sports, and overall are as well rounded as typical high school students. Some are in the in-crowd, but even those who aren't nearly all have a close group of friends that they socialize with at least several hours a week.

○ *Surprisingly few of them are in the genius range of intelligence.*

The vast majority of perfect score students have stellar academic talents, but they don't have intelligence scores that are off the charts. Yes, there may be a few geniuses among them, but this is the exception, not the rule. Perfect score students are very intelligent—don't get me wrong—but they achieve their success because they know how to use their intelligence to the best of their abilities. They find a learning style that works for them and use it to get the most out of their high school courses and to find the best approach to taking the SAT. These are skills that all students can learn, no matter where they fall on the intelligence spectrum.

*Secret 6:*

# They Develop a Social Network of Friends and Family That Gives Them Critical Support

Students who achieve a perfect score place their relationship with their family and friends at the top of their list of what's important to them. These relationships come before academics, before getting into a good college, and before success in a career. This is fascinating news. After all, aren't perfect score students the best and the brightest among us? Aren't they focused primarily on academics?

Most people think that's the case. When I discussed the Perfect Score Study with my friends and colleagues, they wanted to know the secret formula for their own kids to do better on the SAT. They asked me if perfect score students benefited more from the Kaplan or Princeton Review course or whether they hired private tutors. They asked how many times these students took the SAT. They asked whether these high achievers went to foreign-language immersion camps and summer programs for the gifted.

I didn't get a single question, however, asking if my study found that family was important or whether it made a difference who their kids' friends were. No one considered the fact that interpersonal relationships make a big difference in determining how children perform academically and, yes, even how they perform on the SAT.

Yet this is precisely what the Perfect Score Study found. Over and over again, perfect score students cited how important their parents were in their lives. Family was frequently mentioned when students were asked to describe themselves. Sally S. says, "I'm a very independent person and thinker. I'm very academically focused. And I'm family oriented." Perfect score students ranked their parents above their teachers as providing the biggest source of motivation in terms of advice and support. These students said their parents provided them with resources throughout their lives: taking them to the library on a weekly basis, reading to them regularly, getting education materials if their schoolwork wasn't challenging enough, and introducing them to culture through museums and theater.

Parents were unequivocally the most important teachers in the lives of perfect score students. But as these students entered high school, their parents faded into the background of their social lives and friends took over. When I asked the students who achieved a perfect score to rate their interactions and relationships with others, more than 90 percent said they were either "good" or "excellent," and most attributed this to their close friendships. When perfect score students were asked what they did for fun, "hang out with friends" was cited by 71 percent of them.

Without a doubt, parents and friends form the basis of support for perfect score students. They rely on them and lean on them for comfort and self-assurance. "I need my parents and friends to help me relax and not worry," says perfect score student Emily D. "They help take my mind off my academic pressures."

## NATURE VERSUS NURTURE

While it's true that support from family and friends is a top priority of perfect score students, does this support really lead to higher SAT scores? Wouldn't these students have gotten a perfect score anyway, regardless of these relationships? After all, isn't intelligence largely a product of our genes?

Actually, it's not so far off to assume that perfect score students are born to be bright. Most do have natural abilities to learn, but this by no means tells the full story. Plenty of students are born with natural intelligence, yet only 0.03 percent of them achieve a perfect score on the SAT.

In her book *The Nurture Assumption,* developmental psychologist Judith Rich Harris argues that the environment plays a strong role in determining a child's intelligence. Of course, a child's upbringing also plays a role in determining if the child is happy, successful, and well adjusted. Harris writes, "A large number of human characteristics have now been studied with behavioral genetic methods. The results are clear and consistent: Overall, heredity accounts for roughly 50 percent of the variation in the samples of people that have been tested, environmental influences for the other 50 percent. People differ from one another in many ways: some are more impulsive, others more cautious; some are more agreeable, others more argumentative. About half of the variation in impulsiveness can be attributed to people's genes, the other half to their experiences. The same is true for agreeableness. The same is true for most other psychological characteristics."

And I think most experts would agree with Harris that the same is true for intelligence. The Perfect Score Study found that this is probably the case. Perfect score students do, of course, get a portion of their intelligence from their genes. Many parents of these students hold advanced degrees and professional jobs, more commonly in the fields of medicine and engineering. Second, the siblings of perfect score students also tend to score extremely well on the SAT. The average SAT score of perfect score siblings was 1361, far beyond the average score of 1000. Even parents of perfect score students recognize that genes played a role in their child's intelligence. When I asked them what they did for their child academically, several parents answered, "We gave them good genes."

On the other hand, genes don't give the full picture. Being born brilliant won't take you very far if you don't have the resources you need to use your intelligence and fulfill your academic potential. Perfect score students rely on the support network provided by their parents to constantly challenge themselves and feed their intellectual curiosity. Their parents take a keen interest in what their children are learning and know instinctively when their children are bored and need more stimulation. Their parents also know when to encourage their kids and when to step back and let them attempt things on their own. These parents know that even though their child is bright, they could still provide a much needed support system.

Jeff G. wasn't being adequately challenged in school when he entered kindergarten. His parents knew that and took immediate action. Jeff's father recalls that he first realized his son was different "in nursery school, when other kids wanted to go down the slide, while Jeff wanted to play nuclear physicist." He decided to spend more time with his son, reading to him and enrolling him in music lessons. In elementary school, Jeff's parents found a special math program in the area that would give their son more challenging material. "We also put him in some special science programs during the school year and in the summer to make up for a not overly demanding school curriculum," says Jeff's father.

## PERFECT SCORE PARENTING

Of all the factors considered in the Perfect Score research, family stability proved to be one of the strongest in determining SAT scores. A full 90 percent of students who scored 1600 came from families in which neither parent was divorced. In comparison, 69 percent of students who scored 1000 to 1200 were from households with two married parents; that's the same percentage as the national average, according to 2000 U.S. census figures. It's a safe bet to say that having an intact family has a positive impact on SAT scores and academic achievement.

When both parents are engaged and involved in a child's life, they're more likely to have a stronger impact in terms of motivating their child to do well academically. Each parent brings something separate to the table, adding to some particular facet in their child's life. The Perfect Score Study found many examples of this. Sometimes the mother engaged the child in music while the father worked on strategic games. One parent would plan the family vacation to a historic town, while the other would be responsible for making sure the school curriculum was challenging enough.

Charlie and Susan T. are the essence of perfect score parents. Their son, Nathan, goes to a small elite private school in New Orleans and is graduating second in his class. Charlie works for an oil and gas company, while Susan is a stay-at-home mom. As with most perfect score families, Charlie and Susan have divvied up the responsibilities for their child's education. Charlie says, "I know Nathan is bright, and I want to make sure he lives up to his academic potential. I talk with Nathan daily about math and science, his favorite subjects. I enrolled him in the best prep school in the area, because the local schools weren't challenging enough for him. I even took Nathan to work with me to show how math and science are applied in the energy business. I think I got more out of it than he did, but the exposure to real-life applications was good for him."

Susan, on the other hand, is the schoolwork coordinator. She checks with Nathan to make sure his homework is done. "Nathan is a bit lazy," Susan says. "His dad doesn't realize that. So there have been a number of mornings I've had to get Nathan up at 5 A.M. to finish those assignments, which he said he would do on his way to school. No way is that going to happen."

Parents like Charlie and Susan work in tandem to provide the guidance and challenge their children need. Together they are a critical component of academic support and can do more together than any single parent can do. Perhaps this something extra gave Nathan the edge he needed to get a 1600.

The most important thing that perfect score parents give their children is the experience of a normal childhood. Very few perfect score kids were raised as child prodigies. Most led normal lives. As part of this normal childhood, perfect score parents took on four

## FAMILY TIME

Family is a core value in American society, even for young people. In a recent survey conducted by Yankelovich, respondents ages sixteen to twenty-two agreed almost unanimously with the statement that having a good marriage was a sign of success and accomplishment. By comparison, only 24 percent of them said wearing clothes made by a famous designer also was a symbol of success. What's strange, though, is that only 40 percent of these respondents described themselves as family oriented, while 59 percent said they wished their family spent more time doing things together.

Perfect score students had basically the same attitudes about family as the Yankelovich respondents. The difference, however, is that perfect score students actually were family oriented and did spend an optimal amount of time with their families. Family was central to them growing up in terms of activities, reading, trips, and family meals together. Mom and Dad were considered to be the number one providers of academic advice and support. Most important, none of the perfect score students said they wished they could spend more time with their family because they were already satisfied with the amount of time that their family spent together.

major roles that helped maximize their child's success in academics and in the world at large. These roles might be labeled *activity director, motivator, role model,* and *supporter.* All parents can take on these roles regardless of whether they're divorced or married.

In elementary school, parents of perfect score students served mainly as *activity directors,* carpooling, setting up play dates, and arranging music and art lessons. They also *motivated* their sons or daughters to challenge themselves academically. If homework was too easy, these parents gave their kids extra ditto sheets with reading material or math problems. They also communicated with their child's teacher to get more challenging assignments for their overachiever. Some even arranged for their kids to learn in an independent study program. By the time perfect score students reached high school, they were able to take the groundwork laid by their parents and use it to become more independent. Most of them became their own motivators in high school and were able to choose and coordinate their own activities without their parents' input.

Perfect score parents also serve as *role models* for their children. Most perfect score students say they admire their parents the most out of all the people they've met. These students are also influenced in choosing a career based on their knowledge of their parents' professions. Many perfect score parents expose their children to their careers, explaining what they do and taking their kids to work with them on occasion. The parent as role model tends to slip away a bit in high school, as perfect score students become more independent. These students' strong self-identity, however, stems from modeling themselves after their parents and integrating their parents' values and work ethic into their own value system. Perfect score students use these values to push, challenge, and motivate themselves. This enables them to fulfill their potential in school and in all the activities they pursue.

Last but not least, perfect score parents provide a *support system* for their children. This support starts in their child's earliest years and really extends through high school and into college. No matter how independent perfect score students become, they still admit that they rely on their parents for support and encouragement. They may not want Mom and Dad to select their courses or check their homework every night, but they do want their parents to be in the loop, to know when they're struggling with a class and when they have their academic triumphs. They also rely on their parents to tell them when to ease up on themselves, to warn them when they're heading for burnout because they've taken on too many activities or courses. In short, perfect score students still need to be parented throughout their teenage years. They want to know there's a boss looking out for their best interests. Having that security makes these students—and really any student—thrive.

## TWO PERFECT SCORE PARENTS, TWO PERFECT SCORE KIDS

Cal and Ann Bolton are not your typical parents. These two educators took a passionate interest in their children's education, starting from when their older child, Shannon, was still in diapers. They decided to travel from their hometown of Moultrie, Georgia, to Philadelphia to take a weeklong course at the Better Baby Institute. "We learned all the things you can do for your child from infancy on to foster intelligence," recalls Ann. "We became convinced that early reading and a life of literacy is the key to success in life."

When the Boltons returned home, they put into use everything they were taught. They put flash cards all around the house with the names of objects written on them and taught their daughter to recognize the letters and sound out words. Shannon was reading before she turned three. When their son, Patrick, was born, the Boltons did everything they did with Shannon and more. They painted a black-and-white checkerboard on his walls and flicked lights on and off to give him visual stimulation. When he was six months old, they painted over the checkerboard with different colored shapes. Before Patrick could talk, he was able to identify shapes and point to words he recognized. "People thought we were nuts. We thought we were nuts. But we were excited about these learning theories and thought it can't hurt to try," explains Ann.

The Boltons firmly believe that young children are capable of learning anything as long as they receive the proper instruction. During their children's elementary school years, they decided to homeschool Shannon and Patrick because they didn't think the local school would offer them a challenging-enough curriculum. "They called it Camp Bolton," says Shannon. "We received about three hours of instruction each day, and then the rest of the day was set aside for activities. We played every sport, and took music and art lessons. Dad even built a tennis court on some farmland we had on our property." Patrick played tennis as much as he could and entered state and national tournaments in junior high and high school. He earned a national ranking in the top 125 of players under eighteen. "My dad scheduled matches for me and really encouraged me to play because he knew I was talented and that I enjoyed it," says Patrick. "He really wanted me to be committed to it."

What didn't the Bolton kids do? "We pretty much never watched TV or played video games," says Patrick. "My parents were very education focused. They thought we'd be better off reading if we had free time." Shannon remembers reading Nancy Drew books with a flashlight under the covers at night when she was in third grade. By the time she was in sixth grade, her father urged her to read the classics. "He gave me some money after I read *Catch-22* and other books on his reading list," says Shannon.

Both Shannon and Patrick credit their parents' involvement and support with their academic achievements. Shannon, though, decided she had enough of the homeschooling when she reached seventh grade. "I really wanted to make friends, to hang out with girls my own age," she explains. She also wanted to break away a bit from her parents. Ann adds: "We were their coaches, their piano teacher, and their instructors for all school subjects. I was ready and they were ready to branch out and meet other people. They also needed to learn to follow other people's schedules, not just their own."

Shannon says that it took her parents a few months to realize that they wouldn't need to push her in her public school classes. After seeing her first report card, they saw that she was self-motivated and wouldn't need them to be looking over her shoulder. "They pretty much left me alone, though they still always asked me about my classes and what I was learning in school," remembers Shannon. In high school, Shannon became editor of the school newspaper, president of her class, and captain of the tennis team. She had a group of close-knit friends that she hung out with and rarely spent a Saturday night at home.

Patrick, meanwhile, remained in a homeschool environment until he finished seventh grade. Once he entered public school, he flourished academically. He became captain of the academic bowl and of the math team. And he continued to play tennis and piano. However, he had a tough time fitting in socially at the public high school in his small town. "It was hard for him," says Ann. "He wasn't as extroverted as his sister and had a hard time fitting in and finding his group. I think we all feel now that the years of homeschooling made it more difficult for him to adjust."

Patrick decided to switch to a private boarding school in the Atlanta area and quickly found a group of peers he could relate to. He relished his first taste of independence. "I was much happier there," he recalls. "I had to study harder than in public school, but I was with kids who were really into their academics." Patrick enjoyed the challenge of his classes and found he was able to fit in much better than in his high school.

Patrick made local news the first time he took the SAT. "In our newspaper, they had a picture of me shaking my finger at him because he only got a 1590," says Shannon. She got a 1600 on the SAT the first time she took it, while Patrick missed a perfect score by 10 points. He went on to score a 1600 on his third try. "Teachers make a big deal out of a 1600, and I got a nice scholarship to college," says Shannon. "I also got to meet President Clinton, which was cool," she says of the Presidential Scholar award she received. "But I'm not my SAT score. I don't want it to define me." Patrick feels the same way. "After getting the 1590, I only took the test again because I thought if my sister can do it, why not me?" he says. He didn't particularly care about the recognition he'd get from his parents or teachers.

Shannon received a full scholarship to Washington and Lee, a private liberal arts college in Virginia. After completing her degree, she took a job with the Quebec Government Tourism Office based in Washington, D.C., where she uses her fluent French. The twenty-four-year-old's dream is to eventually become a writer. Patrick is in his second year at the University of Texas, also on scholarship, and is majoring in math. He plans to become a math professor or teach high school math. He has found his crowd at Texas and is even rooming with another student who scored 1600. "We met at freshman orientation and totally clicked," says Patrick. "It wasn't until later when we were good friends that we discovered we both got perfect SAT scores."

As for Cal and Ann Bolton, they're applying the education techniques that worked so well with their children to their community at large. "We live in a small agricultural community with some of the lowest reading scores in the country," Ann explains. She and her husband started a nonprofit foundation in Moultrie to encourage all the local residents to get into the habit of reading. They came up with a motto for their town, calling it "the reading capital of the world" and kicked off their reading program by getting thousands of residents to read a million books. "We wanted to see if people could surround themselves with a life of literacy," Ann enthused. "We gave away free books in banks, in hospital lobbies, in doctor's waiting rooms and every other public area. While you're waiting, why not start a book?" When the town reached its million-book goal, 7,500 people filed into the high school football stadium to read a page together from Dr. Seuss's *The Cat in the Hat*.

"We put a lot of hard work into raising and educating our children," says Ann, "and now that they're grown we can see it did them a lot of good. Reading and talking to kids gives them so much more than watching TV. We're now trying to make sure all parents get that message."

## WITH A LITTLE HELP FROM THEIR FRIENDS

Perfect score students may not attribute their perfect SAT scores to their friendships, but these social connections probably did play some role. Let's face it—you can tell a lot about high school students by looking at whom they choose to hang out with. High school is full of cliques: the jocks, the burnouts, the popular kids, the brains. Everyone fits in somewhere, and usually we gravitate toward those we have something in common with.

Friendships help define a person's entire high school experience. You take classes with friends, trade notes with friends, and do homework together. In fact, in many AP classes, group projects are required. And collaborative effort is often necessary to solve problem sets in advanced math and science classes.

Perfect score students take their friendships very seriously. Like other high school students, they tend to gravitate toward those who are most like themselves. "My best friends are those whom I tend to compete with the most academically," says Lucy Z. "But we find it fun to compete with each other, and we're always there to act as a support system for each other." Lucy explains that she and her friends hold study groups together on the night before a test and constantly call each other up with questions about assignments. Did Lucy study with friends for the SAT? "No," she says, "that I had to do all on my own."

Like Lucy, many perfect score students mentioned that it was only their closest friends who understood them or could relate to them intellectually. These friends challenge them mentally and aren't put off by how driven they are because they're also motivated to do well themselves. These high academic achievers engaged in a kind of group therapy with their friends to discuss the pressures of high school and any disappointments they may have experienced along the way. For instance, not getting into a top choice college can be an ego-bruising experience for academic overachievers. The college admissions process can be incredibly cutthroat for all high school students. Even those who ace the SAT often find they've been rejected from a number of top schools. Perfect score students said they relied on friends to help them through this high-pressure experience.

Friends clearly are the heart of high school. And perfect score students are no different from average score students in their dependence on friendships. The vast majority of perfect score students said their social life consisted of going out or just being with friends. Parents were pretty much out of the social life scene when these students hit high school.

When asked which description best characterized them, 54 percent of perfect score students said they were social, while only 18 percent characterized themselves as loners. This is despite the fact that many of these students feel somewhat isolated from their peers because of their intellectual abilities. Those who went to small rural schools still managed to find friends to socialize with even if they weren't on the same level intellectually.

Even the self-described loners put a high priority on their friendships. Nearly 60 percent of these loners had either a boyfriend or girlfriend, and all had at least one or two friends that they went to the movies or did after-school activities with. What's interesting too is that most of the loners were no longer loners when they got to college. Many were thrilled to find that they finally had a group of intellectually stimulating peers.

Art H. is a typical loner among the perfect score students. As he describes himself, "I'm an introspective intellectual. I enjoy outdoor activity. I like spending time alone or with small groups of people I know well." Art grew up in a rural town in the Southwest. He went to a relatively small middle-class public high school. His mother was an insurance adjuster and his dad was a teacher. The two earned a combined income of just $45,000. But lack of money wasn't an impediment to Art academically. Art scored 1600 the first time he took the SAT in his junior year, graduated with a straight-A average, and was third in his class.

While Art admitted he was a loner, he also described himself as an All-around and a brain. He said his social life became much better in his junior and senior years. Even though he only had a handful of close friends, Art said he "developed deep and rewarding friendships with a lot of different kinds of people." He also had a girlfriend for a year. And he admitted that he socialized with friends more than he studied.

Perhaps because he appreciated the time he spent by himself, Art was very introspective and philosophical. "I believe in absolutes, but there are very few. Most things are subjective. Therefore, I believe it is my responsibility to seek out absolutes and define the rest. My personal philosophy is to know myself and what I believe. Then seek the right things."

## SHIFTING DEPENDENCE FROM PARENTS TO FRIENDS

During a child's development, parents start off as the center of their child's universe. By the end of high school, friends have become the social center of a child's world. Of course, this shift from parents to friends prepares a young adult for a life of independence in which romantic love eventually replaces parental love. When does this shift occur? And what can parents do to ensure their children hook up with a group of peers who will have a positive influence on them?

Clearly, a high school student's self-identity is closely tied into the group of friends he or she chooses to hang out with. I believe that parents play a critical role early on in their child's life in shaping and influencing the types of friends their child chooses to make. Children who adopt their parents' values will seek out friends with those same values. Children who aren't given a clear code of ethics may look for friends who break the rules and have a careless attitude about their responsibilities and goals.

So although friends play a central role in providing grounding and stability in high school, parents set the groundwork for what type of friends their child chooses to identify with.

## *Stage One: Grade School Years*

Parents are most directly involved in their child's upbringing before age twelve. Perfect score students say their parents were extremely involved in their lives during their preschool and elementary school years. Although they had friends, these friendships were peripheral to their lives at this age. Their parents provided most of their social activities when they were younger. They remember their parents coaching their Little League games, taking them to music appreciation class, and reading to them for at least a half hour every day. They also remember their parents engaging them in conversation rather than talking above them.

Mary Y. is typical of a perfect score parent. "I took Ethan to story hour before he could read," she says, "where they read books and did arts and crafts. Ethan also did swimming lessons." She recalls both she and her husband managed to do a lot of one-on-one activities with Ethan even though both of them worked. They tried to arrange their schedules so he could have significant quality time with at least one parent in the morning and in the evening. Other parents use family activities, such as vacations and trips abroad, as a way to broaden and stimulate their children's intellect and curiosity. But for the most part, perfect score parents were involved with their kids on a day-to-day basis, providing them with educational resources such as books, brain quizzes, puzzles, and other activities to stimulate their minds.

The father of perfect score student Josh F. says, "We encouraged Josh to think freely and gave him a lot of opportunity to engage in the world. I would bring home a book with solutions to math problems that were creative or unusual. As a result, he had exposure to problem solving from multiple perspectives." Josh's mother adds, "We provided a lot of family time when Josh was growing up. We focused on a few activities for Josh, which included music, chess, religious school, and dance. Family needs were important. We had a strong commitment to our relationship with each other." These sentiments are echoed again and again by perfect score parents.

## *Stage Two: The Junior High School Years*

For most perfect score students, junior high school marked the shift away from their parents and toward their friends. This is probably true of most children at the brink of adolescence. Perfect score students, however, had to contend with another issue, namely, the fact that they were much brighter than most of their peers. This issue came to the forefront during the junior high school years. At the same time, perfect score parents found that their kids relied on them less and less for academic input. Ken A.'s father says, "We were good role models overall, but starting from the beginning of junior high school, our role wasn't as great. We insisted Ken do his homework, although we didn't have to. Since it only took him five minutes to do, he always did it."

When perfect score students didn't perform up to their expectations, their parents usually took action. Ryan L.'s father says, "I expected Ryan to do well. Sometimes in eighth and ninth grades, he didn't do so well on courses he didn't like. Therefore, we would discipline him a little. We would make him do his homework and not let him play on his computer. After a while, we made a deal with him: if he got all As on his report card, we would leave him alone."

By and large, perfect score students recognized in junior high that they were bright and could do the work with varying degrees of effort. Most say their parents helped them to recognize their abilities and instilled in them a determination to do well. By this time, these students began to motivate themselves and became less reliant on their parents for motivation. Parents generally agreed to let their budding teenagers take care of their own schoolwork responsibilities as long as the kids did well. Some students described pacts that they made with their parents, similar to Ryan L.'s. Basically, this was an informal agreement that they could organize their own schoolwork responsibilities as long as they kept up their grades.

If the pact was broken, parents stepped in to reassert control. Usually, perfect score students got back on track in order to regain the control that their parents had taken away. Gradually, the parental role shifted from direct involvement in elementary school to cheerleader and champion by the time these students were ready for high school.

### Stage Three: High School and Beyond

Stage three, the high school years, is the first taste students have of academic independence from their parents. They are largely self-motivated and know where they want to go and how to get there. They are primed to develop deep friendships because they no longer need their parents for self-identity. They know deep down that their happiness will now be tied to their friendships as much as, if not more than, their relationship with their parents.

In order for students to enter stage three successfully, they have to pass completely through the first two stages. Perfect score students, for the most part, enter stage three within the first two years of high school.

However, other students, who may be less successful academically, can stagnate in stage one or two and find that they still rely on their parents for academic motivation through their high school years. I've seen far too many high school students who are prodded and pushed by their parents to complete homework and essay assignments, and I think this is because their parents never really let go and failed to give their children a chance to motivate themselves and assert some control over their academic goals.

Students who have successfully moved into stage three find that both their parents and their friends do, indeed, play a critical role in their lives—even if it's not to motivate them to succeed. Perfect score students said over and over again that their parents provided academic guidance and support during high school. Their friends gave them emotional support and fulfilled their social needs. These students also used their friends to challenge themselves academically, matching wits against wits. Perfect score students do set certain boundaries for their parents and friends. They gather input and listen to the opinions of their closest confidants, but they also rely largely on themselves in making important decisions. Very few perfect score students say they selected a college based on where their friends were going or where their parents wanted them to go.

The Perfect Score Study suggests that there's an ideal way to pursue friendships in high school and beyond. Seeking out friends with the same values is important, but so is maintaining one's identity within those friendships. Some high school students allow their friends to dictate their lives and become beholden to their friends, making life choices based on what's best for their friends rather than on what's best for themselves. Perfect score students manage to keep their own needs at the forefront and learn to integrate their friendships into their lives, rather than integrating their lives into their friendships.

When I interviewed Eric N. it was clear how naturally connected he was to his friends and family. When I ask about his social life in high school, Eric replies, "It's excellent. I have a lot of good friends who I have been close to for a very long time. My girlfriend is really nice. We've been going out for a year and a half." Eric says his relationships are not shallow or short-lived. He has friends from kindergarten that he is still close to.

He adds that his parents are strict but give him complete freedom over his academics as long as he performs up to his potential. "Up until high school, my parents were crazy about grades. Then in high school, Mom and Dad wanted me to be responsible, and unless I got bad grades, I was on my own." The more responsibility his parents gave him, the more Eric vowed not to let them down. He says his parents are the people he most admires and who influence him the most.

Eric considers himself very family-oriented. In fact, one of the things he likes doing most is spending time with his family. He details the trips he took to Europe and Asia with his family when he was growing up. When questioned about his biggest fear, he responds, "Not fulfilling my or my parents' expectations." It is evident that Eric's friends and family give him stability. Could he have done as well in school and on the SATs without this support? I think it's highly unlikely. Would he have been as happy? Definitely not.

# Secret 7:
# Their Real Goal Isn't
# to Ace the SAT—
# but to Succeed in Life

In a scene from Monty Python's *The Meaning of Life,* a group of fish are swimming around a tank and greeting one another good morning. Suddenly, one fish says to another, "Hey, look, Howard's being eaten!" All the fish look out of the tank and watch a waiter serving a large grilled fish to a man at a table. A second fish says, "Makes you think, doesn't it? I mean . . . what's it all about?" A third fish says, "Beats me."

As high school students get caught up in the whirlwind of AP exams, college applications, an overloaded course schedule, a battery of extracurricular activities, and, of course, the SAT, they often neglect to take a step back once in a while. To take a brief moment to consider what's it all about. To think about what they really want out of life and how they define success.

This type of philosophical reflection is seen by many to be an unaffordable luxury. Who has time to sit around and map out a life plan? Any free time that high school students have is precious, and it's understandable that they'd want to spend it hanging out with their friends. Yet all the effort that these students put into doing whatever it takes to get into the college of their choice really means nothing if they don't have a clue what their life is all about or how to obtain success.

Perfect score students have figured out the secret to themselves, what makes them tick and where their place is in the world. This may explain why they, more commonly than average students, report that they want to make a difference, to do something positive that will make an impact on the world.

When perfect score students are asked to describe themselves in three sentences, most can pinpoint precisely who they are. Charlotte B. says, "I'm all about math, physics, and writing." Daniela A. says, "I'm very academically focused." "I'm smart, funny, and athletic," responds Nava L. "Intelligent, caring, considerate, good," says David Z.

Many define themselves in terms of family and friends. "I have a very close relationship with my best friend and my family," answers Tim A. "I'm a leader, an athlete, but most important, a good friend," says Mark D. Some focused in on their drive or intellectual curiosity. "I get passionate about things when I get involved in something," says Frank H. "I'm someone who is eager to learn," responds Pin C. "Since I'm from New Mexico, I like to stay active and do outdoor activities," says Robert L.

Perfect score students freely discuss themselves and their definition of success, when the SAT doesn't even merit a mention. Even when asked to name their strengths, none of the perfect score students mentioned the SAT by name, and only three named their talent for test taking.

## Top Strengths Listed by Perfect Score Students

- academic potential
- self-confidence
- a talent for science
- perfectionism
- strong work ethic
- logical mind
- honesty
- fair-mindedness
- good memory
- willingness to take risks
- consideration for others

Obviously, the SAT isn't the defining moment in the lives of most who ace it. Despite the fact that these students achieve what 99.97 percent of all other students cannot, they don't see their perfect score as a life-altering accomplishment or even as one of their most important strengths. They're far more focused on the deeper meaning of their lives and on finding the path to happiness.

What's fascinating, though, is that this focus on the big picture, which enables perfect score students to put the SAT into perspective, is a major factor in helping them achieve a perfect score in the first place. Students who can think more globally have an easier time comprehending SAT questions, which deal with material relating to life and the world at large. They may be better equipped to quickly get a firm grasp on the critical reading section. And they may have better reasoning skills, which help them tackle the logic questions in the math section. From a psychological standpoint, they may be more relaxed during the test and able to focus on the test questions rather than on their fear about how they're going to do.

None of the perfect score students think that an SAT score should be used to define a person. "It feels great to do well on a standardized test, especially when there's so much preparation involved," says Lucy Z. "But then the excitement wears off. It's a one-shot deal."

These students take the tack that life goes on, regardless of academic achievements. No test can ever make or break you. Daniela A. expresses the sentiments of many perfect score students when she says, "It's important to set goals and figure out what you're good at and then achieve it, but it's also important to maintain balance with friends and family." Shuva M. takes an even more optimistic approach to life: "Live your life so that when you die you are smiling. When you are old you can look back and see your life was enjoyable and honorable."

How do perfect score students define themselves? What's most important to them? Knowing this gives us a clue about their philosophy of life and how they put into motion plans that propel them toward success.

The three most important things to perfect score students are academics, friends, and family. According to the Perfect Score Study, more than 70 percent of perfect score students name these three things as being extremely important. Social life is next, with 40 percent citing its importance. In comparison, sports are not nearly as important to perfect score students. Only 14 percent say sports are extremely important, while 37 percent say sports are not important at all. Money is also not a major priority for perfect score students: only 14 percent rate it extremely important. About 31 percent say religion is extremely important to them, 28 percent say it is somewhat important, and 41 percent say it is not important at all.

## WHAT'S MOST IMPORTANT TO PERFECT SCORE STUDENTS (%)

|  | Academics | Social Life | Extra. Curr. | Sports | Religion | Comm. Serv. | Family | Friends | Peers | Money |
|---|---|---|---|---|---|---|---|---|---|---|
| Extremely Important | 77 | 40 | 25 | 14 | 31 | 17 | 70 | 73 | 14 | 14 |
| Somewhat Important | 22 | 59 | 70 | 48 | 28 | 66 | 27 | 26 | 81 | 66 |
| Not Important | 1 | 1 | 5 | 37 | 41 | 17 | 4 | 1 | 5 | 23 |

The values of perfect score students become clearer when they are asked to rank these categories in order. Nearly half of all perfect score students say family is most important, while 70 percent consider family either first or second most important to them. Friends come just behind family, followed by academics. What's interesting is that even though these are the brightest students in the nation, they still put family and friends ahead of school in terms of what means the most to them, as seen in the following chart.

## TOP 3 IMPORTANCE RANKINGS FOR PERFECT SCORE STUDENTS (%)

|                   | Family | Friends | Academics | Religion |
|-------------------|--------|---------|-----------|----------|
| Most Important    | 43     | 21      | 16        | 13       |
| 2nd Most Important| 27     | 27      | 12        | 6        |
| 3rd Most Important| 11     | 24      | 23        | 7        |

Despite all their schoolwork responsibilities and extracurricular commitments, perfect score students invest a lot of time and energy in their personal relationships. This gives them a broader outlook on life that has helped them become loving, compassionate human beings. Acing the SAT certainly doesn't require students to become bookworms who memorize SAT review books for fun. In fact, just the opposite: those who lead fuller lives actually do better on the test. Having the thoughtfulness of life experience does count when it comes to figuring out the exam questions.

The control group of average-scoring students have very similar rankings in terms of the importance of friends and family. One difference is that a somewhat higher percentage of average-scoring students report that religion is very important to them. About 17 percent rank religion as the most important, 15 percent rank it as second most important, and 11 percent rank it as third most important.

## DEFINING LIFE AND THE PURSUIT OF SUCCESS

Many of us have become so jaded that we don't even think about the purpose of our lives. We don't think in terms of whether we've achieved success or are living by our values. Satirists have been able to turn these philosophical musings into comedy. In the words of Woody Allen: "What if everything is an illusion and nothing exists? In that case, I definitely overpaid for my carpet."

Unfortunately, far too many high school students today have a morally relativistic outlook. They're not exactly sure what's right and what's wrong or what's good and what's evil. They think that it all depends on your own perspective, a philosophy that's often taught in today's public schools. (After September 11, we saw this in the media over and over again, as some journalists tried to excuse the actions of terrorists by explaining the rationale behind what compels men to hijack planes and drive them into buildings, killing themselves and everyone else on board.)

This moral relativism may lead to utter confusion. Students aren't quite sure what to believe. They don't believe in absolute rights and absolute wrongs—everything falls into a gray zone, and they're left with a big question mark about the meaning of their own lives. They don't really know if they have values or, if they do, whether they'll stick with them no matter what happens in their lives. Many believe that it's futile to define who they are or what they want to become. They can't even say what they plan to do to achieve success, because they have no idea how to define success for themselves.

Perfect score students don't hedge when asked about their own philosophy of life. Most take a moment to think before responding to questions about who they were or what they wanted out of life. All, however, are able to formulate concrete responses, knowing exactly what gives their life meaning. Though I found these responses varied widely from student to student, they did fall into some distinct categories. Some perfect score students really are looking for meaning in life, and this search forms their identity and directs their activities. Others define themselves by what they are good at and what they accomplish. The outlooks of perfect score students can be grouped into five distinct philosophies on life:

1. **Searchers**—Life is looking for meaning.
2. **Dreamers**—Life is wanting to have an impact.
3. **Doers**—Life is what you do.

4. **Socializers**—Life is your relationships and interactions with other people.
5. **True Believers**—Life is your religion and relationship with God.

What distinguishes each of these types? Let's look at five perfect score students who each hold a different outlook on life.

### Tim W., the Searcher

Tim W. is a thoughtful, inquisitive type who often answers questions with a question of his own. He says he is looking for meaning in life, a life that has been spent in an upper-middle-class neighborhood in Seattle, where his father is a doctor and his mother is a business manager. "I'm an extremely curious person who loves seeking information about the world. I'm constantly searching to understand myself, those around me, and my place in the universe. I consider myself to be someone who is always striving to be the person I want to be, whatever that is, which I haven't decided yet."

Curly-haired and attractive, Tim describes himself as a loner and a brain. From his tone, he sounds like a brooding type, approaching life with thoughtfulness rather than ebullience. "I'm fairly reclusive," he says, "yet at the same time, outspoken. I'm not everyone's cup of tea. I'm a philosopher at heart." Tim is still searching for himself, now that he is in college. "I hope the next few years in college will at least point me in the right direction of who I am and what I want to do."

### Nancy N., the Dreamer

Nancy N. says she wants to make the world a better place, and she believes that she, personally, can change it. She went to public high school in a middle-class neighborhood outside of Boston, and she was class valedictorian. The daughter of Chinese parents, she says she was raised with a sense of obligation, not only to her family, but also to humankind in general.

"I'm someone who cares deeply about the impact I can have in the world," says Nancy. "I want to do right by my family and all the other people whom I care about. I'm always interested in learning new things, but I always think about how that knowledge could be used. I care about values and morals. I care about how people treat others, and especially how I treat other people."

Nancy devotes seven hours a week to a meals-on-wheels organization that delivers food to AIDS patients. "It's not a lot, and I'm no saint, but it is consistent with what I hope to do long-term," she says.

## Jane S., the Doer

Jane S. is a bundle of energy. She defines herself by what she does. With striking black hair and a gregarious nature, Jane is incredibly organized and a great time manager, which is how she juggles her membership in several school clubs. She comes from a large middle-class family in Texas and says her biggest problem is not having enough time to do what she wants to do. She enjoys her friends immensely but spends time with them largely in the context of her other activities. "I'm constantly trying to find the proper balance between doing things and going too far. In high school, I was vice president of the debate team, president of the Latin club, and a member of the Key Club and National Honor Society. By the end of high school I was taking nine classes. I just burned out, so I have learned to find a balance."

Jane got into all seven colleges she applied to, and she decided where to go based on the place that had the most to offer in terms of diversity of majors and activities. "In college, I still take one more class than most students, but now I am more aware of it." Jane says she works hard at balancing her schoolwork, activities, and social life and finds herself paring down her list of activities so she can focus on the one or two that really mean the most to her.

## Drew M., the Socializer

Drew M. is a friend's friend. His life revolves around his interactions and relationships with other people. He excels in English and math but is most interested in how people think, talk, and act. He is a natural politician and is secretary of his class. He also plays shortstop on his high school baseball team. Drew's house is the local gathering spot, and on any given day, a dozen or more of his closest friends will be hanging out in the kitchen.

"I like being around new people from different backgrounds and who have different interests," says Drew. "I enjoy discussions in which varying opinions are expressed and well defended. I love having fun, and I know people enjoy being with me."

### Matt H., the True Believer

Life to Matt H. is his religion and relationship with God. Matt grew up in a religious household in the Midwest and attended a private Christian high school. He views school as an extension of his home. He says his family is not wealthy in terms of money, but they are "rich spiritually." Matt gives you the impression that he has very firm convictions that he won't sacrifice for anyone or anything. He sees his education and his perfect SAT score as a way to serve and advance the Lord's work. And he gives God credit for his talents and his academic success.

"I have different areas of life: education, home, and religion," explains Matt. "I enjoy being at home, and I enjoy people, being with them and talking with them. I enjoy schoolwork and learning new things and seeing how things get together. But I also realize it's important that we recognize that there is a God and that we direct our lives accordingly. My goal is to do my best for other people and for God."

When I posed the same questions to each of these students with their varying philosophies, I was struck by how their answers consistently followed their individual philosophies on life.

### What are your hopes and fears?

*Nancy N., the Dreamer:* My hope is to leave a mark on the world and make my family proud. My only fear is not having enough time to do everything I think I should do.

*Tim W., the Searcher:* I hope to make something useful of my life. To do something nobody has done before. My fear is the opposite—that is, making something less of my life by taking things as they come.

*Matt H., the True Believer:* My hopes are to be successful in college and in industry, and to be one with God. Fears? None.

*Jane S., the Doer:* I hope to be happy and successful and I'm afraid that I won't be, which I guess is a fear I've imposed upon myself.

*Drew M., the Socializer:* My hopes are for success in academics, future jobs, and social contacts. My fear is dying young.

## Whom do you most admire?

*Tim W., the Searcher:* Thomas Edison

*Nancy N., the Dreamer:* my grandmother

*Jane S., the Doer:* my mother

*Drew M., the Socializer:* my parents

*Matt H., the True Believer:* St. Thomas

## How would you define success?

*Jane S., the Doer:* Live life to the fullest. Try to experience everything. Learn as much as you can.

*Drew M., the Socializer:* Try to treat everyone with respect. Do whatever will make you the happiest.

*Tim W., the Searcher:* The point is to figure out why you're here. So you should always be analyzing, exploring, and experiencing as much of life as you can.

*Nancy N., the Dreamer:* Do the best you possibly can. Never leave without having made a difference.

*Matt H., the True Believer:* I believe there is a God who has made moral standards, and I believe we should live by them.

### How important is the SAT to you?

*Drew M., the Socializer:* not at all important

*Jane S., the Doer:* somewhat important

*Matt H., the True Believer:* somewhat important

*Nancy N., the Dreamer:* not at all important

*Tim W., the Searcher:* very important

What's obvious from these various philosophical approaches to life is that perfect score students have a strong sense of who they are. Their SAT scores haven't altered their way of thinking about life. They all have a vision of what success means to them and how they want to conduct their lives. The question is: do these values—which vary from student to student—actually help perfect score students achieve a higher score on the SAT?

The perfect score study suggests the answer is yes. That's because the beliefs held by perfect score students have altered their choices about how they're going to lead their lives. In wanting to have an impact on the world or to do right in the eyes of God, these students always put their best foot forward. They guide themselves wisely through life when it comes to choosing friends, taking on a challenging course load, and, yes, even preparing for the SAT.

They don't define success in terms of money. Most would rather have an impact on the world than become a multimillionaire. Success means happiness and fulfillment, whether it's through a rewarding career or through the love of friends and family. Success can also be some tangible goal like a space shuttle mission, a house filled with a loving spouse and three kids, or a Nobel Prize. Regardless of how perfect score students define success, they are confident that if they put forth the effort they will achieve whatever it is that will make them successful in their own eyes.

## TRANSLATING PHILOSOPHY INTO SUCCESS IN LIFE

From watching *Dawson's Creek,* you would think that every teenager's life revolves around dating, problems with teachers, fights with friends, and lack of money to buy the coolest clothes. You'd never think teenagers worried about such meaningful things like personal satisfaction with life, whether they're giving back to their community, or what they want to achieve academically.

To understand the social attitudes and values of American consumers, Yankelovich surveyed a national representative sample of 2,500 adults to get their opinion on everything from how they define success and accomplishment to what they do for fun. This research, called the Yankelovich MONITOR®, provides a good pulse on the thinking, attitudes, and values of today's consumers. I decided to compare the attitudes of 326 Yankelovich survey participants, ages sixteen to twenty-two, with the attitudes of perfect score students. I wanted to see if the perfect score students' pursuit of meaning and success in life affected their attitudes and overall goals.

### *Money versus Education*

Having a lot of money is a sign of success and accomplishment for 45 percent of the young adults who responded to the Yankelovich survey, while 43 percent view an advanced degree as a sign of success and accomplishment. Perfect score students put a higher premium on education and a lower premium on money than the average young adults: 94 percent of the 1600 kids say they plan to go to graduate school and see a graduate degree as a way to achieve success. This compares with 70 percent of the average-scoring students who participated in the Perfect Score Study. One reason for this difference is that perfect score students come from families where graduate degrees are the norm. Moreover, they tend to choose fields of study such as medicine, law, or physics that require graduate degrees in order to pursue a career in that field.

Most perfect score students prefer to advance their learning or education rather than focus on accumulating money. Only 25 percent of the perfect score students worked during high school, versus 62 percent of the average-scoring control group. When asked about their greatest hope, 12 percent of average score students say they wanted to be financially comfortable. None of the perfect score students list this as their greatest hope. When asked about their greatest fear, 6 percent of average score students say they fear a poor economy or not having enough money. None of the perfect score students list this as a fear.

What's apparent is that perfect score students put more stock in succeeding in their careers than in making a lot of money. This is consistent with their broad vision of wanting to make a positive impact on the world and of feeling a responsibility for doing something worthwhile with their talents. There is, however, another possible reason for why perfect score students think little about money. They generally come from families who have higher incomes, which means they may worry less about money. A full 17 percent of perfect score students say their family is upper class, compared with none of the average score students. Just 7 percent of perfect score students fall into the lower-middle- or lower-class categories, compared with 14 percent of average score students.

## SOCIOECONOMIC STATUS

|  | 1600 | 1000–1200 |
| --- | --- | --- |
| Upper Class | 17% | 0 |
| Upper-Middle Class | 41% | 42% |
| Middle Class | 35% | 44% |
| Lower-Middle Class | 6% | 8% |
| Lower Class | 1% | 6% |

## SOCIOECONOMIC STATUS (continued)

| Family Income | 1600 | 1000–1200 |
|---|---|---|
| Above $100,000 | 45% | 22% |
| $76,000–$100,000 | 22% | 17% |
| $51,000–$75,000 | 21% | 28% |
| $26,000–$50,000 | 8% | 28% |
| Below $25,000 | 4% | 5% |

While it's true that those who have the most money tend to obsess about it the least, this doesn't completely explain why perfect score students care little about how much money they're going to earn. Even those perfect score students whose families earn less than $50,000 per year place money low on their list of priorities. These students are just as likely as wealthier perfect score students to choose careers with prestige over those with earning potential.

## THE SECRET TO HAPPINESS AND SUCCESS

Peter K. encompasses nearly all the 7 Secrets that are the trademark of perfect score students. He pursues his tennis passion by playing on the varsity team in high school. He gives back to society by volunteering at a local soup kitchen three hours a week. And he creates his own luck by using his natural learning talents to ace easier courses and applying a driving learning style for his more challenging course work.

Peter is also incredibly self-motivated. "It's all about priorities," Peter says. "I can't argue that my parents didn't have a big influence on me, but in the end, I gave my schoolwork a high priority. My parents provided the stimulation and they expected a lot. But I took it from there." Peter says his family means a great deal to him and describes himself as "family oriented, yet independent."

Peter also has a definite idea of what he wants out of life and what he needs to do to be successful. He defines success as "doing something important." He hasn't figured out yet what this important thing is that he should do, but he says, "I know it's not about money, but it is about doing something I want to do, being happy, and hopefully having an impact on other people." Peter values having an impact on the world far more than he values money. He also values his own happiness. His philosophy of life: "Do what you can do, what is right for yourself and for others."

Getting a perfect score on the SAT is certainly not the ticket to happiness in life, though many students may think that it is. Just as rich people aren't necessarily happy, neither are smart kids. However, perfect score students seem to be happier than most students—probably due to their 7 Secrets, rather than the test score itself.

As part of the Perfect Score Study, students were asked to rate how happy they were at various times in their lives: before high school, during high school, and in college. I wanted to see if Lisa Simpson, the daughter on the animated TV show *The Simpsons*, had it right when she observed that there's an inverse relationship between intelligence and happiness. Was it true that the brightest students were also the least happy?

As mentioned, the Perfect Score Study proved Lisa Simpson wrong. Perfect score students are, on the whole, very happy. Based on a 7-point scale, with 1 being not happy and 7 being extremely happy, the 5.6 average happiness score of perfect score students is the same as that of average SAT score students.

## STUDENTS' HAPPINESS RATING

|             | 1600 SAT Score | 1000–1200 SAT Score |
|-------------|----------------|---------------------|
| Growing Up  | 5.6            | 5.5                 |
| High School | 5.3            | 5.1                 |
| College     | 5.8            | 6.1                 |

KEY: 1 = NOT HAPPY; 7 = EXTREMELY HAPPY

Even though perfect score students study more and socialize less than their average score counterparts, they're just as happy, at least in part because these students have a sense of purpose in life. They know they are working for a larger cause beyond a good high school transcript or acceptance to a top college. They know they will eventually make an impact on the world, so the efforts they make now won't go to waste.

Even more key to their happiness, perfect score students pursue those things they're good at and those things they enjoy. Usually, these two things are intertwined. So if a student has a passion for math equations and spends every afternoon pursuing this passion on the math team, he's likely to find happiness. If that same student is pushed to practice the clarinet instead, his happiness will decline. Perfect score students generally are given the independence to pursue their natural talents and passions—for the pure joy of it. Perhaps this is why these students can wax philosophically about wanting to change the world. Their happiness with life gives them motivation to want to make others happy.

Just like any other students', perfect score students find that their happiness does vary over time. As with average score students, for them high school is generally a less happy time than elementary school, junior high, or college. Students may feel awkward or uncomfortable in high school, with the pressures of adolescence, peers, and the college admissions process. Still, the overall happiness rating of the perfect score high school students drops only a little— slightly less, in fact, than the happiness rating of average score students.

To no great surprise, happiness peaks for both perfect score students and average students during their college years. Almost all the perfect score students report that they're adequately challenged in college. And most say they formed close friendships with people they could relate to. In the words of Jake S., "I love college. I hang around with interesting yet diverse people. There's plenty of opportunity to try new things. It's freer in that I don't have the requirements of high school. I like being on my own. In short, I like the independence . . . and having my own car."

I think the main lesson we can learn from perfect score students is that those who have a general life plan usually find that the rest falls into place. They may not make a career choice at seventeen or decide on the age for marriage and kids. But they do have some sense of self-identity: they know who they are and where they want their life to go. They know what's most important and what can be chucked out with the trash. They feel their life has a purpose, even if they're not sure what that is. All of these things bring a sense of optimism. And optimism is the sister of happiness and success.

Students who can embark on their pursuit of success in high school will be ready for the freedom and independence that college life brings. Ted L. acknowledged that he now savors his college experience: "I'm happier in college because of all the things I'm learning. People are nicer. Nobody bothers you. For me it was a chance to start over, do new things, and really be myself."

Sounds like a path to success that most students would want to follow.

# PART III

# Raising SAT Scores:
# Practical Advice and
# Learning for Life

# SAT Advice from Perfect Score Students: What Works, What Doesn't

The Perfect Score Study offers a life plan that works for the highest academic achievers in this country and can work for any student. This study also reveals what these perfect score students do specifically when it comes to preparing for the SAT. Do they take review courses? How much do they study? Are they stressed out or relaxed before taking the test? How many practice exams do they take?

You'll be surprised by some of the answers. For example, review courses and private tutors are the exception, not the norm. And for the most part, these students are pretty relaxed going into the test. What's more, this advice is just as relevant for the new SAT since the 7 Secrets and the tips that follow directly address the new material on the test.

Part III will give you all the answers you need to know about how those who ace the SAT get ready for this test. Still, it's important to emphasize that students shouldn't expect to get the full benefits of the information uncovered in the Perfect Score Study without incorporating the 7 Secrets. Short-term solutions are fine, but a lifelong approach gives you far more bang for your buck in the long run.

## SAT STUDY HABITS OF PERFECT SCORE STUDENTS

If you take the top ten students in any high school class and compare their study habits, the differences are striking. At least one or two students get A+ on every test and assignment while studying very little. At the other extreme, there are two or three students who also manage to ace their exams and assignments, but they study and work on their academics nonstop to the exclusion of all extracurricular activities. The other five or six students fall somewhere in between these two extremes.

The Perfect Score Study found these same trends hold true for those who scored a 1600 on the SAT. Some students breeze through the standardized test, getting a 1600 on their first try without any preparation. Others take the SAT three or four times, attend two or three review classes, and take a dozen or more practice exams. The bulk of perfect score students fall in the middle of this group, taking the exam once or twice with a fair, but not excessive, amount of preparation.

Here's how the statistics break down from the Perfect Score Study:

○ 39 percent of perfect score students ace the SAT on their first try

○ 37 percent take the SAT two times

○ 24 percent take the SAT three or more times

A significant 35 percent of the perfect score students took the exam in the seventh grade, with an average score of 1207 (scores ranged from 990 to 1500). Most of the students who took the SAT before high school did so to qualify for a gifted and talented program offered by a local high school or college—rather than as early preparation for the SAT. Less than 10 percent of perfect score students took the SAT in eighth or ninth grade, but their scores rose rapidly compared with those who took the exam in seventh grade. The average scores for eighth graders was 1321, for ninth graders 1450.

Of course, the vast majority of perfect score students take the

SAT in their last two years of high school, which is the typical time to take the test. The Perfect Score Study showed that 92 percent of perfect score students take the SAT in their junior year, with 75 percent of them scoring 1600 on their first or second try. The rest score 1600 in their senior year. In terms of studying for the SAT, 77 percent of the perfect score students do some preparation, while only 23 percent do no preparation whatsoever. Most take timed practice exams, followed by a class and/or review.

I can't overemphasize the importance of SAT review. While the Perfect Score Study finds that 23 percent of perfect score students don't prepare for the SATs, it also finds that a whopping 58 percent of students who score 1000 to 1200 do no preparation. The comparison chart below shows that earning a perfect SAT score depends more on preparation than brains or pure luck.

### SAT PREPARATION STRATEGIES OF PERFECT SCORE STUDENTS VERSUS AVERAGE SCORE STUDENTS (BY %)

|  | Perfect Score Students | Average Score Students |
|---|---|---|
| Timed practice tests | 29 | 2 |
| Class or private tutor | 13 | 20 |
| Review materials on own | 12 | 4 |
| Kaplan/Princeton Review class | 11 | 12 |
| Prep books | 8 | 2 |
| Computer program | 4 | 2 |
| None | 23 | 58 |

So, how hard is the SAT? Slightly more than 50 percent of perfect score students find the SATs to be of moderate difficulty, compared with 44 percent who feel they are easy. Those with average SAT scores feel that the test is more difficult: about 75 percent find the SAT to be of moderate difficulty, and 25 percent say the test is very difficult. None of the average students reported that the SAT is easy.

## ADOPTING A PERFECT SCORE ATTITUDE

I believe the reason that perfect score students do so well—not only on the SAT but in all areas of academics—relates to these students' core set of beliefs about themselves. These beliefs center around thinking, curiosity, and hard work. They might be summed up in three self-descriptions:

1. I think, therefore I am.
2. I am curious.
3. I work hard and play hard.

Most perfect score students have a blending of these three belief sets. They come by them from their parents' values and from their high school experiences, and these beliefs really drive these students to ace the SAT. It isn't so much that they want to be the best among the nation's high school students. They might compete with their friends for fun, but the competitive edge doesn't drive them. Rather, they seem to want to remain true to themselves. The three students profiled below personify each of these attitudes. If all high school students adopted these kinds of attitudes, their SAT scores would naturally rise as a result.

### I Think, Therefore I Am

This belief focuses on the process of thinking as an end in itself. Acing the SAT is not the goal; rather it is an outcome of always thinking deeply about everything, always analyzing academic challenges.

"Why me? Where do I go from here? What's the hardest way to get there?" That's how Carl P. describes his approach to life. He took the SAT five times before he got a 1600. Unlike most of the perfect score students, Carl got a 990 his first time taking the test—though he was in seventh grade at the time—and then he worked his score up the hard way. "What preparation did you do?" I asked. Carl replied, "Just taking the test again and again."

Carl's widespread activities show that he clearly is not a linear thinker. Like other perfect score kids, he's on the math team and the computer science team and participates in science fair and public speaking. But he also performed in theater and played on several sports teams. And he read—a lot. "Mostly classics and science fiction," he says, "and some math and political science books thrown in for diversion."

When Carl explains his philosophy on life, he says, "The point is to figure out why you're here, so you should always be analyzing and exploring and experiencing as much of life as you can." He says he had one teacher in particular who challenged him to think deep thoughts. "I had this high school computer science teacher who, interestingly enough, was a real intellectual. He introduced me to a variety of fields, such as Hegelian philosophy and biblical history. He would tell me his opinions and, equally important, would listen to mine."

Carl is interested in anything and everything. He reads a lot of Russian literature and French existentialism and never misses an episode of *The Simpsons*. He typifies the "thinking as being" attitude that many perfect score students have.

### *I Am Curious*

The second approach describes students who are fascinated by the world around them and everything in it. These students are curious about how and why things work. They are always probing beyond the first question and seeking multiple layers and levels of understanding. This attitude is exhibited not only by perfect score students who excel in math and science but also by those who excel in English and humanities.

When I called Charles K. to interview him for the Perfect Score Study, I could hear him struggling to carve out a time to speak to me. He listed his schedule for the next two weeks and was unable to find a free hour to talk. He promised to call me back in two weeks, and he did.

I could see why Charles was so busy. He has an insatiable curiosity and can't resist trying various activities to learn more about the world and himself. In high school, he participated in sports and took music lessons, typical for many students. But he was also concertmaster in his school orchestra and played in a rock band. And once a week, he attended Latvian language classes to learn the language and culture of his parents. Even with all this on his plate, he still had time to volunteer four hours a week as a tutor at the local Boys and Girls Club.

"School-wise, I never had a problem," says Charles. "I went to an upper-middle-class suburban high school and got straight As. But I wasn't at the top of my class. Maybe I could have graduated valedictorian or salutatorian, but that's not what really motivates me. I was more interested in trying new things. I also like being around people from different backgrounds and interests. And I like to have fun."

Charles told me he was more interested in being well rounded in a lot of different activities than becoming valedictorian and getting the chance to tell everyone on high school graduation day to "be bold, venture forth, and do the things I've never done." Charles is a doer, not a talker. He feeds his curiosity by trying new things. This allows him to approach the SAT as a new and exciting challenge, rather than as a stressful standardized test.

### I Work Hard and Play Hard

Balancing studying with a social life can be a challenge for even the brightest students. Yet most perfect score students manage to do it. They work hard in school, put effort into their extracurricular activities, study intensely for the SATs, but also know how to have fun.

Ray J. clearly makes this balance work for him. He worked hard to maintain a 4.0 GPA and earn a place in the top 10 in his class of 500, and he got into eight of the nine colleges to which he applied. He took a lot of practice tests to achieve his perfect SAT score. Ray admits that he loves to learn, but he also says that he loves good music and makes an effort to have an active social life. "It was good in high school because I got into a lot of activities and made a lot of new friends. I am able to connect with people one on one. I am someone people can count on to help as a friend." He says he cherished his relationship with his high school girlfriend, whom he dated for a year before heading off to college.

Ray fondly remembers the good times he had. He played tennis and was second-chair violin in the orchestra. He also practiced the piano fifteen hours a week because music is his passion. He is just as happy reading his favorite books as he is socializing at a party with friends. He works hard and plays hard because he gets an intense excitement out of life. It's that kind of excitement and joie de vivre that is the real secret behind the perfect SAT score.

## TOP TEN TIPS FROM PERFECT SCORE STUDENTS

Most of us would expect the perfect score students to offer three tips for getting a perfect SAT score: study, study, study. Yet two of the top three suggestions of perfect score students—reading and relaxation—had little to do with studying. Apparently, scoring well on the SAT is more than just an academic exercise. We asked perfect score students to offer their top three pieces of advice for doing well on the SAT:

### Top 10 SAT Tips

1. Read everything: 50% (5% specifically mentioned reading the classics)
2. Buy SAT books, take practice tests: 42%
3. Relax, don't stress about it; it's only a test: 41%
4. Memorize vocabulary: 20%
5. The night before the test, don't study—get a good night's sleep: 14%
6. Pace yourself: 9%

7. Identify and focus on weaknesses (use PSAT and review what you get wrong): 8%

8. Double-check your work: 7%

9. Study early (preferably one year before taking the SAT): 7%

10. Take a prep course: 5%

### Tip 1: Read Everything

No surprise here. Reading is fundamental for both doing well in school and acing the SAT. While extensive reading may be difficult to do two weeks before taking the test, students who have a few months before the SAT or who plan to take it again can definitely benefit from the books, magazines, and newspapers they read. Ideally, challenging reading material is better than trashy romances or quick-read best-sellers. Reading sophisticated periodicals like the *New York Times* or *Harper's* magazine or classic books by such authors as James Joyce, Mark Twain, or Charles Dickens can both expand vocabulary and help improve critical reading skills. But above all else, students should just read, read, read whenever they can.

### Tip 2: Buy SAT Books, Take Practice Tests

Simple but valuable advice. Review books can help students understand the test and benefit from test-taking tips and shortcuts. These tips are generally simple and easy to put into practice—such as remembering to skip difficult questions and come back to them, since the SAT is a timed test. A few hours spent learning how to take the SAT could significantly increase a score. Practice tests will help students familiarize themselves with the exam. Short-term, this kind of review is the most important thing students can do to get a high SAT score.

### Tip 3: Relax, Don't Stress Out; It's Only a Test

Staying focused and calm during the test is a necessity for doing well. The best relaxation technique is preparation. Those who are prepared will be relaxed. They'll also get hassled less by their parents. That alone makes it worthwhile to study, as my children will attest to.

Having a fair share of confidence can also help students. Those who think they won't do well probably won't. They should take comfort in the notion that as long as they prepare as much as they can and put forth their best effort on the exam, that's all their parents, teachers, and most of all, themselves, can ask.

### Tip 4: Memorize Vocabulary

Ignore the naysayers who question the utility of memorizing arcane words that they claim you will never use again. A good vocabulary never hurt anyone, and in the case of academics and the SAT, there's no question that it helps. Some perfect score students learned Latin and Greek roots to help increase their vocabulary. Others found that reading helped. But nothing takes the place of the old-fashioned method of memorizing, repeating, and using new vocabulary. Flash cards, anyone?

### Tip 5: The Night Before the Test, Don't Study—Get a Good Night's Sleep

Cramming may help on most school exams. For instance, studying all night before that big history or physics final may help with short-term memory and improve a student's grade. This doesn't work, however, for the SAT. Unlike most school exams, which assess knowledge of specific material, the SAT can't be learned in a single night.

The day before the SAT should be spent doing fun, relaxing things. Students need to have peace of mind just before they head in to one of the most important exams of their lives. Even taking a practice exam is verboten; students can psyche themselves out right before the test if they don't do well on the practice exam. If they haven't prepared enough, a day before the test isn't the time to find out or to start hurriedly jamming in review. Students are better off going to bed early and getting eight hours of shut-eye. This will improve their concentration and mental speed for the test.

Perfect score students also recommend eating breakfast on the morning of the test to prevent hunger and grogginess. A growling stomach can be a huge distraction during an important exam. To avoid slumping in the middle of the exam, eat a meal that contains a combination of carbohydrates, protein, and some fat, such as a cheese omelet with a piece of toast or yogurt with a piece of fresh fruit.

### Tip 6: Pace Yourself

The current SAT is three hours long. When the new SAT is instituted in 2005, the test will be forty-five minutes longer. In addition, the questions advance from easy to more difficult. So it is important for students to recognize that they have anywhere from 45 to 72 seconds per question. They need to keep track of time and avoid getting hung up over questions they don't understand or can't do. They can skip them, circle them, and then come back to them at the end if they have extra time.

### Tip 7: Identify and Focus on Weaknesses (Use PSAT and Review What You Get Wrong)

Students usually know which subjects they're good at. These subjects, which come more easily, are usually the ones they spend the most amount of time on. On the other hand, perfect score students recommend focusing on weaknesses. For a small fee, the PSAT will send a breakdown of which questions a student got right and wrong. This is extremely worthwhile, because it identifies areas of weakness. While it may not be pleasurable memorizing those ten words a day or reviewing math problems, it can have a huge impact on an SAT score.

## Tip 8: Double-check Your Work

About one-third of the perfect score students finished the SAT early and therefore had time to recheck their work. Even if students don't finish early and are pressed for time, they should take a few extra seconds on each question to go over calculations and prevent careless mistakes. Students should also give themselves a little extra time to consider trick questions, which usually come near the end of each section. Remember, there's about a minute allotted for each question, so taking five extra seconds here and there to avoid mistakes shouldn't cost too much time overall.

## Tip 9: Study Early (Preferably One Year Before Taking the SAT)

I think this is the best advice from students who aced the SAT. No music student would expect to become proficient at the piano in two weeks. By the same token, no student should expect to become a whiz at taking the SAT in a short amount of time. Reviewing two or three years of high school math and English may take a few months, not a few hours on the weekend before. Not all perfect score students start studying six months in advance. Not all of them need to. In general, however, the earlier students start preparing for the SAT, the more ingrained the test will be in their mind-set, and the higher their eventual score will be.

## Tip 10: Take a Prep Course

Students who are naturally structured and self-disciplined can skip this tip. Most students, however, aren't such strong self-starters. They don't know where to begin or how to discipline themselves to learn the rules of the SATs and take timed practice exams. Prep courses provide this structured approach to learning how to take the SATs, and they're usually given weekly at a set time, so students are forced to put in the review and not save all their preparation for the last minute.

## PREPARING FOR THE SAT IN SIX MONTHS OR LESS

While it's best to fit SAT preparation into a lifetime of good academic strategies like those embodied in the 7 Secrets, I realize that parents and students reading this book may also need short-term solutions if the SAT is looming just around the corner. Here's how perfect score students spend their months leading up to the SAT.

### *Strategy 1: Evaluate Your Strengths and Weaknesses, Determine Your Needs, and Then Devise a Personalized Study Plan*

When it comes to creating a test-study action plan, one size does not fit all. Some students may feel they just need to familiarize themselves with the format of the test. Others might take a dozen sample tests under real-life testing conditions with a stopwatch to time themselves. Some students might opt for a Princeton Review or Stanley Kaplan class, though many students chose that path. Still others may discover that they can make the best use of their time by working with a parent or study partner or studying alone. Some students might not even take a single practice test but will spend hours memorizing vocabulary words by the hundreds, reviewing math and problem-solving skills, and practicing reading comprehension.

The first step is for students to know what they do well and what they don't. Lucy Z. recalls, "I always excelled in math, so I didn't spend much time reviewing SAT math problems. I knew my vocabulary was weak, though, so I studied flash cards." Few of us are equally adept at both math and English, even those students who score 1600. Therefore, perfect score students recommend conducting an honest assessment of a student's strengths and weaknesses, based on classroom grades, test scores, interests, and past experiences in school.

The first basic question is: do I need to focus on English, math, or both?

At the same time, students need to understand the test itself—what kinds of questions will be asked, the time limit to complete each section, specific instructions, and so on. Taking a practice SAT exam is one of the best ways to get a feel for the test and is great for identifying areas that a student needs to work on.

Almost all perfect score students said they read the prep booklet prepared by the College Board, reviewed the instructions for the SAT, and looked over the kinds of questions being asked. Most went further to understand the logic and rules of the test. For example, the test is designed so that two out of the four or five answers are clearly wrong. Logic would dictate that students should eliminate those answers right off the bat. Understanding this will help save time and help raise a score.

These rules also are important, since it pays to understand whether or not guessing is productive. Partial deductions are made for wrong answers, so it may pay to guess. The logic and rules of the SAT are usually summarized in the first fifteen pages of any SAT review book, such as those published by Stanley Kaplan or Princeton Review. Once perfect score students understand the format, logic, and rules of the SAT, they then focus specifically on those areas in math and English where they are weak or can improve. This becomes their personalized study plan.

Some students actually write this plan out to help them get organized. They make a checklist of what they need to do to achieve a perfect score. This can include: reading the College Board test book, buying an SAT review book, taking practice tests, taking a prep course, memorizing vocabulary words, hiring a private tutor, and studying with friends for a certain amount of time each week. If, after taking the test, perfect score students didn't achieve a perfect score, they went back to the drawing board. Many took another two or three practice exams or even another prep course before taking the SAT again.

## Sample SAT Review Plan

1. Sign up for a six-week review course
2. Buy a SAT prep book.
3. Take a practice exam.

4. Spend four hours a week reviewing the material that was weak on the practice exam. (Make up flash cards and review them, practice math problems, work on critical reading, and so on.)

5. Two weeks before the SAT, take another practice exam. Time it with a stopwatch.

6. Practice areas on the exam that you didn't have time to complete to improve speed.

7. One week before the SAT, go to the library or bookstore and browse through SAT review books. Make a list of any rules or tips that may have been missed.

8. On the day before the SAT, go to a movie, eat a relaxing dinner, and go to bed early.

9. On the day of the SAT, eat a light breakfast and leave extra time to get to the exam.

### Strategy 2: Understand the Structure and Pattern of the SAT

Imagine going into a final exam without ever having attended class, read the book, or seen a previous test given by the teacher. This would be academic suicide. Yet this is exactly what students do when they forgo any preparation for the SAT. More than 50 percent of the average academic achievers in the Perfect Score Study reported that they didn't prepare for the SAT at all. I think this is a colossal mistake.

While experts debate whether the SAT is coachable, since it is designed to be an aptitude test, there is no question that basic familiarity with the test helps improve scores. Both Kaplan and Princeton Review offer money-back guarantees on some of their products if students don't raise their scores significantly.

Most of the perfect score students found that basic preparation helps and that they couldn't have aced the SAT without it. Since the SAT is a timed test, it pays to know how long you can or should spend on each question. It is also helpful to know that the questions go from easy to hard, so that answers are far more obvious earlier on than later in the section. Students should also spend less time on earlier questions since they will need more time for difficult ones.

Perfect score students also try to put themselves in the heads of the question developers. What are these developers really asking? Is it a trick question? If I step back and look at this logically, can I eliminate wrong answers with certainty? Can I sidestep traps? Should I complete the test more quickly to give myself time to go back and check my answers? These are all questions that perfect score students asked themselves.

They also tried to look for patterns in SAT questions to keep themselves from getting tripped up by specific questions. In this vein, the same types of questions are used over and over again from one test to the next. This is especially true in the math section, where only the numbers change. Thus, if a student understands the basic questions and formulas, it is easier to recognize the question, since it is familiar, and more quickly determine the correct answer.

### Strategy 3: Be Confident in Your Abilities; Be Calm; Don't Panic

As we've seen, students who scored 1600 have a good perspective on the SAT and its importance. They know that the test is important, but it is not the be-all and end-all of life. Most students who scored 1600 said the test was only moderately important to them. Putting the SAT into a proper perspective helps make students more relaxed and less pressured, and this enables them to perform better.

We see this example in any kind of performance, from sports to music. When athletes or musical performers are tight and stressed out, they tend not to perform to their highest ability. I was struck by this watching the open auditions on the TV reality show *American Idol*. So many of the singers performed horrifically, and you could tell they were nervous. Some assured the judges that they really were good singers—in the privacy of their own homes. Nerves, however, can shatter even the best voices. Performance anxiety can be a huge roadblock that lowers SAT scores. Students need to remind themselves to relax, concentrate, and just do their best.

This mental component to standardized test taking is often dismissed by high school students, who assume that all but the smartest students are going to be nervous. The truth is, any student will be nervous if he or she goes into a test unprepared. Perfect score students prepare for the test until they feel confident they can get the highest score that's within their ability. This makes them more confident and self-assured going into the test. Are they nervous? Of course, but it's a nervous kind of energy that gets the adrenaline pumping, not the kind of nervousness that breaks concentration.

## ADVICE FROM THE STUDY PREP EXPERTS

More than 40 percent of the perfect score students recommend using SAT study prep guides. In addition, two-thirds of them suggested that students gain an understanding of the test and how to take it correctly. As part of the Perfect Score Study, I decided to look at six popular SAT prep books to see how similar to or different from their advice was that of the perfect score students. I reviewed:

1. Stanley Kaplan's *SAT & PSAT*
2. The Princeton Review's *Cracking the SAT*
3. Barron's *How to Prepare for the SAT I*
4. *The SAT I for Dummies*
5. *Up Your Score: The Underground Guide to the SAT* (written by five students who aced the SATs)
6. The College Board's *10 Real SATs*

Two of the books, *Up Your Score* and *The SAT I for Dummies,* provide a good basic overview, some basic tricks, and practice examples. They employ humor to make their guides informative and readable. Both are good starting points. Three of the guides, Kaplan's, Princeton Review's and Barron's, also offer test-taking strategies, but are far more problem-intensive and specific. These books are designed for students who are serious about spending time and effort preparing for the SATs. Kaplan's *SAT and PSAT* even offers a high-score guarantee. The final book, which is actually recommended by the other five, is the College Board's own *10 Real SATs*. This book has ten actual SAT exams, with an answer key and explanation of the answers.

### The Similarities

There is definitely some overlap between the advice offered by the guides and the advice offered by perfect score students. Let's take this advice by category: those pieces of advice recommended by all; those recommended by some guides and perfect score students; those recommended by at least one guide and perfect score students. I think it's safe to assume that the strongest advice is that recommended universally by the experts and the perfect score students.

## Advice Recommended by All Guides and Perfect Score Students

○ Take practice exams.

○ Pace yourself.

○ Do the subsections in the best order (from easiest to hardest).

○ Know the test setup.

○ Use educated guessing.

○ Learn vocabulary words.

## Advice Recommended by Most of the Guides and Perfect Score Students

○ Set a realistic goal.

○ Know the directions.

○ Eat well before the test.

○ Use a calculator selectively.

## Advice Recommended by a Few Guides and Perfect Score Students

- ○ Take the test multiple times.
- ○ Use College Board services.
- ○ Dress comfortably and in layers.
- ○ Learn memory and concentration skills.
- ○ Use flash cards.
- ○ Double-check your work.
- ○ Learn relaxation techniques.
- ○ Use scratch paper.
- ○ Transfer answers in groups.
- ○ Be confident, go with hunches.
- ○ Get a good night's sleep.
- ○ Don't overthink the test.
- ○ Read everything.
- ○ Learn word roots.

### The Differences

Perfect Score students, to the exclusion of the SAT guides, also recommend:

- ○ Take good classes and do well in high school.
- ○ Study early (one year before the exam).
- ○ Play a musical instrument.
- ○ Write a lot.
- ○ Go to math competitions.
- ○ Do crossword puzzles and brain teasers.

## COMPARING THE ADVICE GIVEN IN SAT GUIDES WITH THE ADVICE OF PERFECT SCORE STUDENTS

| | Up Your Score | SAT for Dummies | Princeton Review | Kaplan | Barron's | Real SATs | Perfect Score Students |
|---|---|---|---|---|---|---|---|
| Take practice tests | X | X | X | X | X | X | X |
| Take test multiple times | X | X | | | | | |
| Use College Board services | X | X | | | | | |
| Set a realistic score goal | X | X | X | | X | X | X |
| Make a study schedule | X | | | | | | X |
| Study with friends | X | | | | | | |
| Pace yourself | X | X | X | X | X | X | X |
| Do the subsections in the best order | X | X | X | X | X | X | X |
| Know the test setup (learn tricks) | X | X | X | X | X | X | X |
| Know the directions | X | | X | X | X | X | X |
| Educated guessing | X | X | X | X | X | X | X |
| Dress comfortably and in layers | X | X | | X | X | | |
| Eat well | X | X | X | X | X | | X |
| Learn memory and concentration skills | X | | X | X | | | |
| Learn vocabulary | X | X | X | X | X | X | X |
| Use flash cards | X | X | X | X | X | X | |
| Double-check your work | | X | | | | | X |
| Learn relaxation techniques | X | X | | X | | X | X |
| Use scratch paper | | | X | X | X | X | |
| Transfer answers in groups | | | X | X | | | |
| Answer less, get more right | | X | X | | X | | |

## COMPARISON OF ADVICE FROM SAT GUIDES TO
## PERFECT SCORE STUDENTS (continued)

| | Up Your Score | SAT for Dummies | Princeton Review | Kaplan | Barron's | Real SATs | Perfect Score Students |
|---|---|---|---|---|---|---|---|
| Use calculator selectively | X | | X | X | X | X | X |
| Read everything (with a dictionary) | | X | | | X | X | X |
| Be confident, go with hunches | | | X | X | | | X |
| Sleep | | | X | X | X | | X |
| Go to math competitions | | | | | | | X |
| Identify weaknesses | | | X | X | X | | X |
| Take good classes, do well in HS | | | | | | X | X |
| Study early (at least one year before) | | | | | | | X |
| Spend 20–30 hours studying | | X | | | | X | |
| Prep course | | | | | | | X |
| Crossword puzzles, brain teasers | | | | | | X | X |
| Don't overthink the test | | | X | X | | | X |
| Play a musical instrument | | | | | | | X |
| Learn word roots | | | X | X | X | | X |
| Write a lot | | | | | | | X |
| Learn to read fast | | | X | X | | | X |

Overall, I think study prep guides are a good investment of time and money. They do an excellent job of providing practical advice, vocabulary lists, and sample questions. They are very useful if a student has six months or less to prepare for the SAT. And they are helpful if a student's primary objective is to raise his or her SAT score. The guides are limited, however, in one respect: they can do little to improve a student's overall academic abilities or to teach the kinds of life lessons that perfect score students have already learned. The perfect score students, on the other hand, offer long-term advice that can teach students to excel in school, on the SAT, and in life in general.

Almost every student can benefit from studying and preparing for the SAT. Mapping out a study plan is a good idea for those who are starting the SAT review process. This can help students get organized and manage their time, so they're not cramming a week before the exam.

The Perfect Score Study suggests that perfect score students aren't just born to ace the SAT. They work hard at it and prepare until they feel confident that they understand the exam and know the material. All but a small percentage of these students say they studied or reviewed for the SAT. All understood their strengths and their weaknesses and where they could stand to improve. And all had a healthy perspective on the test. They knew it was important and could help them get into a good college, but they also knew that their academic achievements wouldn't be defined solely by their SAT score. These students view the SAT as part of a long academic journey rather than just as a final destination of a perfect score.

# Frequently Asked Questions About the SAT

Whether you're a parent helping your child study for the SAT, or you're a student getting ready to take the test, chances are you have some pressing questions about the exam and the best way to prepare. Through speaking with parents and students about the results of the Perfect Score Study, I found the same questions cropping up again and again, and I decided to devote a chapter to answering them. With luck, this chapter will lay some concerns to rest and offer some practical information about the complex process of SAT preparation.

I divided the questions into those geared for parents and those geared for students. I found that the pressing issues on parents' minds differ greatly from the issues on their children's minds. For instance, parents tend to ask broader questions, such as whether they should send their child to private school as opposed to a public school. Students tend to focus on the moment at hand with questions like "I am a junior and the SAT is in two weeks. Is it too late for me to start studying and get a good score?"

Other questions from parents and students are similar but come from very different perspectives. Parents ask, "What should I do to help my son or daughter achieve a high score on the SAT when he or she doesn't seem to care?" Students put the question differently: "What should I do if my parents are driving me crazy about studying for the SAT?"

So, read through the questions that apply to you and show the rest of the questions to your child or parent—as the case may be.

## QUESTIONS FREQUENTLY ASKED BY PARENTS

*Question 1: When should my child start preparing for the SAT? In high school? In junior high school? Or even earlier?*

Preparing to do well on the SAT is like preparing to do well in sports. Tennis pro Andre Agassi's father reportedly hung a tennis mobile above his crib and gave him a racquet when he started walking. But this is the extreme. For most students, preparation for the SAT should begin early in life, though that doesn't mean studying for the exam itself or taking practice tests at age five. As in sports, the early years of your child's life should focus on discovery and stimulation.

The Perfect Score Study found that parents should take a holistic approach to their child's educational development. Perfect score parents reported reading to their children at a young age, having plenty of books and other educational resources around the house, engaging their kids in stimulating, intellectual conversation, and so on. The research also shows how important it is to provide a supportive network for your child and to encourage him or her to develop close friendships.

A major theme of this book is that doing well on the SAT doesn't involve focusing solely on school classes, SAT review, or the math team. Having a healthy perspective on school and the SAT is far more important than setting a singular goal to ace the exam. So, yes, providing a supportive learning environment for students should begin as early as possible. Parents should monitor and motivate their children through elementary school. And it's also critical for parents to oversee their kids' school progress and make sure they don't get offtrack in junior high school.

There is, however, a point when children need and want to take responsibility for their academic progress and achievement. Try making a pact with your child similar to the one made by perfect score parents: "As long as you do well, we'll leave you alone." Once in high school, your child should be encouraged to take challenging courses. This will be especially relevant with the new SAT, which will tie the exam more directly to classroom work.

The Perfect Score Study indicates that focused SAT review shouldn't begin until the first semester of eleventh grade, or the summer before. Kids have more important things to do in ninth and tenth grades, such as indulging their passions, than to take practice SAT exams.

### Question 2: I care a lot about the SAT and school, but my child doesn't seem to show any interest or concern. What should I do?

This really depends on how old your child is. If your child is in eighth or ninth grade and he or she isn't thinking about the SAT or getting into a good college, it should be neither surprising nor disturbing. In fact, I would be concerned if the SAT were a primary focus at this age. If anything, it is normal for most kids, perfect score students included, to put off preparing for the SAT until much, much later. If your child is in the eleventh grade and is scheduled to take the SAT in two weeks and has done nothing, then we need to talk.

More than three-quarters of the kids who scored 1600 say they did some preparation for the SAT, but none started preparing until eleventh grade. If your child is a junior or senior, it's time for him or her to start thinking about the SAT. You can emphasize the importance of the SAT by explaining that they are a determining factor in college admission. At Harvard, the average SAT score is 1485; at NYU it's 1334, and at Boston University it's 1290.

Of course, these are averages, and it doesn't mean that all students need to meet that average. Students with exceptional talents in other areas might not need as high a score. Still, the better a student's score, the greater the chance of admission. You can try setting up a meeting with your child's guidance counselor. Or you can try to enlist one of your child's college-bound friends to take up the cause. The main thing is to keep an open line of communication with your child that allows the two of you to agree on an appropriate amount of SAT preparation. But keep in mind that the ultimate decision on how much to prepare is your child's. You can't force your child to study or review flash cards, just as you can't force him or her to apply to a specific college.

*Question 3: How many extracurricular activities should my child participate in? I believe a child should be well rounded, joining a number of clubs, playing on sports teams, and taking up at least one or two instruments. Am I wrong?*

Less is more. Parents often assume that they're neglecting their child's needs if their daughter doesn't play soccer, take piano lessons, study French, and take a dance class or if their son doesn't play baseball, take clarinet, study Spanish, and learn tae kwan do. This desire to program a kid's every waking hour speaks more about a parent's wish fulfillment than it does about the kid's desire or interest. We all have certain interests, but do kids really want or need that many activities?

Surprisingly few of the perfect score students say they were involved in half a dozen or more activities in high school. Most concentrated on one or two activities at a time and focused on doing them well. Some activities were nonacademic, such as reading science fiction books, joining a sports team, playing music, or enjoying the outdoors. Other activities were more academically focused, like the Math Olympiad, Model UN, French club, and the debate team. Regardless, perfect score students really talk more about the focus and depth of their interests rather than their breadth.

Encouraging your child to pursue one or two talents will enable passions to emerge. This will allow your child to develop these passions into his or her self-identity. In high school, these passions become particularly important in helping to develop attention span and fulfill goals, the exact skills a student needs to prepare for the SAT.

### Question 4: How much parental involvement is enough and how much is too much? My child and I disagree.

Lincoln was once asked how long a man's legs should be. He replied they should be long enough to reach the ground. The same is true with parental involvement. Perfect score parents recommend that parents do enough to help their kids reach their academic potential. The issue then becomes who defines that potential and what constitutes help. In this case, good judgment and common sense should prevail. For the perfect score students, most of their parents felt that earning anything less than an A was not living up to their child's ability, *and* their child generally agreed. These students knew that they could do well, and they did. In fact, perfect score students, rather than their parents, became the driving force behind their own success.

There were a few cases where perfect score students didn't live up to their potential, and the students admitted that they had a hard time dealing with it. Their parents wanted them to get straight As in all their subjects, while the students wanted to excel only in the subjects that interested them. At first, these parents tried positive reinforcement, rewarding their kids with a new electronic game or higher allowance if they pulled up their grades. This failed miserably. Then these parents tried negative sanctions, such as grounding, which also didn't work. Finally, these parents learned to accept the fact that their child was going to accomplish only what he or she was able or willing to achieve. They had to accept As in some subjects and Bs and Cs in others.

The lesson in this, I believe, is that parents should encourage their children's best efforts but accept the fact that their expectations and desires may differ from their kids'. In the end, the Perfect Score Study found that parents can encourage motivated students to do well. However, too much pressure doesn't produce the desired results.

### Question 5: Since the SAT tests math and English skills, should I focus my child's energies on developing those particular skills?

Perfect score students do excel in math and English. That is no surprise. But at the same time, more than 97 percent of perfect score students rank in the top 10 percent of their class, which means they must also do well in their other courses. One of the defining characteristics of these high academic achievers is that they are multidimensional. They are motivated to learn, regardless of the subject matter, and they are curious about a lot of things, from politics to astronomy to quadratic equations.

Yes, some subjects come easier than others. But all learning can help build skills necessary for the SAT. While math and English skills are critical, focusing on them to the exclusion of other academic and interpersonal skills clearly is not wise. It's obvious from the Perfect Score Study that well-balanced skills promote higher academic achievement.

Some focus on honing math and English skills is definitely a good idea. Far too many students—more than half of the average SAT scorers in the Perfect Score Study—go into the SAT cold, without any preparation. Moreover, developing these math and English skills not only will help boost SAT scores, but will also help improve academic performance overall.

### Question 6: How much studying or preparation is enough for the SAT? In other words, when can I stop bugging my kid about studying vocabulary and taking practice tests?

Before the Perfect Score Study, I assumed that a student couldn't overprepare for the SAT. I was convinced that I was right and would direct my kids to study as much as they possibly could. My son Ted, however, had a different answer. Like the students who scored 1600, he intrinsically knew when he had prepared enough. Basically, students should study until they feel comfortable that they know the material, and that's enough. For some perfect score students, that means taking one or two practice tests. For others, it means taking twenty practice tests and a Kaplan or Princeton Review course. The truth is, taking a single practice test or the PSAT will indicate how much more students need to prepare. Find out whether your child's SAT score practice exam score is good enough to meet the requirement for your child's first-choice college. Most college guides list the SAT scores required for admission to a particular college alongside other criteria.

Supporting and encouraging your child as he or she prepares can be beneficial. Pushing and pressuring is not. Listen to your child when he or she says *enough*. Your child may be right on the money.

### Question 7: You say that social networks are important—especially among friends and family. Should I make family dinners mandatory? Should I encourage my child to go out with friends instead of studying? Are these social networks really that critical?

The lesson of the Perfect Score Study is crystal clear: Friends and family really do matter. The importance of friends and family was frequently mentioned by perfect score students throughout their interviews. These social factors are difficult to ignore.

But does this mean it is necessary to eat together every night? Not necessarily. You just have to do enough to make your child feel connected. One perfect score parent said that family meals were important. Another perfect score mom said she stayed at home with her child until he was in kindergarten. A third parent said he discussed issues and problems with his child every night before bed. What is important is not the specific kind of interaction, but whether there is substantive engagement.

Both studying and socializing are important. Generally, parents should encourage studying more than socializing. The truth is, perfect score students do study more than they socialize. However, all work and no play definitely makes for a dull student. So, yes, you should encourage your child to go out and have fun after the work is done.

### Question 8: I realize reading is important, but does it matter what my child reads? And how much is enough?

Reading is to educational achievement what the brain is to the body. It is critical. Without it, there is little or no academic learning. Almost without exception, perfect score students say they love to read. They developed this love at a very young age, when their parents read to them. And these students report reading almost twice as much for school as average academic achievers.

As for what your children read, the evidence suggests that it really doesn't matter all that much—as long as they're reading a lot, of their own volition, and enjoying it. The reading lists of perfect score students are as varied as the books in the library. No one book stands out as a must-read. However, these students all gravitate toward books that challenge them both in terms of ideas and vocabulary. Some prefer the classics, while others seek out best-selling authors like Toni Morrison or John Irving. Some students say they read books, magazines, and newspapers, or whatever their parents have lying around the house. One student says he reads *The New Yorker* and *The Economist,* two magazines that his father subscribes to. The truth is, though, children will read what they enjoy. Parents don't have to push Dickens or Tolstoy. What's most important is that children read, and read often.

### Question 9: If I want my child to do well on the SAT, should I take him out of public school and send him to a private school?

One of the great myths is that private school education is the only road to academic success. Many of us have an idealized view of elite private schools—that their programs are better, the classes are smaller and more challenging, and students get more individualized attention. We assume that those who go to private schools get higher SAT scores in large part due to this higher-quality education.

Think again. More than 80 percent of the students who score 1600 go to public schools. While it's true that private school classes are smaller, public school students tend to take more AP courses. So the real issue is not where students will get a better education, but which kind of education better meets your child's needs.

### Question 10: I know my child is no Einstein. How much do these 7 Secrets really apply to her, since the perfect score students are all brilliant? Also, can my child really score 1600?

I'll be the first to admit that my kids aren't geniuses either. They are intelligent, social, and lovable. The point is not whether they will or need to score a 1600 on the SAT. The real issue is that they should do the best they can. Would I like them to score 1600? Of course, but that is for me and not for them. Will I become an overbearing stage dad to enable them to do that? Not anymore. I learned that lesson from my son.

That being said, the chance of any one child scoring 1600 on the SATs is extremely small. Is it possible for your child? Of course. Is it likely? No. However, your child can maximize his or her SAT score by adopting the 7 Secrets of perfect score students. In the same vein, few of us will ever be a great athlete like Shaquille O'Neal or a great cellist like Yo Yo Ma, but most of us can improve and become more proficient at whatever we work hard at. The same discipline, determination, and practice that professional athletes, musicians, and dancers follow can help all motivated students to do better.

The Perfect Score Study found, without a shadow of a doubt, that there's no one prototypical student who aces the SAT. The perfect score students I interviewed came from all over the United States. They attended different kinds of schools—public, private, and religious. They were interested in areas as diverse as string theory and origami. They differed in the amount they needed to study to achieve a high class rank and in the amount they needed to prepare for the SATs.

While perfect score students differed in many ways, they all shared seven traits in common, which formed the 7 Secrets of success. They all had passions, a strong family support system, a love of reading, and a love of life. They were all curious and motivated to do well. They all had a mind-set that they wouldn't settle for less than their best.

Very few of us reach our potential the first time. Most of the perfect score students took the test more than once, and most prepared for it. Your child may never win a professional championship or score 1600 on the SAT, but few students can't improve or do better than what they're doing now.

## QUESTIONS FREQUENTLY ASKED BY STUDENTS

### Question 11: When should I begin preparing for the SAT?

Ideally, you should probably start to think about the SAT at the beginning of eleventh grade, about six months to a year before you take the exam. That's when you should send away for or pick up the SAT booklet and application and have some preliminary discussions with your parents and a guidance counselor.

But this is the real world. If you only have two or three months to prepare, so be it. Take heart and realize that all is not lost. First, think about it. You are going to spend four years of your life in college. It might as well be the best four years of your life. So a little planning, a little studying, and a little preparation will go a long way to making this happen. Two things are clear from the Perfect Score Study. Preparation helps, so you should definitely prepare. And the amount of preparation you need to do depends on you and how ready and confident you feel about the material.

Some of the perfect score students felt they needed to just read the booklet the night before (this was a small minority), while others spent over one hundred hours studying. You decide. It's your future.

You should also realize that the SAT is a means of helping you get into the college of your choice. So any effort you spend preparing for the SAT is worth it in the long run. The earlier in your junior year that you prepare, the better.

### Question 12: I'm totally stressed out about the SAT. What should I do?

Keep repeating to yourself: It's only a test. It's only a test. It's only a test. Stressing out won't help. I realize that's easy for me to say, because I'm not the one taking the test. However, like sixty million other Americans, I did take the test. Twice. One of the 7 Secrets of perfect score students is that they keep the test in perspective. One of the most common pieces of advice that these students can offer to students taking the test is to relax and be confident in your own abilities. They also recommended getting a good night's sleep on the night before the test and eating a decent breakfast that morning.

The SAT is important, because it will help determine your choice of colleges. On the other hand, there is only so much preparation you can do. Assuming you've done your best, that's an accomplishment in and of itself. Even those who scored a 1600 realize that they'll need more than a perfect SAT score to get into college. These students rated the SAT as "somewhat" important, because they realize it is just one of a number of factors that colleges use to assess students. They also realize that it doesn't help to be stressed out. So they accept the SAT as an academic challenge that they're going to take on, rather than as a source of stress and anxiety.

### Question 13: I'm in my junior year of high school and my parents are driving me crazy about taking the SAT. What can I do to get them off my back?

One of the immutable laws of nature is that parents are convinced that they know what is best for their teenagers and that teenagers are convinced that their parents know nothing. The truth probably lies somewhere in between.

Parents can get pretty demanding. Even if you're a straight-A student, ace the SAT, and get into Yale, your parents can still find room for improvement. One parent of a perfect score student complains that her son's room is always messy even though she constantly reminds him to clean it up. Another perfect score parent remarks, "My daughter is very obstinate. She has to do everything her way. That's probably why she got 1600, but it also makes her difficult to live with."

Your parents want you to do well on the SAT because it is important to get into college. But they may be applying too much pressure. On the other hand, they may have a right to be concerned if you keep telling them "I'll study next weekend because I've got a date tonight and I'm going shopping tomorrow. Anyway, the SAT is three months away. Give me a break." Lessons from the Perfect Score Study point to compromise as the way to go. In order to reduce conflict or disagreement, perfect score students and their parents generally try to reach a pact on what constitutes acceptable performance. Show your parents your study plan for the SAT: what you plan to do and when. Then, stick with this plan. This will give your parents peace of mind and get them off your back. You'll be able to prepare for the SAT in an environment of domestic tranquility.

### Question 14: How many times should I take the SAT? On the one hand, my scores may improve each time, but what if I do worse? And if I take the SAT more than once, will all scores be reported to colleges?

Take the SAT as many times as you like, until you get the score you want. Just 39 percent of the perfect score students scored 1600 on the first try. And 24 percent took it three or more times. This latter group was determined to get a 1600 and they felt they had a reasonable chance after getting a high score the first time around. (Taking the test five or six times, though, may be excessive. At some point, you have to just accept your score.)

In order to set your goal score, you first need to decide where you want to go to college and which schools you'll realistically have a shot at with your GPA. If you have a B average, Harvard is a long shot, even if you do get a perfect score. Just to give you some idea, the average SAT scores for Ivy League colleges and other top-tier schools range from 1270 to 1580, according to *U.S. News & World Report.* Average SAT scores for top regional schools are between 770 and 1370. The better your SAT score, the better your chances of admission, assuming that the rest of your academic record is competitive for that school. If you score high enough to meet the requirements of your top-choice colleges, there's no need to retake the SAT.

Scores generally improve each time you take the SAT, since you become more familiar with the test each time you take it. The College Board says that most students improve by about twenty points. On the other hand, there is the chance your scores will decline. Be aware that all scores will be sent automatically to the schools you name—and that each school sets its own policy about which scores to consider. About 90 percent of colleges will take your best score for math and for English from all the times you've taken the SAT. Only 10 percent will look only at your most recent test. It's best to check out the policy of the college you are most interested in attending and then decide how many times to take the test.

### Question 15: Should I take an SAT prep course? If so, should I take one given by an established name like Kaplan's or the Princeton Review, or should I take one offered by my school or church? Is it worth it to hire a private tutor?

This is a potentially expensive question. Not quite one quarter of the kids who scored 1600 took a review couse offered by Kaplan, Princeton Review, or anyone else for that matter. On the other hand, most perfect score students are very disciplined and self-motivated and may not need the structure of a course. Still, most of these students did some preparation. The first question you need to ask yourself is what kind of preparation you need. If you don't understand the test, don't do well on standardized tests, need structure and discipline, or feel that you need an expert's advice on doing well on the SAT, you should by all means take a review course.

I can't tell you which review course to take. You and your parents need to do a bit of research to see what's available in your area and what's offered at convenient times. Affordability may be an issue, and a private tutor can get pricey, charging $50 to $100 an hour—though they can be helpful if you need extra help in one particular area. Well-known courses like Princeton Review often charge $800 for one six-week course and tend to be more expensive than courses offered by local schools or parishes. On the other hand, the more expensive courses may hand out better advice and materials for review. I can't say this for certain. You have to compare the materials yourself, or ask to sit in on a session.

You should also consider other options to help you review on your own, such as prep books and computer programs. Or you can get together and review with a friend—provided the two of you are committed to not breaking a weekly study date. Bottom line: worry less about what review class to take, and focus your efforts on doing some preparation. Chances are whatever you do to prepare will improve your score as well as your academics.

### Question 16: What courses should I take in high school, and will taking APs help me do better on the SAT?

The answer is that you should take the hardest, most challenging courses available, provided you can do the work. This is the advice of perfect score students who aced the exam. They also recommend taking AP and honors courses. Any course that challenges you and forces you to consider difficult issues and problems will help you learn and improve your analytical and reasoning skills. This also will help improve your SAT scores.

But there's another question that directly impacts your score: what can I do in general to improve my SAT scores? The answer lies in the 7 Secrets of perfect score students. These secrets all deal with identity building, finding out who you are and what makes you tick. So pick challenging courses, but not because they will improve your SAT scores. Rather, choose courses because they are interesting, motivating, and thought provoking. If you pick things you truly want to learn about, then you will be rewarded with a better education—and probably a higher SAT score as well.

### Question 17: I'm not really good at taking standardized tests like the SAT. What should I do?

Very few people are good at everything. Some perfect score students are horrible at doing art projects. Some are not athletes. Based on my experience, kids who don't do well on the SAT either don't know the material or freeze and choke on standardized tests. The Perfect Score research offers two insights.

First, even kids who ace the SAT don't know it all. Most study very hard, and most prepare for the SAT. Therefore, you can learn how to take the test, the logic behind the exam, and the kinds of questions that will be asked. Since the revised SAT due out in 2005 will be more directly related to what is taught in school, this advice is even more relevant. The bottom line is that you can learn how to take the exam and can learn the material in it.

The second insight is that almost everyone is nervous in competition, whether it's academic or athletic, and especially when the stakes are high. Coaches advise athletes to relax. In fact, in the best-selling book *The Inner Game of Tennis*, W. Timothy Gallwey advises tennis players to find that "state of relaxed concentration" and "to focus your mind to overcome nervousness and self-doubt."

## Question 18: Regardless of whether I study or not, I'll still get the same score. So why study?

Some students use the argument that the SAT isn't meant to be studied for, so they don't need to bother preparing if they can't improve their scores. With this attitude, they don't do as well as they could. It becomes a self-fulfilling prophecy.

You *can* prepare for the SAT, and this preparation can raise your score. I know I've said this again and again, but there's a misconception out there that students don't need to study for the SAT. Like any test, the SAT has its nuances and rules. It's organized a certain way. The questions are phrased in a certain way to get specific information. Students have to learn the art of taking this test.

SAT studying and preparation do help improve scores. The Perfect Score Study confirms it. So do studies conducted by the Princeton Review and Stanley Kaplan. Some of these prep courses even have guarantees that students will improve by a certain number of points. Even the College Board concedes that SAT coaching produces some improvement in scores, though not as much improvement as the prep courses claim. There is no data to negate the beneficial effects of SAT preparation.

## Question 19: Students who earn a perfect score are geeks, like the guy in my math class who gets straight As, aren't they? Why would I want to turn myself into a geek?

Everyone knows a really smart kid who is an absolute nerd. She studies all the time, has no friends, and seems afraid of her own shadow. You might also know a great football player in high school who can't do simple arithmetic. Then, there is this really quiet loner who is antisocial and who seems like the type to bring a machine gun to school one day. You might know students like that, but is it fair or accurate to generalize? Are all football players stupid because one individual can't do academics? Are all loners dangerous because of some isolated cases? Are all high academic achievers geeks and losers?

The answers to all these questions is quite simply no. The Perfect Score Study shows that perfect score students are anything but geeks and nerds. They do well academically, have good social lives, and have strong bonds with friends and family.

### Question 20: Is my life ruined if I don't do well on the SAT and get into an Ivy League college?

The SAT is important. You should prepare for it and do your best. But will it ruin your life if you don't do well? No way. None of the perfect score students defined their lives in terms of the SAT (although some of their parents did). In fact, few of these students even mentioned the SAT when asked to describe who they are as individuals.

Many of us get caught up in high SAT scores and Ivy League and elite colleges, but at the end of the day, most of those who ace the exam hope not for high SAT and college admission scores, but rather for happiness and success in life. Those are probably your hopes as well. Success is a personal goal that cannot be defined by college, money, or social status. Lives are not made or ruined by the SAT and college admission, even though these may seem like the most important things in the world when you're in high school.

Success for the perfect score students is defined by hard work and doing your best. These are the factors you can control. Chances are that few people will ever ask you what you got on your SAT after you are accepted into college. It's not something you put on your résumé when you go into the workforce and look for a job.

# Learning for Life

We are in the midst of an education crisis in this country. In an attempt to improve the public school system, the federal government has mandated that states put more demands on their school districts to raise national standardized test scores. The states that meet these demands are being given more federal money for education. The school districts that meet their state's requirements by raising scores are being given more money for books, salaries, and other resources. Thus, teachers, principals, and superintendents all feel pressure to get their students to perform. As a result, they frequently teach to the test in an effort to get students to make the grade above all else.

Far too many high schools focus obsessively on the SAT and other standardized tests, running review courses from ninth grade onward and basing their curriculums on the material given in the SAT IIs, AP exams, and other national exams. Yes, it's important to do well on these tests, but not to the exclusion of a teacher's creativity in presenting the curriculum. How often do teachers teach by giving their students test-taking tips for the specific national or state-wide exam given at the end of their course? How often do they forgo interesting topics or class discussions in their urgency to get students to learn the test?

This push to improve test scores may seem excessive, but the intentions are in the right place. The U.S. government recognizes that its public school system fails miserably when compared with schools in other Westernized countries throughout the world. European and Asian high school students far surpass American students when it comes to their knowledge of math, science, geography, history, and foreign languages. The United States narrows this gap on the college and graduate school level, where course work is often more rigorous than in other countries. Still, there's a sentiment out there among American educators that our system has got to improve.

In a broad sense, everyone from the president of the United States to high school administrators and teachers has an opinion on how best to improve learning in this country. Congress is considering enacting legislation for national standardized testing and private school vouchers. In a personal sense, we, as parents and students, strive to get the best education possible for our children or ourselves, factoring in where to go to school, what courses to take, how to spend free time, and what to do academically.

There's also the issue of how to deal with students who fall at either end of the academic spectrum. Schools often fail to accommodate the needs of the brightest and weakest students, choosing to have a one-size-fits-all curriculum that satisfies the bulk of the students who land in the middle. Critics of public schools say that large class sizes make it impossible to give personalized attention to all students. They maintain that private schools are the way to go, with their smaller class sizes and smaller student-to-teacher ratios. The answer, they say, lies in school tax vouchers that allow families to choose their own schools—public, private, or religious—at the government's expense.

Perhaps this system would work in an ideal world, but it's extremely costly and probably not necessary. I think the answer lies in improving public schools. And yet these schools must have something to offer, since 80 percent of perfect score students attended them.

I think a more pressing issue concerns defining the goals of education in terms of preparing a student to be a productive member of society, and defining the value of standardized testing within this framework. The fundamental purpose of a high school education is to prepare students for college, technical school, or the workforce. Since I assume everyone reading this book is a college-bound student or a parent of a college-bound student, let's just address the goal of preparing students for college.

In their critically acclaimed book *The Shape of the River,* William Bowen and Derek Bok, former presidents of Princeton and Harvard respectively, say that colleges assess three things when determining whether to accept or reject a student's application for admission: a student's academic potential, whether a student will add to the school diversity, and whether a student has the potential to make significant professional or societal contributions after college.

Academic potential is defined not only as the ability to excel in course work and take advantage of all that the university has to offer, but also to contribute to the education of fellow classmates. School diversity refers to the need to admit students with varied backgrounds, experiences, and talents. Minority recruitment is one part of this diversity, but so is the need to recruit athletes, musicians, and other gifted individuals who can contribute and build the university community. Finally, professional and societal contributions mean recruiting individuals who will make a mark on the world, either by doing well in their chosen profession or adding something positive to the society they live in. This is often assessed by the essay portion of the application, which gives admissions officers a more personal glimpse of the student. Grades and standardized test scores like the SAT are also used to determine if students meet these three criteria.

This raises the question: Does the SAT really help admissions officers achieve their goal of admitting the best and the brightest? Or, as some critics maintain, does the SAT taint this process because the test is inherently biased and doesn't provide a useful measure of other kinds of intelligence beyond math and English skills?

As we've seen, perfect SAT scores are linked with academic success and success in life. Let's review the results from the Perfect Score Study.

1. It is clear that the perfect score students do extraordinarily well not only on the SAT, but also in their high school subjects. The fact that 40 percent were valedictorians and that 97 percent fell into the top tenth of their class leaves little doubt in this area. This satisfies one criteria for academic potential.

2. The Perfect Score Study found that perfect score students take more AP courses and honors classes than average academic achievers, not a great surprise. But, equally important, perfect score students participate in more school clubs, both academic and nonacademic, than their peers. And they tend to hold more leadership positions. So it is evident that perfect score students do take greater advantage of the total school experience, a sign that they will take advantage of all their college has to offer.

3. Perfect score students contribute to the education of others. Very few of these high achievers describe themselves as isolated or inwardly focused. More than 95 percent talk extensively about their close relationships with friends and their involvement in school activities. And many volunteer at soup kitchens or do other activities to help those less fortunate. One of the most common types of volunteer activities mentioned was tutoring younger students from poor neighborhoods.

4. What about diversity? Well, perfect score students are very diverse. They come from a variety of socioeconomic backgrounds, and many are the children of first-generation immigrants. Some are even immigrants themselves and had to learn English as a second language.

5. The Perfect Score Study suggests that perfect score students do, indeed, have the potential to make significant contributions to society. They have the intellectual capability, the social consciousness, and the motivational desire to make an impact.

Many of them expressed a desire to make an impact on the world or to use their intellectual talents to give back to society. Nearly 80 percent currently do community service, so this desire to contribute is consistent with their actions.

Bowen and Bok's criteria for higher education are certainly useful, since they offer a blueprint to define the purpose of high school. High schools should produce students who meet the general criteria that colleges are looking for. The large majority of perfect score students have met them with flying colors—and they also aced the SAT. So, the SAT probably can be a real predictor of success in college. No, the test shouldn't be used as a sole assessment of future potential. But when SAT scores are provided alongside grades, an application, references, and an essay, college admissions officers get a pretty good idea of how well a student will do at that school.

## GETTING A GOOD EDUCATION

What does it really mean to get a quality high school education that will prepare students for the rigors of college life? How can we use our nation's obsession with test preparation for larger and more useful goals? And how can we truly educate our children to deal with all of life's tests—not just the standardized ones—and thus give them their best shot at valuable careers and happy lives? What do educators, parents, teachers, and students need to do?

The Perfect Score Study reveals both common themes and wide diversity in approach and thought to the issue of getting a good high school education. On one hand, the 7 Secrets of perfect score students reveal common patterns and lessons exhibited by perfect score students that we can all learn from. It is critical that we take a proactive approach to learning. The best students study hard, prepare for the SAT, and actively seek out challenges. The lesson for parents and teachers is that they must motivate and encourage all students to do this. The lesson for educators and community leaders is that they must provide the opportunity and the atmosphere where this type of proactive learning is encouraged.

The good news is that it is not critical for students to go to an elite private school or even an upper-middle-class public high school in order to get a quality education and do well on the SAT. While rich students may have somewhat of an academic advantage, money and economic class are not necessary requirements for academic achievement.

On the other hand, the study also shows that perfect score students exhibit a great diversity in their approaches to getting a good education. Some of them are extremely driven and study long hours to do well, while others spend far more of their time participating in clubs or sports, or just hanging out with friends. Some of these high achievers know exactly what they want to do after college, such as medicine, engineering, or teaching, while others still are searching for who they are and what their life means.

Although I support the notion of the SAT and its use as a college assessment test, I think that our nation has become obsessed with standardized testing and that we could all learn a lesson on this from perfect score students. These students have a healthy perspective on the importance of SAT. They use the test as a means of entry into college, but they aren't fixated on it and don't define themselves by their SAT scores.

Putting the SAT into its proper perspective is critical, since this test isn't going to disappear anytime soon. Even if it's eventually replaced, it will probably be replaced by another standardized test. Most calls for reforming the current education system involve some form of standardized testing—for instance, achievement instead of aptitude testing—rather than abolishing testing altogether. Creating more opportunities, both academic and nonacademic, and then channeling student efforts in these directions offer far more promise than either increasing pressure on students to study for the SAT or abolishing the test entirely.

The debate over the SAT puts learning for a lifetime into focus.

Richard Rothstein, educational editor for the *New York Times*, argues that the debate over whether the SAT predicts academic success has overlooked a deeper issue—namely, how do we define broader goals for college graduates? He wrote, in a recent opinion piece, "Most people agree that universities should train students for economic, political, intellectual and moral leadership. These require academic skills, but also more. But nobody knows if these [SAT scores] can predict later college grades or completion, or character, creativity, civic engagement, religious leadership or business acumen."

I believe the Perfect Score Study directly addresses the issues of character, creativity, civic engagement, and follow-through. Students who score 1600 have demonstrated all of the above and more. Evidence is clear that the achievement of a perfect SAT score is not due to happenstance or just good genes. A number of factors, including teachers' expectations, parental encouragement, support of friends, and personal characteristics such as intelligence and inner motivation, enable perfect score students to do so well. In all but a few cases, perfect score students have a combination of all of these factors. Most average academic achievers, on the other hand, have some—but not all—of them.

Many schools do not create an environment conducive to fostering high academic performance. Many parents don't provide intellectual stimulation and encouragement for their children. Many students don't use their social networks or work hard enough to fulfill their academic potential. High academic achievement and high personal success don't just happen to those who were born lucky. Perfect score students create their own luck.

The Perfect Score Study sounds a clarion call for educators, parents, and students to take a more active and broader approach to improving education and promoting higher achievement. Throughout the book, I've discussed specific steps that parents and students can take for improving education and maximizing SAT scores. Here are some vital lessons from the Perfect Score Study for students, parents, and school educators. These suggestions are purposely broad based. They are meant to guide and focus our efforts. They should stimulate discussion and debate. Clearly, there is room for improvement that can benefit students throughout the country.

## LESSONS FOR STUDENTS

*Lesson 1: Never let them see you sweat.*

The pressure on kids to excel academically has never been greater. Some of this pressure comes from colleges, which raised their standards for admission. Students need to get higher grades and, yes, higher SAT scores than ever before. This occurred because more high school students are applying to colleges in 2003 than ever before. College enrollment is expected to increase further, with 17 million students expected to enroll in college in 2011, compared with 15 million this year, according to the U.S. Department of Education.

Students may feel additional pressure when they hear that they'll earn more with a college degree. The Census Bureau reports that college graduates will earn almost a million dollars more over their lifetimes than high school graduates. Getting into a good college is only that much more important.

Parents, of course, can add to this pressure. They tell their kids that good grades and high SAT scores are tantamount to success. Even with the best intentions of looking out for their child's best interest, parents can instill fear, and this fear can paralyze children and set them up for failure.

My own son Ted taught me a lesson on parental pressure. When he was sixteen and getting ready to take the SAT in his junior year in high school, I became an overanxious, stressed-out parent, as many parents of college-bound students are. I went into automatic pilot and started spouting the self-help advice that I had been collecting during the Perfect Score Study. I quickly told my son, much to his dismay, that I was the world's foremost expert on scoring 1600 on the SAT, based on my preliminary research. Thus, I was qualified to "help" him.

I went out and bought an SAT computer program (actually, two programs) hired a math tutor, and told my son to take practice tests—a lot of them. Based on my "expertise," I was certain this would help raise Ted's SAT scores, and I told him so.

While my son hadn't seen my research yet, he was already living the life of a high academic achiever. He was self-motivated and had been self-motivated throughout high school. He knew exactly how much work he needed to do to succeed academically. Ted proceeded to take two practice SAT exams, never opened the computer programs, and went to the math tutor for half an hour. He then proclaimed to me that he was finished studying for the SATs.

I told him he was nowhere near done. Ignoring all of my research and better judgment—after all, I was an anxious parent first and a researcher second—I threatened the wrath of God and an inferior college education. Ted insisted, "Dad, I'm done. I've finished my prep work." I said, "Ted, you should take more practice tests. I'm sure the tutor can help you sharpen your math skills. And the computer programs definitely will increase your test-taking speed." Ted replied, "Dad, feel free to do any additional preparation that you would like to do, but I'm done, finished, end of discussion."

As I've described, Ted trusted his own instincts and refused to yield to parental pressure. He stood his ground and entered the SAT relaxed and confident. His resulting score of 1500 put him in the top one percent of U.S. students. He then walked around the house for a week calling himself "the genius."

I explained that he wasn't a genius until he'd scored 1600 and made it into my book. I told him there was still plenty of time for him to study to achieve a perfect score. Now that Ted knew what he got wrong, he could focus on those areas and raise his score a hundred points. "A few practice tests, a few hours with the tutor, and you will be set to go," I said all-knowingly. Ted informed me he was finished taking the SAT. He said, "I got the score I wanted. It's good enough to get into the college I want, and that's it." Ted was right.

Ted followed one of the core lessons that perfect score students use when preparing for the SAT: Never let them see you sweat. Ted chose not to be stressed out about the SAT. He figured he would do the best he could, and that would have to be good enough. As a result, he was able to focus and plan his preparation. He also knew when he had prepared enough—when he could enter the test confident that he would be living up to his potential.

This relaxed state of concentration enabled Ted to use his time wisely on the exam and answer the questions without the burden of stress breaking his concentration. Perfect score students agree that it's important to be relaxed during the exam. John C. gave this advice to students preparing for the SAT: "Studying is important, but don't overdo it. Give yourself a time limit for each question, but don't rush. Don't panic. Don't let the pressure get to you. Think of the SAT as a challenge."

### *Lesson 2: Recognize that hard work pays off.*

Most students believe that those who ace the SAT are so smart that they don't need to do anything to prepare for the exam, or they believe that these students are nerdy and spend months or even years studying for the SAT. Both beliefs provide a rationale for most students to do little preparation.

Nice try, but the data from the Perfect Score Study doesn't support either assumption. Most perfect score students do have to study to do well on the SAT, as well as in school in general. Very few are so naturally gifted that the SAT is a snap for them. In fact, fewer than 5 percent of the perfect score students said the SAT was very easy. On the flip side, an equally small number of perfect score students reported that all they did was study for the better part of their junior and senior years. Overall, the vast majority of 1600 kids worked hard for their perfect score. But they also were passionate about what they were interested in outside of academics, participating actively in clubs, sports, and social life. Stuart H. summed up his perfect SAT score this way: "I worked hard my whole life. I learned as much as I could, and I read a lot of everything."

All students need to work hard to improve academic performance both in school and on the SAT. Students need to focus their effort, so hard work pays off. Finally, students need to realize that their reward is in the effort as much as it is in the end result.

### Lesson 3: Believe, as Homer Simpson (once) said, that "it's cool to be smart."

Students should resist the urge to hide their intellect from their peers. Yes, I realize that in high school smart and cool often don't mix. The fact that Homer Simpson said "it's cool to be smart" when he became smarter for one episode shows how our society mocks the smartest among us. The truth is, in college, it *is* cool to be smart. Think of the admiration and honor that are reserved for the best and brightest on college campuses. And by the end of high school, students look up to those who get into the top colleges in the nation. So students should celebrate their academic talents and seek out those who challenge them to think, not conform with the crowds.

Students can also take comfort in the fact that perfect score students are anything but eggheads. They don't have hair like Einstein. They don't dress like Urkel. And they don't walk like John Nash. What they were able to do is clearly articulate who they are, what their philosophy in life is, what's important to them, and why they are generally very happy. The Perfect Score Study found out that just because you're smart doesn't mean you're unhappy. If anything, perfect score students are both smart and happy. Not a bad combination.

### Lesson 4: Develop passions and pursue them.

What excites you so that you want to get up in the morning? Lance Armstrong is passionate about cycling. After a bout with cancer, it was questionable whether Armstrong would live, let alone compete professionally in cycling. Yet cycling was Armstrong's life. He trained and not only regained his strength, but also competed professionally. He won the Tour de France five times *after* he was diagnosed and treated for cancer.

Like Armstrong, perfect score students have one or two passions that they pursue with intensity. These range from jazz to cross-country running to complex mathematical problem solving to Shakespearean literature. The critical element is not whether their interest is academic, but rather whether they take the time and effort to pursue it.

For example, one perfect score student who loved music was in three different music groups: the high school orchestra, a jazz ensemble, and a rock band. He also composed music and continually attended concerts of all different types. Will he become the next Arthur Rubinstein, Dizzy Gillespie, or Bruce Springsteen? There's no guarantee. But the discipline and focus with which perfect score students pursue their interests carry over to their academic studies, and vice versa. These outside interests generally complement and reinforce their studies. The same intensity that they apply to their passions also makes them successful at school and on the SATs. Describing her SAT prep experience, Sarah P. said, "I was passionate about the material and the practice tests. I also worked on thinking logically about the questions."

All students need to focus on an interest and then develop it to the best of their abilities. It may not be the first thing they're interested in and it probably won't be the last. But the best ballplayers, musicians, and students are serious about their work. They also enjoy it. Students should experiment in a few different areas, take some lessons on a particular instrument, and check out martial arts or whatever else piques their interest. They can then identify where their real passion is and pursue it.

### Lesson 5: Accept help from your parents when you need it.

I'm not saying that parents should be dictators over their submissive children. I'm all for raising the independent child, since I raised three independent kids of my own. However, parental support, encouragement, and advice are crucial in order for high school students to excel academically and to maximize their SAT scores.

As a parent, I found that my children, for the most part, did their work and were focused on tests and assignments. However, they also needed my encouragement and positive support, and I happily gave them kudos for a job well done. Sometimes, however, they needed my discipline, which meant telling them that they needed to get their schoolwork and studying done before they could head off to the movies with friends.

Perfect score students and their parents manage to achieve a balance between independence and responsibility. The students wanted complete freedom to determine when and how their work should be done. Perfect score parents wanted assurance that their children would complete their work in a timely manner and would put forth their best efforts. And, yes, even the brightest students can screw up. Some of their parents reported having to cajole, threaten, bribe, and take away the computer until the studying or project was completed. The trick is knowing when to use this form of discipline.

Students should make the most of their parents' advice, both solicited and unsolicited. Parents sometimes do know what they're talking about (as I constantly remind my kids). Even if parental advice isn't helpful, students might want to give it a try before rejecting it out of hand. My son gave his SAT math tutor a whirl before telling me he didn't need the instruction. After all, the more students are able to work cooperatively with their parents, the better off everyone is. And guess what? Students who respect their parents often find they get the same respect in return.

### Lesson 6: Put the SAT into perspective.

The SAT is a rite of passage from high school to college. Like most rites, it is always deemed to be more important before you do it than after you're done. Yes, the SAT will be a challenge, but it's certainly not the first or last challenge of a student's life. In fact, most perfect score students find that the importance of the SAT fades far from their memories once they face the academic rigors of college life.

One message that came up over and over again in my interviews with perfect score students is that they took the SAT seriously, prepared for it, did well, and then went on with their lives. They didn't dwell on it. They didn't boast about it, even though they achieved a flawless score. They went on to their next challenge or activity. In short, they put the test into perspective.

Jacob H. put it this way: "A lot of doing well on the SAT is the attitude you go in with. Remember, it's a nationwide test. If you're above average in school, you'll do well. Don't freak out over it." Charles K. gave these pieces of advice to help students put the SAT into perspective: "Be confident in your abilities. There are patterns you can see in every SAT exam. But most of all, keep in mind that it's only a test."

At the same time, the perfect score students didn't ignore the test or underestimate its importance. At the end of the day, though, the measure of perfect score students is not their perfect score, but who they are as individuals, what they have done in life academically and socially, and what they hope to achieve. The same can be said for any high school student. Students should put time and effort into preparing for the SAT in order to do their best. But they need to realize that success is not acing the exam, rather it is what a good score enables each student to achieve in college and later in life.

### Lesson 7: Learn material for the SAT for the sake of the challenge.

For the most part, perfect score students relished the challenge of taking the SAT. They saw it as a puzzle or strategic game, something to figure out and learn how to win. "I knew the material on the SAT was very limited and that the thinking behind the questions was specific," says Anthony S. "I thought I could learn the test. I also knew my vocabulary was weak, so I studied lists of five hundred words that are often used on the test. In the end, I emerged with a lot better vocabulary, and I'm happy about that. I still use some of the words I learned."

Most students can figure out what they need to do to improve their SAT scores. If they apply themselves and evaluate their performance on practice tests, they can easily find their weak spots and work on those. The trouble is, many students sell themselves short. If they've always maintained a B average, they figure they'll have to make do with an 1100 or 1200. And that may be the case, or they may be able to increase their score by 100 to 200 points by accepting the SAT as a challenge that they're going to take on with gusto. Like anything else, students will get out of the SAT what they put into it.

## LESSONS FOR PARENTS

Perfect score students also had some advice for parents. They noted that their own parents helped them immensely when it came to laying down a strong foundation for learning and then stepping back to give their children the independence they needed to succeed.

### Lesson 1: Be supportive, but not dominating.

Parents should take the advice of Austin Powers: "Oh, *behave.*" There are limits to what parents can and should do to and for their sixteen-year-old child, especially when it comes to preparing for the SAT. Yes, parents provide the first push toward giving their child a love of reading, encouraging his or her curiosity, and providing enough intellectual challenges. By the time a child is near the end of high school, however, it's time for parents to take a step back and offer support without forcing their own agenda in terms of how their child should study and complete assignments. This definitely goes for SAT preparation. Perfect score students mentioned again and again the pacts they had made with their parents. Their parents agreed to leave them alone as long as the students did well and fulfilled their academic potential.

This, of course, enables these high academic achievers to become self-motivated, fueled by the steam of their own engines. None of the perfect score students checked with their parents to see if they needed to clock in more hours for SAT preparation. These students knew in their gut that they were ready, and that's when they stopped studying.

### Lesson 2: Allow kids to choose their own activities.

Yes, perfect score students get involved in extracurricular activities, but they generally don't have lists of things they do that run two or three pages long. Far too many parents sign up their kids for every sports team, music class, and club that's offered in their area. They have their kids' lives booked every minute of the day.

What does this have to do with the SAT? Actually, quite a lot. Perfect score students said they often focused on one particular interest at a time and pursued it with a passion. They may have dabbled in other things or switched passions from one year to the next, but usually they knew where to focus their attention. So when it came time for studying for the SAT, these students were able to make that study time into a passion for a few months. They were able to focus singularly on the task at hand rather than letting their attention wander off into other things.

Lucy Z. admits that she always honed in on one particular interest at a time in high school and went all out for the activity until she met her goal, whether it was writing a short story or preparing for a competition for the math team. "When it came time to prepare for the SAT, I let everything else go for a few months. I studied intensely and made hundreds of flash cards to learn vocabulary words."

I think the message here is that parents need to give their kids a chance to really pursue an activity to its fullest, rather than giving them something new for each day of the week. Kids in today's world often have short attention spans and have a hard time seeing things through to the finish. With any activity that children are involved in, parents should set a particular goal and make sure their children meet that goal before allowing them to get involved in something new. This will help them in the long run write lengthy term papers, study for finals and, yes, even prepare for the SAT.

## Lesson 3: Put the SAT into perspective, for your own sake and your child's.

Parents can be far worse than their children in playing up the importance and omnipotence of the SAT. I, myself, waited breathlessly each day for my daughter's SAT results to arrive. When I thought the results were due, I called home twice a day to see if they had been delivered. When the letter finally came, I just looked at it. I was afraid to open it. My daughter grabbed the envelope away from me and told me to stop making such a big deal out of it.

All parents fall into the trap of defining their kids by their grades and SAT scores. Perfect score parents were far more likely to talk about their children's perfect scores than the students themselves. Many of these parents cited the perfect score as the thing they were most proud of. What's interesting is that perfect score students managed to put the test into perspective even though their parents often weren't able to do so.

Parents need to put some emphasis on the SAT. It is, after all, an important entrance exam for college. However, too much pressure will have the opposite effect. At the end of the day, parents need to recognize who's taking the test and whose life it will ultimately affect.

## A COURSE OF ACTION FOR SCHOOLS

### Lesson 1: Schools can do more to motivate high-achieving students.

Students who score 1600 are generally positive about their total school experience. They recall that their classes were fairly interesting, they participated in a lot of clubs, and they had good friends. And they excelled. Yet few say high school was extraordinarily challenging, either academically or intellectually. Only 6 percent mentioned that extra special teacher, a Mr. Holland or Mr. Escalante, who changed their lives and took their thinking to a new level. The truth is, schools did a good job but not a great one for these high-performing students. They didn't stimulate creative or innovative thinking. They didn't force students to reexamine their lives or existence. It wasn't until college that perfect score students finally felt really challenged.

Is it the purpose of high schools to challenge these highly gifted few? If we believe that schools have the responsibility to help each student reach his or her potential, then it is the duty of schools to challenge each and every student. It is not that most schools are doing a bad job, but why must we settle for mediocre? Schools need to develop a specific strategy for high academic achievers that addresses the quality of teachers, course work, special programs or activities, support for academic clubs or teams, and so on. How many schools have such a strategy or plan in place? Not enough.

### Lesson 2: Schools can find ways to create more opportunities for all kids to participate in nonclassroom academic activities and clubs.

Perfect score students benefit greatly from academic clubs like the math team, Science Olympiad, or debate club. In fact, 70 percent of the perfect score students say they participated in such clubs and that they were important for enabling them to explore different ideas and to make new friends. Clearly, these activities also helped these students achieve academically.

Yet only 46 percent of the average academic achievers participated in academic clubs. Does this mean that the average academic achievers are not interested in doing academics after school, or are they shut out of these opportunities because they feel intimated by the brighter students who take charge of these clubs? I would venture a guess that schools are much more likely to encourage their highest achievers to participate in academic clubs rather than those in the middle of the class. This does a great disservice to the average achievers who can contribute to these clubs and may discover that they find a new passion.

Schools need to consciously develop academic activities for average students and encourage them to join. These activities need to be recognized and students rewarded for participation in them, for example, by recognizing students at an awards assembly. Teachers and administrators need to take a more active role in motivating all students to try out one of these clubs. Schools actively encourage all students to participate in sports—why not academic clubs?

### Lesson 3: Schools should do more to foster curiosity and creativity.

It is interesting that the characteristics and traits that distinguish highly creative people also define perfect score students. It also is significant that school was not reported to play a major role in shaping highly creative individuals, according to research by Mihaly Csikszentmihalyi. Schools, on the whole, are not the breeding ground for creativity.

It's true that there are summer programs for the gifted that encourage creativity, such as TIP (Talent Identification Program). In this program, students study selected topics in areas like politics, psychology, and physics. But these programs are only offered to those at the top of their class.

Schools need to think about how to incorporate such programs into their regular curriculum so that all students can benefit from them, not just the top 2 or 3 percent from their class. For example, DeKalb County in Georgia has a Science Tools and Technology program, which is an advanced science program taught by college professors to high school students in weeklong modules. The subjects range from astronomy to advanced biology to geology. This program fulfills the course requirements for a regular science course but is taught in a totally different and creative way and—best of all—it's offered to a wide range of students. There is no reason this can't be done in high schools throughout the country.

### Lesson 4: Schools should set aside part of their budget to offer assistance for all students for tutoring for the SAT (especially in low-performing schools and for low-performing students).

One criticism of the SAT is that students who can afford to take costly prep courses can raise their scores unfairly in the process. This puts poor students at a disadvantage and exacerbates inequality in the educational system. Because of this unfairness, critics suggest that the SAT be dropped as a requirement for college admission.

Real problem, wrong solution. I believe, as do 80 percent of the colleges in the United States, that the SAT does provide valuable data about academic performance. It correlates highly with other measures of academic performance. Finally, it assesses thinking and reasoning skills, which are important and valuable for college and beyond. This is especially true with the revised version of the SAT, which includes a writing sample.

The solution to the problem that coaching creates inequity is not to drop the test but rather to expand coaching to lower-income students. Freeman Hrabowski, president of the University of Maryland, Baltimore County, puts it succinctly in an op-ed column in *USA Today:* "To support all students, especially low-income and minority students, schools should be encouraged to offer SAT preparation courses, and families should be encouraged to become even more involved in the process. All students should have an opportunity for coaching—which, when done right, is no different from teaching—to provide them with a chance to focus on math word problems and on reading and writing. Bottom line: We should be holding all students to high standards. At the same time, we should be giving them the support they need to achieve those standards."

*Lesson 5: Teachers and superintendents can become leaders in spearheading the debate over the purpose of education.*

American businesses engage in elaborate planning processes with one-, three-, and five-year time horizons. They look at all aspects of business, even raising fundamental questions about what business they are in and/or what business they should be in. Companies devote significant resources and energy to this planning endeavor, which can take up to six months every year. If businesses don't reexamine the fundamentals of their business each year, they may no longer be in business in the future. How many schools or school systems do the same?

The research on perfect score students shows that schools must do a better job of examining the fundamentals and purpose of education. These students certainly are capable of doing far more than they were asked to do in high school. It is not until college that many of these students get the academic challenges they need. This gap exists not only for the highly gifted. The average academic achievers also received a subpar education that could have used a great deal of improvement.

What's clear is that schools are too narrowly focused. Sometimes, schools do teach to the test, not because students demand it, but rather because it is easier to offer an eight-week prep course than question the fundamental business they are in or should be in. This debate needs to involve parents, students, and teachers, not just administrators. And if schools learn from the practice of successful businesses, strategic planning should be an ongoing process that is continually reviewed and improved upon. Unlike businesses, schools generally will continue to operate year after year, regardless of whether they engage in strategic planning. But like businesses, if they don't continually reevaluate their purpose and operations, their output will never improve.

## FINAL THOUGHTS

The SAT is a critical part of our nation's education system. It is vital for assessing the performance of high school students and the performance of teachers and the schools themselves. And it will remain a key to education reform. Over the next year, the latest version of the SAT will be introduced, and it will more closely follow the curriculum taught in our high schools. Plus, it will contain a written essay, so students can express their unique ideas in their own words.

What this means is that the long-term approach to learning uncovered by the Perfect Score Study will be more important than ever for doing well on the SAT. The 7 Secrets of perfect score students will teach students how to learn to the best of their abilities and how to become stronger academic achievers through high school, college, and beyond.

Each of the secrets plays a vital role in creating success for perfect score students. Having a win-win combination of self-confidence, self-effacement, and self-motivation enables these students to believe in themselves and to drive themselves to succeed without thinking that everything is going to come easily. They know they need to work, but they know their efforts will pay off in high grades, high SAT scores, and admission to their top-choice school.

The reason perfect score students strive to learn is that they are intellectually curious. They want to learn everything they can about what interests them. They aren't satisfied with unanswered questions. They lead themselves down roads less traveled and seek out the unknown. Creativity springs forth from these explorations. Perfect score students take their new ideas and mold them to create something out of nothing, whether it's writing a poem, composing a piece of music, or solving a challenging math equation in an elegant way. They know that creativity is the essence of being human. And they want to prove to themselves that they can make some unique mark on the world.

What truly opens up the minds of perfect score students is their thirst for books. They read quickly and voraciously, consuming the classics or the latest sci-fi novel with equal gusto. They also devote many hours a week to assigned reading material, spending more than twice as much time reading for school as average students. They often go beyond their assignments, reading extra books or articles recommended by their teacher. These reading skills help perfect score students enormously on the verbal section of the SAT. Their vocabulary is far more extensive, and their critical reading skills are sharper than those students who read less.

Satisfying their curiosity and learning about the world through books enables perfect score students to figure out what turns them on. They develop one or two passions that they pursue eagerly, and they excel within them. Many work on their particular talent for years, honing their skills until they're ready to enter competitions. They don't give up when the work gets tedious, because they know they were meant to become proficient in their passion. They know their passions are part of their identity, and they're proud of this unique part of themselves.

Just as they vary in the books they read and in the passions they pursue, perfect score students approach learning in different ways. Some learn naturally and easily and don't have to study much to get all As. Others need to work extremely hard to maintain a high GPA and spend many months preparing for the SAT. The largest portion of these students, however, find they fall somewhere in the middle, having to put in a moderate amount of studying to achieve academic success. The point is, though, that perfect score students do what they need to do to get the results they want. They don't wait for good grades and high SAT scores to happen to them. They create their own luck and take a proactive approach to success. And they know how to make adjustments if they aren't achieving the goals they set for themselves. Ultimately, the buck stops with them. If they want to excel, they have to make it happen.

Perhaps the most vital trait of perfect score students—and the most surprising finding to come out of this research—is that they rely on a strong network of friends and family for support. These students place their parents, friends, and other family members as the top priorities in their life, more important than academics. They have active social lives and spend a good deal of time hanging out with their friends, going to the movies, and dating—just like their peers. But these high achievers also know how to balance their social lives with their school responsibilities. They won't let late-night phone calls preclude them from studying for a big exam. These students also have a strong relationship with their parents—one based on mutual trust. Their parents serve to support and advise them both emotionally and academically, and they do this without pressuring or pushing their kids.

All of the traits and behaviors that are commonly shared by perfect score students add up to one thing: a healthy perspective on life. Perfect score students know that the SAT is just a test and isn't something that should define them. They don't brag about their 1600 score and are eager to move beyond the test. Yes, they know their score will help them get into a good college, but they also understand that it's one stepping-stone on the pathway to success. They'll have to keep on facing challenges and working hard if they want to meet their goals and establish the life for themselves that they envision.

Although the Perfect Score Study initially focused almost exclusively on academics, it turned out to be about so much more. The study uncovered the secrets of the most successful students in our nation. These students have what it takes to achieve, not just on the SAT, but also in high school, in college, and in life.

The keys to this success often involve doing the opposite of what you might think. Most parents assume that the more their children study, the better they'll do. They think if one SAT review class is good, three must be better. They think their kids must be pushed, cajoled, and bribed in order to reach the highest echelons of academic achievement. And they expect their kids to excel in all areas from sports to art to music. The result from all these efforts? Often, it's a burned-out teenager who wants to throw in the towel.

The Perfect Score Study shows that parents need to chuck many of their natural inclinations. They need to take a step back and let their child take the initiative in terms of schoolwork, studying, and finding one or two passions. Those students who achieve the most, both socially and academically, are the ones who manage to find balance in their lives. They balance homework with extracurricular activities. They balance their study time with an active social life. They balance their love of parents and family with their strong relationships with their friends. And they balance their pursuit of learning with their need to give back to those less fortunate in their community.

It is this balance that creates a well-rounded student who is happy in school and happy in life. This student learns for the sheer joy of it, not to get a perfect SAT score or to get into a good college. All parents want to infuse their children with this love of learning. It is a sign that their children will continue to seek out learning experiences and expand their knowledge even after schoolwork is behind them. They have taught their kids to learn how to learn and have sent them on their way. Success now rests in their children's hands.

# Bibliography

Arenson, Karen W. 2002. "To Raise Its Image, CUNY Pays for Top Students." *New York Times*, 11 May, sec. A, p. 16.

Armas, Genaro C. 2001. "Nation's Schools Face Flood of Teens." *Atlanta Journal-Constitution*, 23 May, sec. A, p. 12.

Asinof, Lynn. 2002. "Hard Lesson: Applying to College Costs More, Too." *Wall Street Journal*, 28 February, sec. C, p. 1.

Atkinson, Richard C. 2001. "Standardized Tests and Access to American Universities." Paper presented at the 83rd Annual Meeting of the American Council on Education [on-line], 18 February, in Washington, D.C. [cited 4 December 2001] www.ucop.edu/news/sat/speech1.html.

Barnes, Julian E. 2002. "The SAT Revolution." *U.S. News & World Report*, 11 November, 51–58.

Berger, Larry, Michael Colton, Joe Jewell, Manek Mistry, and Paul Rossi. 2000. *Up Your Score: The Underground Guide to the SAT*. New York: Workman Publishing.

Bowen, William G., and Derek Bok. 1998. *The Shape of the River: Long-Term Consequences of Considering Race in College and University Admissions*. Princeton: Princeton University Press.

Briggs, Tracey Wong. 2001. "Financial Aid System Crams More Costs onto Collegians." *USA Today*, 24 October, sec. D, p. 7.

Burton, Nancy W., and Leonard Ramist. 2001. "Predicting Success in College: SAT Studies of Classes Graduating since 1980." *College Board Research Report No. 2001-2*. New York: College Board.

Camara, Wayne J., and Gary Echternacht. 2000. "The SAT I and High School Grades: Utility in Predicting Success in College." *College Board Research Notes RN-10*. New York: College Board.

Chall, Jeanne S. 2000. *The Academic Achievement Challenge: What Really Works in the Classroom?* New York: The Guilford Press.

Claman, Cathy, editor. 2000. *10 Real SATs*. 2nd Edition. New York: College Entrance Examination Board.

Cloud, John. 2001. "Should SATs Matter." *Time*, 17 February, 62.

"College Applications up Sharply." 2002. *CNN.com* [on-line]. Glassboro, New Jersey: Associated Press, 22 November [cited 22 November 2002]. www.cnn.com/2002/EDUCATION/11/12/college.application.ap/index.html.

"College Board Revamps the SAT." 2002. *MSNBC.com* [on-line]. New York: Associated Press, 27 June [cited 28 June 2002]. www.msnbc.com/news/773367.asp.

Corliss, Richard. 2002. "Does Divorce Hurt Kids?" *Time.com* [on-line], 28 January [cited 24 January 2002]. www.time.com/time/magazine/article/0,9171,1101020128195302,00.html.

Csikszentmihalyi, Mihaly. 1996. *Creativity.* New York: HarperPerennial.

Curry, Jack. 2002. "For Glavine, Throwing the Baseball Is an Everyday Job." *New York Times*, 3 June, sec. D, p. 1.

Davis, Alisha. 2001. "How to Ace College." Interview with Richard J. Light. *Newsweek*, 11 June, 62.

DeBarros, Anthony. 2003. "New Baby Boom Swamps Colleges." *USA Today*, 2 January, sec. A, p. 1.

della Cava, Marco R. 2002. "The Race to Raise a Brainer Baby." *USA Today*, 25 June, sec. D, p. 1.

Dorans, Neil. 1999. "The Effects of SAT Scale Recentering on Percentiles." *College Board Research Summary RS-05*. New York: College Board.

Edelman, Marian Wright. 1998. *The Measure of Our Success: A Letter to My Children and Yours.* New York: HarperPerennial.

Eisenberg, Daniel. 2002. "The Softer Side." *Time, Inside Business*, February.

Elias, Marilyn. 2002. "Boomer Echo: College Freshmen Look Liberal." *USA Today*, 28 January, sec. D, p. 5.

"Expected Record Enrollments Continue at Elementary and Secondary Schools, Colleges and Universities This Fall." 2002. *Office of Educational Research & Improvement* [on-line]. Washington, D.C.: U.S. Department of Education, 20 August [23 August 2002]. www.ed.gov/PressReleases/08–2002/08202002.html.

Freeman, Mike. 2001. "Creating a Yale Receiver the Pros Can Love." *New York Times,* 9 November, sec. C, p. 15.

Gallwey, W. Timothy. 1997. *The Inner Game of Tennis.* New York: Random House.

Gardner, Howard. 1993. *Multiple Intelligences.* New York: Basic Books.

Geiser, Saul. 2001. "UC and the SAT: Predictive Validity and Differential Impact of the SAT I and SAT II at the University of California." *University of California,* 29 October.

Ghezzi, Patti. 2002. "Westminster Seniors Shrug Off Perfect SATs." *Atlanta Journal-Constitution,* 8 May, sec. B, p. 1.

Gibbs, Nancy. 2001. "What Kids (Really) Need." *Time,* 30 April, 49.

Gladwell, Malcolm. 2001. "Examined Life: What Stanley H. Kaplan Taught Us about the S.A.T." *The New Yorker,* 17 December, 86.

Goleman, Daniel. 1995. *Emotional Intelligence.* New York: Bantam Books.

Goode, Erica. 2002. "Exploring Life at the Top of the Happiness Scale." *New York Times,* 29 January, sec. D, p. 6.

Green, Sharon Weiner, and Ira K. Wolf, Ph.D. 2001. *How to Prepare for the SAT I.* New York: Barron's Educational Series, Inc.

Harris, Judith Rich. 1998. *The Nurture Assumption: Why Children Turn Out the Way They Do.* New York: Simon & Schuster.

Haynes, V. Dion. 2001. "Study: SAT Good in Gauging College Success." *Atlanta Journal-Constitution,* 5 May, sec. B, p. 5.

Healy, Michelle. 2002. "Divorce Detrimental to Kids' Academics." *USA Today,* 4 June, sec. D, p. 7.

"How to Boost Babies' Brain Power." 2002. *CNN.com* [on-line]. 14 November [cited 14 November 2002]. www.cnn.com/2002/HEALTH/parenting/11/14/smart.babies/index.html.

Hrabowski, Freeman A. 2002. "SAT Remains Key Measure." *Commentary* [on-line]. New York: College Board. 26 June [cited 20 July 2002]. www.collegeboard.com/about/newsat/commentary.html.

Kantrowitz, Barbara, and Donna Foote. 2001. "The SAT Showdown." *Newsweek,* 5 March, 49.

Kantrowitz, Barbara, and Pat Wingert. 2002. "The Right Way to Read." *Newsweek,* 29 April, 61.

Kaplan, Inc. Staff. 2001. *SAT & PSAT.* New York: Simon & Schuster.

Kirn, Walter. 2001. "What Ever Happened to Play?" *Time,* 30 April, 56.

Kolata, Gina. 2001. "Admissions Test Courses Help, But Not So Much, Study Finds." *New York Times,* National Section, 25 March, p. 14.

Leman, Nicholas. 1999. *The Big Test: The Secret History of the American Meritocracy.* New York: Farrar, Straus, & Giroux.

———. 2001. "What Do These Two Men Have in Common?" *Time,* 12 March, 74.

Levine, Mel. 2002. *A Mind at a Time.* New York: Simon & Schuster.

Lewin, Tamar. 2002. "College Board Revises SAT after Criticism by University." *New York Times,* 23 March, sec. A, p. 10.

———. 2002. "New SAT Writing Test Is Planned. *New York Times,* 23 June, National Section, p. 26.

———. 2002. "College Board Announces an Overhaul for the SAT." *New York Times,* 28 June, sec. A, p. 12.

McCarthy, Sheryl. 2001. "Instead of Scrapping SATs, Focus on Raising Black Scores." *Atlanta Journal-Constitution,* 13 March, sec. A, p. 11.

Marklein, Mary Beth. 2001. "Why Was My Child Rejected?" *USA Today,* 3 April, sec. A, p. 1.

———. 2002. "Could the SAT Be on the Bubble?" *USA Today,* 28 January, sec. D, p. 5.

———. 2002. "SAT Exam up for Big Revision." *USA Today,* 26 June, sec. A, p. 1.

———. 2002. "College Board Adds Written Essay to SAT." *USA Today,* 28 June, sec. A, p. 3.

———. 2002. "SAT Erases Some Old Standbys." *USA Today,* 1 July, sec. D, p. 6.

———. 2002. "Love It or Hate It, the SAT Still Rules." *USA Today,* 27 August, sec. A, p. 1.

Manuel, Marlon. 2002. "SAT Doesn't Always Add Up to Success." *USA Today,* 13 September, sec. E, p. 1.

"Minorities on Campus." 2002. *USA Today,* 11 April, sec. A, p. 10.

Mollison, Andrew. 2000. "College Is Costing More." *Atlanta Journal-Constitution,* 17 October, sec. A, p. 3.

Morse, Jodie. 2001. "Flying without the Test." *Time,* 12 March, 71.

Nasar, Sylvia. 1998. *A Beautiful Mind: The Life of Mathematical Genius and Nobel Laureate John Nash.* New York: Simon & Schuster.

Nathan, Julie S., and Wayne J. Camara. 1998. "Score Change When Retaking the SAT I: Reasoning Test." *College Board Research Notes RN-05.* New York: College Board.

Olenchak, F. Richard. 2002. "Being a Gifted Boy: What We Have Learned." *Duke Gifted Letter,* Vol. 2, Issue 4, 1.

Owen, David. 1999. *None of the Above: The Truth Behind the SATs.* New York: Rowman & Littlefield Publishers, Inc.

"Path to College Shifts as SAT Changes Form." 2002. *USA Today*, 28 March, sec. A, p. 12.

Perez, Christina. 2002. "Grades Are a Much Better Measure of How a Student Will Do in College." *USA Today*, 28 March, sec. A, p. 12.

Powers, Donald E., and Wayne J. Camara. 1999. "Coaching and the SAT I." *College Board Research Notes RN-06*. New York: College Board.

"Quick Fixes Not the Way to Increase SAT Scores." 2002. *Atlanta Journal-Constitution*, 29 August, sec. A, p. 19.

Robinson, Adam, and John Katzman. 2002. *Cracking the SAT*. New York: Random House.

Rothstein, Richard. 2001. "The SAT Debate Ought to Be Broader." *New York Times*, 28 March, sec. A, p. 17.

———. 2001. "Dramatic Voucher Findings Fall Short." *New York Times*, 9 May, sec. A, p. 26.

———. 2001. "The SAT Scores Aren't Up. Not Bad, Not Bad at All." *New York Times*, 29 August, sec. A, p. 17.

"SAT and Gender Differences." 1998. *College Board Research Summary RS-04*. New York: College Board.

"The SAT: Questions and Answers." 2001. *FairTest* [on-line]. Cambridge: The National Center for Fair & Open Testing. 28 August [cited 3 October 2001]. www.fairtest.org/facts/satfact.htm.

"SAT's Changes Ought to Raise Bar." 2002. *Atlanta Journal-Constitution*, 11 July, sec. A, p. 13.

Schouten, Fredreka. 2002. "25-Minute Exercise Will Test Students, Graders Alike." *USA Today*, 17 September, sec. D, p. 9.

Schouten, Fredreka, and Larry Bivins. 2002. "A Substitute for an Education." *USA Today*, 23 December, sec. D, p. 6.

Simmons, Kelly. 2002. "College Entrance Test Due Changes." *Atlanta Journal-Constitution*, 28 June, sec. C, p. 1.

Steinberg, Jacques. 2001. "Most Colleges Are Expected to Continue to Use the SAT." *New York Times*, 24 February, sec. A, p. 6.

———. "Usefulness of SAT Test Is Debated in California." *New York Times*, 17 November, sec. A, p. 6.

———. "Challenge Revives SAT Test Debate." *New York Times*, 19 November, sec. A, p. 14.

Sternberg, Robert J. 1996. *Successful Intelligence*. New York: Plume.

———. 1997. *Thinking Styles*. New York: Cambridge University Press.

Strauss, Robert. 2001. "The Masterminds behind the SAT." *Los Angeles Times,* 27 March, sec. E, p. 1.

Tofig, Dana. 2003. "Test Czar Aims to Up SAT Scores." *Atlanta Journal-Constitution,* 28 March, sec. E, p. 1.

"UC President Richard C. Atkinson Calls for Ending SAT I Test Requirement At UC." 2001. *Office of the President News Room* [on-line]. Oakland: Regents of the University of California. 16 February [cited 4 December 2001]. www.ucop.edu/news/sat/satarticle1.htm.

U.S. News & World Report. 2002. *America's Best Colleges.* 2003 Edition. New York: U.S. News & World Report LP.

Vlk, Suzee. 1999. *The SAT I for Dummies.* 4th Edition. New York: Hungry Minds, Inc.

Whitaker, Barbara. 2001. "University of California Moves to Widen Admissions Criteria." *New York Times,* 15 November, sec. A, p. 20.

Wilgoren, Jodi. 2000. "National Study Examines Reasons Why Pupils Excel." *New York Times,* 26 July, sec. A, p. 14.

Winter, Greg. 2003. "College Loans Rise, Swamping Graduates' Dreams." *New York Times,* 28 January, sec. A, p. 1.